The Complete Guide to Self-Discovery & Emotional Healing

Enneagram, Inner Child, and Shadow Work

(3 Books in 1)

Relove Psychology & Sofia Visconti

The Enneagram

A Guide to Determining Your Personality Type, Unlocking the Power of Personal Growth and Self-Discovery

Relove Psychology

TABLE OF CONTENTS

Introduction

The Enneagram can help us break free from our unconscious patterns and live more consciously and authentically. —Sandra Maitri

Have you heard of personality tests like the Myers-Briggs Type Indicator (MBTI) and DISC? They are often used in organizations and personal development for understanding our own behavior and improving our interactions with others. But have you heard of the Enneagram? It's a more comprehensive and fascinating tool that measures our psychological patterns and motivations at cognitive, emotional, and behavioral levels.

We all have different personality traits, and Enneagram helps us understand why we behave and feel the way we do. When we are in a balanced state, we make productive and purposeful decisions. But, when we are stressed or imbalanced, we can become reactive, and our defense mechanisms kick in. The Enneagram helps us identify our potential and shows us how to actualize our best selves.

So, how can we apply the Enneagram in our lives? By becoming more self-aware and practicing self-management, we can make informed decisions and avoid becoming driven by our personality patterns. We can identify our strengths and weaknesses, and work towards our goals by aligning our actions with our higher purpose beyond our ego structure. By doing so, we can overcome challenges and lead a more fulfilling life.

As you read in the quote by Sandra Maitri, the Enneagram can help us break free from our unconscious patterns and live more consciously and authentically, but how? When we have a deeper understanding of ourselves, we can make more conscious choices and live a more fulfilling life.

One way the Enneagram helps us break free from our unconscious patterns is by uncovering our defense mechanisms. These mechanisms are often rooted in childhood experiences and are used to protect ourselves from perceived threats (Booth, 2022). However, these defense mechanisms can become unconscious patterns that limit our ability to grow and develop.

For example, if we have a fear of abandonment, we might develop a pattern of people-pleasing to avoid rejection. This can become an unconscious pattern that limits our ability to assert our own needs and boundaries. By understanding this pattern through the Enneagram, we can work on becoming more self-aware, and break free from this limiting behavior.

While the Enneagram can be a powerful tool for personal growth, there are some common complaints and problems that people may encounter when learning about or using it. One of the most common issues is difficulty identifying their own Enneagram type. The Enneagram is a complex system with nine different types, and it can be challenging to determine which type best describes our personality and motivations.

Another issue is feeling limited by their Enneagram type. While the Enneagram can provide valuable insights into our behavior and patterns, it's important not to box ourselves into one type, or to use it as an excuse for our behavior. We are all complex individuals with unique experiences, and the Enneagram is just one tool among many for self-discovery and growth.

Are you curious about the Enneagram and how it can help you understand yourself—and others—better? If so, this handy guide is packed with valuable insights, practical tips, and powerful tools for exploring the fascinating world of the Enneagram. Whether you're a seasoned Enneagram enthusiast, or you're just getting started, this book has something for everyone. With clear explanations and real-world examples, you'll learn how to identify your Enneagram type, understand your unique strengths and weaknesses, and cultivate greater self-awareness and personal growth.

In this Enneagram book, you'll find a wealth of information on the nine different Enneagram personality types and how they interact with each other. You'll learn how each type approaches life, relationships, and work, and how they respond to stress and challenging situations. You'll also discover how your Enneagram type influences your communication style, decision-making process, and emotional patterns. With practical exercises and insightful advice, you'll be able to apply the

Enneagram to your own life and see tangible results. Whether you're looking to improve your relationships, boost your career, or simply deepen your self-awareness, this Enneagram book is the perfect place to start. So, what are you waiting for? Let's begin!

UNDERSTANDING THE ENNEAGRAM

Chapter 1:
The Nine Enneagram Types

Discovering your personality type can provide valuable insight into your inner workings, including your motivations and how you engage with others. One commonly used theory for determining personality type is the Enneagram system. Identifying your Enneagram type not only piques your curiosity, but also grants you a greater comprehension of the driving forces behind your actions.

However, determining your Enneagram type is only the beginning of the journey. It's equally important to gain a comprehensive understanding of the various types within the Enneagram system. In the following chapter, we will delve into each type and its significance within the Enneagram framework.

According to a study published in the American Journal of Psychiatry, the Enneagram system is characterized as "a personality theory that outlines nine distinct strategies through which the psyche constructs a perspective on the world and interacts with oneself and others" (Alexander & Schnipke, 2020). Psychiatrists have employed this system since the 1970s, and researchers indicate that the theory suggests individuals establish a primary personality strategy to deal with external circumstances by the time they reach adulthood.

The Enneagram system defines nine unique worldviews and motivations, with one of them having the greatest influence on an individual's personality type. These types are not assigned arbitrary numbers; rather, they are categorized into three groups based on the three core aspects of human nature: head types, heart types, and body types. Each group, also known as a triad, is characterized by a central emotion, and driven by a specific center of intelligence (The Nine Enneagram Types [Complete Descriptions], n.d.). While individuals possess traits from all three aspects, the group their personality type belongs to has a greater impact on their life.

To work with the Enneagram, one needs to consciously observe their thoughts, emotions, and behaviors, similar to how mindfulness practices enhance awareness of the present moment. Through this observation of where attention and energy are directed, one can gain valuable insights into their automatic patterns of thinking, feeling, and acting.

The Enneagram can be beneficial in several ways.

First, it can help individuals understand themselves better by shedding light on their motivations, desires, and fears. This self-awareness can lead to personal growth and development, as individuals can begin to identify and work on their areas of weakness and challenge.

Second, the Enneagram can improve interpersonal relationships by increasing empathy and understanding. When individuals understand the motivations and perspectives of those around them, they can communicate more effectively, resolve conflicts more easily, and build stronger relationships.

Third, the Enneagram can be used as a tool for professional development. By understanding their own strengths and weaknesses, individuals can choose careers that align with their values and abilities. They can also identify areas where they need to improve and seek out training or mentorship to develop those skills.

Overall, the Enneagram can provide valuable insights into one's personality, relationships, and career path. By gaining a deeper understanding of oneself and others, individuals can live more fulfilling and meaningful lives.

The Enneagram system outlines nine core types, each with a unique basic fear, basic desire, and typical behavior during times of stress and security. By analyzing these fundamental fears and desires, the Enneagram is able to explain the driving forces behind the behavior. This allows for a comprehensive understanding of each type, which can provide valuable insights into an individual's psychological well-being.

Type One: The Perfectionist

Type One individuals—also known as the "Perfectionists" or "Reformers"—are recognized for their rationality and ethical principles, often working diligently while disregarding their own wants. They harbor a strong desire to be righteous, accurate, and flawless, focusing on values and morality. Furthermore, they are prone to idealize the future, and aspire to improve the world. They may take on the role of a moral compass in their social circles or workplace, guiding others to do the right thing and upholding the values they hold dear. Their dedication to self-improvement and personal growth can be admirable, but it can also become a source of anxiety and stress (Bernes, n.d.).

Type Two: The Helper

Type Twos in the Enneagram—also known as the "Helpers"—possess an inclination to feel helpful and provide assistance to others. They display warmth, affection, and enthusiasm in their approach to supporting others, but in doing so, they can easily disregard their own necessities. These individuals usually exude an amicable and optimistic demeanor; however, they may struggle with overemphasizing the opinions of others. They may struggle with setting boundaries and saying no, as they fear that they will be seen as unhelpful or unlovable if they do not constantly put others first. This can lead to feelings of burnout and resentment if their efforts go unappreciated or unreciprocated (Bernes, n.d.).

Type Three: The Achiever

Type Three, commonly referred to as the "Achievers," are primarily driven by the desire to attain acknowledgment through their accomplishments. Their success is closely tied to their image and public perception. These individuals are goal-driven, competitive, and action-oriented, often pushing themselves excessively to gain the approval of others. They thrive on recognition, praise, and they are highly attuned to the opinions and perceptions of others. This can sometimes lead them to prioritize their public image over their inner feelings and needs. Despite their drive and ambition, Threes may struggle with feeling a sense of inner emptiness or lack of fulfillment. They may struggle to connect with their own emotions, and may use their achievements as a way to compensate for this feeling of inadequacy (Bernes, n.d.).

Type Four: The Individualist

Enneagram Type Four, also referred to as the "Individualists," are recognized for their self-sufficiency and unconstrained nature, which can result in them feeling misunderstood by others. They are recognized as the "seekers" within the Enneagram system, openly contemplating profound inquiries related to their existence, identity, and overall being. Possessing imaginative and analytical traits, these individuals can often experience melancholic tendencies. Fours are often drawn to creative pursuits such as art, music, or writing, as these allow them to express their innermost thoughts and emotions. Their self-sufficiency and individualistic nature can sometimes lead Fours to isolate themselves from others, as they may feel misunderstood, or like they don't fit in. They may also struggle with comparing themselves to others and feeling like they are lacking in some way (Christian, 2021).

Type Five: The Investigator

Type Five, also known as the "Investigators," are inclined towards being curious, analytical, and solitary individuals. They can come across as detached from others, but it's primarily because they treasure privacy and personal space. This type holds a keen interest in discussing topics they are knowledgeable about, emphasizing self-sufficiency and logic as core values. They tend to be logical and objective, using reason and analysis to understand the world around them. At times, Fives may struggle with feelings of inadequacy or fear of not having enough resources, including time, energy, and emotional support. This can lead them to withdraw even further from others, creating a cycle of isolation (Christian, 2021).

Type Six: The Loyalist

Enneagram Type Six, also known as the "Loyalists," demonstrate a high concern for safety and security within the world. Their tendency to anticipate potential mishaps may lead to a perception of being fearful. However, they can exhibit significant courage when it comes to causes that they are passionate about. These individuals are characterized by their sense of loyalty, albeit often coupled with anxiety. They may be prone to self-doubt and second-guessing, constantly seeking reassurance and guidance from others. They may also struggle with decision-making, as they are often highly aware of the potential risks and consequences of each option. Sixes also tend to be highly attuned to social dynamics and the expectations of others. They value structure and hierarchy, often seeking out clear rules and guidelines to follow. They may be prone to conformity and may struggle to assert themselves in situations where they feel uncertain or unsupported (Christian, 2021).

Type Seven: The Enthusiast

Enneagram Type Seven, commonly referred to as the "Enthusiasts," possess a buoyant and vivacious nature, driven by their yearning for joy and delight. These individuals are inclined towards spontaneity, hold a distaste for feeling restricted or confined, and they are always full of energy. They evade emotional distress or discomfort by engaging in activities that bring them pleasure and satisfaction, often keeping themselves occupied. They may struggle with negative emotions, preferring to focus on the positive and avoid anything that might bring them down. This can sometimes lead to a sense of restlessness or dissatisfaction. Despite their carefree and adventurous nature, Sevens may also struggle with commitment and follow-through, due to their desire for new experiences and their tendency to quickly lose interest in ongoing pursuits. They may have a tendency to start new projects or relationships with enthusiasm, only to lose interest or become distracted when things become challenging or less exciting (Booth, 2022).

Type Eight: The Challenger

Enneagram Type Eights are known for their directness, assertiveness, and strength. They tend to have a strong will and desire to be in control, often taking charge of situations and people. This type values independence and self-sufficiency, and they may become confrontational when they feel threatened. They can also display a protective nature towards those they care about, but at times, this may come across as domineering or intimidating (Booth, 2022). Despite their tough exterior, Eights can have a sensitive side, and they desire deep connections with others.

Type Nine: The Peacemaker

Enneagram Type Nines, also known as the "Peacemakers," possess a remarkable ability to consider various perspectives and mediate conflicts. However, they often prioritize others' needs at the expense of their own, sometimes without even realizing it. They tend to go along with the status quo to maintain harmony, even if it means compromising their own desires. Nines may struggle with decision-making, as they tend to see multiple perspectives and fear making the wrong choice. This type values simplicity and stability, preferring a routine and predictable life. They can be easygoing and agreeable, but may struggle with assertiveness and speaking up for themselves (Booth, 2022).

Chapter 2:
The Enneagram's Structure
and How It Works

Over the last decade, the Enneagram, a unique geometric structure with nine points, has gained popularity in the fields of personality testing and career coaching. This system connects the nine points with underlying aspects of the psyche, such as the unconscious mind, to identify fundamental motivations, fears, virtues, fixations, desires, and temptations (How the Enneagram System Works, 2014). If you find this explanation vague, I can help clarify the Enneagram process for you.

The Enneagram unveils the idea that each of the nine personality types holds a unique fundamental belief about the world, which profoundly impacts their motivations, fears, and overall perspective. While these core beliefs are not necessarily incorrect, they can limit our understanding by creating biases and narrow viewpoints. By delving into our Enneagram type and its influence on our perception, we can expand our outlook and approach situations with greater effectiveness. Understanding someone's Enneagram type provides valuable insight into their behavior, as each type possesses distinct core beliefs that consistently drive their actions and decisions. It helps us make sense of behavior that may initially appear puzzling or inconsistent.

In addition, the Enneagram provides insight into how people respond to stress. By detailing how each Enneagram type adjusts and reacts to both stressful and supportive circumstances, the Enneagram highlights avenues for personal growth and establishes a basis for comprehending others.

The Basic Structure

According to Verywell Mind, the Enneagram is represented by a nine-pointed geometric symbol with an outer circle and an irregular hexagon connecting the points, as well as a triangle between points 9, 3, and 6 (Cherry, 2019). The circle represents human wholeness and unity, while the other shapes illustrate how it is divided. The Enneagram includes wings, which are related personality styles that individuals can adopt to develop new facets of themselves. Understanding the influence of wings can add nuance to one's self-understanding. Additionally, each Enneagram type is connected to two other types by lines that represent the person's repressed childhood type and a type they may grow into with further development. These connections illustrate how each type has strengths and challenges, and how personality can change under different circumstances.

In addition to the basic structure of the nine points, wings, and connecting lines, the Enneagram also includes a few other important elements.

For example, each Enneagram type is associated with a deadly sin or passion, which is believed to be at the root of the personality's motivation and behavior (Bayside Church, 2016). These passions are:

1. Type One: anger
2. Type Two: pride
3. Type Three: deceit
4. Type Four: envy
5. Type Five: avarice
6. Type Six: fear
7. Type Seven: gluttony
8. Type Eight: lust
9. Type Nine: sloth

Understanding these passions can help individuals gain greater insight into their own motivations and tendencies.

Another key aspect of the Enneagram is the concept of levels of development. Each Enneagram type has nine levels of development, ranging from healthy and integrated at Level One, to unhealthy and disintegrated at Level Nine. Understanding the levels of development can help individuals recognize their own progress and growth, and identify areas for improvement (How the Enneagram System Works, 2014).

One essential concept in the Enneagram is the idea of integration and disintegration points. These points represent how each type can move towards growth or towards stress, depending on their circumstances. The integration point is the point that a person moves towards when they are healthy and growing. It's the type that they can take on some of the positive qualities of when they're in a good place (Storm, 2020). For example, a Type Five, who tends to be analytical and reserved, might move towards Type Eight , which is more assertive and confident, when they're feeling secure and self-assured.

On the other hand, the disintegration point is the type that a person tends to take on some of the negative qualities of when they're under stress (Storm, 2020). For example, a Type Two, who typically wants to be helpful and supportive, might move towards Type Eight when they're under stress, becoming more aggressive and confrontational. Knowing your integration and disintegration points can be helpful in understanding your patterns of behavior and how to work towards personal growth. By recognizing when you're moving towards one of these points, you can start to make conscious choices to move towards integration and away from disintegration.

The Enneagram also includes a set of subtypes or instinctual variants, which describe how individuals prioritize three key instinctual needs: self-preservation, social connection, and one-on-one relationships. Each Enneagram type can have a different dominant subtype, which can further influence their behavior and motivations (How the Enneagram System Works, 2014).

The Enneagram also includes the concepts of "holy ideas" and "virtues." The holy ideas represent the highest, most enlightened state of each Enneagram type. These ideas are not meant to be religious in nature, but rather spiritual or philosophical. Each type has a unique holy idea that represents its highest potential and serves as a guiding principle for personal growth (Cloete, 2022).

The virtues, on the other hand, represent the positive qualities that each Enneagram type can cultivate in order to move towards their holy idea. Each type has a specific virtue that is associated with their core motivations and fears. By developing this virtue, a person can begin to transcend their core type and move towards a more integrated and balanced state (Cloete, 2022).

Here are the holy ideas and virtues associated with each Enneagram type:

1. The Reformer: Holy Idea—Perfection; Virtue—Serenity

2. The Helper: Holy Idea—Freedom; Virtue—Humility

3. The Achiever: Holy Idea—Hope; Virtue—Truthfulness

4. The Individualist: Holy Idea—Origin; Virtue—Equanimity

5. The Investigator: Holy Idea—Omniscience; Virtue—Non-attachment

6. The Loyalist: Holy Idea—Courage; Virtue—Faith

7. The Enthusiast: Holy Idea—Wisdom; Virtue—Sobriety

8. The Challenger: Holy Idea—Truth; Virtue—Innocence

9. The Peacemaker: Holy Idea—Love; Virtue—Action

It's important to note that the holy ideas and virtues are not meant to be seen as fixed or absolute. Rather, they are aspirational goals that a person can work towards in order to become more integrated and balanced. By cultivating the virtues associated with their Enneagram type, a person can begin to move towards their holy idea and reach their highest potential (Cloete, 2022).

Overall, the Enneagram is a complex and multi-faceted system that offers individuals a comprehensive framework for understanding their personalities, motivations, and opportunities for growth.

How Does it Work?

The consensus among major Enneagram authors is that *everyone is born with a dominant personality type*, which is determined by temperament and other prenatal factors. Each individual emerges from childhood with one of the nine types dominating their personality.

The Enneagram's basic personality type has several noteworthy characteristics.

1. Individuals do not transition from one basic personality type to another throughout their lifetime.

2. The descriptions of the personality types are universal and apply equally to both genders. No type is inherently masculine or feminine.

3. A person's behavior and attitudes may fluctuate between the healthy, average, and unhealthy traits that define their personality type. Not everything in the description will apply to them at all times.

4. Numbers are used to designate each of the nine types, as they are value-neutral and do not imply anything positive or negative. Unlike psychiatric labels, numbers provide a

shorthand way of indicating a lot about a person without being pejorative.

5. The numerical ranking of the types is not significant. A larger number does not equate to a better type, and no type is inherently better or worse than any other.

6. Although some types may be perceived as more desirable in certain cultures or groups, it is important to recognize that each type has unique strengths and weaknesses. The goal should not be to imitate another type's assets, but to become the best version of oneself.

The Enneagram is structured as a 3 x 3 grid that groups nine personality types into three centers based on the predominant way each type processes information. The Centers are the Instinctive, Feeling, and Thinking Centers, each containing three types that share common traits and tendencies of that Center (Enneagram Centers of Intelligence, 2020). For instance, the Feeling Center includes the types that have distinctive strengths and weaknesses in relation to their emotions, such as Type Four. Similarly, Type Eight is in the Instinctive Center, as it has its own set of strengths and weaknesses related to its instincts, and so on for all nine types.

Every person has a unique combination of their basic personality type and one of the two types adjacent to it on the Enneagram's circumference. This combination is known as the person's "*wing*." While the dominant type shapes a person's overall personality, the wing complements it and adds additional, sometimes contradictory, elements to a person's character. Understanding someone's wing is essential to gain a better insight into their personality (How the Enneagram System Works, 2014). For instance, if someone is a type Nine, they will have either a One wing or an Eight wing, and their personality can be best understood by blending the traits of the Nine with either the One or the Eight. However, some people may show little influence from either wing, or may be strongly influenced by their basic type.

The Enneagram traditions differ on whether a person can have one or two wings. Technically, everyone has two wings, as both the types adjacent to their basic type are present in their personality. However, some proponents of the two-wing theory believe that both wings operate equally in everyone's personality. For example, a Type Nine would have an equal amount of both their Eight and One wings.

The Enneagram also recognizes that individuals within each type can be at different *levels of development.*

As I previously explained, the levels of development within each Enneagram type are commonly referred to as the "Levels of Integration" and "Levels of Disintegration," which describe the degree to which an individual has developed the positive or negative traits associated with their type (How the Enneagram System Works, 2014).

The Levels of Integration for each type are:

1. Reformer: Becoming more spontaneous, joyful, and accepting of imperfection.

2. Helper: Developing healthy boundaries and learning to take care of themselves.

3. Achiever: Becoming more compassionate and empathetic towards others, and developing a sense of inner peace.

4. Individualist: Learning to accept themselves as they are and finding a sense of purpose.

5. Investigator: Developing a sense of connection with others and learning to express their emotions.

6. Loyalist: Learning to trust themselves and their instincts.

7. Enthusiast: Developing a deeper sense of meaning and purpose in life.

8. Challenger: Using their strength and power to help others and protect the vulnerable.

9. Peacemaker: Becoming more assertive and learning to express their own needs and desires.

The Levels of Disintegration for each type are:

1. Reformer: Becoming rigid, dogmatic, and losing touch with their own emotions.

2. Helper: Becoming manipulative and resentful towards others and neglecting their own needs.

3. Achiever: Becoming competitive, arrogant, and losing touch with their own values and beliefs.

4. Individualist: Becoming self-absorbed, moody, and losing touch with reality.

5. Investigator: Becoming paranoid, isolated, and losing touch with their own emotions and relationships.

6. Loyalist: Becoming anxious, indecisive, and losing trust in themselves and others.

7. Enthusiast: Becoming scattered, impulsive, and losing touch with their own emotions and relationships.

8. Challenger: Becoming controlling, abusive, and losing touch with their own vulnerabilities and emotions.

9. Peacemaker: Becoming passive-aggressive, stubborn, and avoiding conflict and change.

It is important to note that these levels of development are not fixed or static, and individuals can move up or down the levels throughout their lives, depending on their experiences and personal growth.

While the Enneagram is an incredibly flexible and constantly evolving system, it is important to note that it does not encompass the entirety of human complexity. Each individual has their own unique and often unpredictable traits and behaviors that cannot be fully explained or understood by any single theory or framework. However, the Enneagram can offer valuable insights into certain aspects of an individual's personality and behavior, providing a starting point for deeper understanding and growth.

Chapter 3:
The Enneagram's Origins and Evolution

Despite the unclear origins of the Enneagram, it is evident from all available evidence that it has a rich and intricate history spanning across different cultures and regions. Its roots can be traced back to various mathematical, philosophical, and spiritual traditions (Wagner, 2010).

The Enneagram model as it exists today is a fusion of traditional wisdom and modern psychology. In the following chapter, I will aim to pay tribute to the numerous brilliant minds that contributed to the development of this influential and groundbreaking tool.

A Brief History of the Ancient Roots of Enneagram

The word "Enneagram" is derived from the Greek words "ennéa," meaning "nine," and "gramma," meaning "figure."

Fragments of the Enneagram symbol have been traced back to ancient Greece, where the numerical patterns of three, seven, and nine appeared in epics, myths, philosophy, and mathematical science, emphasizing the significance of this sequence of numbers in ancient works and thought (Wagner, 2010).

Some scholars argue that variations of the Enneagram symbol can be found in the sacred geometry of Pythagorean mathematicians and mystical mathematics (Cloete, 2010).

Pythagoras himself claimed that his theory of numbers, the key to understanding the universe, came from his teacher in Egypt. Respected Enneagram expert Russ Hudson also lectures on the origins of the Enneagram, noting how the Egyptian Enneagram and metaphysical powers and numbers are linked to the origins of the Enneagram .

The founder of Neoplatonism, Plotinus (270 CE), described nine divine qualities that manifest in human nature. His work would later greatly influence Western and Near-Eastern thought through subsequent thinkers such as St. Augustine of Hippo, the Cappadocian Fathers, St. Thomas Aquinas, and Pseudo-Dionysius the Areopagite (Cloete, 2010). The early Greek concepts of vice and virtue were standardized by Christian monks into the seven deadly sins, which became widely recognized.

The first recorded use of a symbol resembling the Enneagram is attributed to Ramon Llull, a Catalan philosopher and theologian. In his work, Ars Magna (1305), Llull posited that there were fundamental truths underlying all fields of knowledge, and that these truths could be understood by studying combinations of elemental principles (Cloete, 2010). He created a diagram consisting of nine sets of aspects in concentric circles, with one of the circles mapping to the Vices of the Enneagram.

Evolution to Its Modern Form

The current understanding of the Enneagram is much clearer than its earlier evolution. George Gurdjieff, a Christian mystic, spiritual teacher, and philosopher of Armenian descent, used the Enneagram and three centers to describe the perpetual motion of creation. Gurdjieff considered movements or sacred dances an essential part of his teachings and referred to himself as a "teacher of dancing." Although he alluded to being introduced to the Enneagram in the 1920s during a visit to an Afghan monastery, he never provided further details on its origin (Cloete, 2010).

The Enneagram gained influence in the 20th century through South American philosopher Oscar Ichazo, who connected the symbol to different personality types through his school, the Arica Institute (The Enneagram Institute, 2014b). Chilean psychiatrist Claudio Naranjo, known for integrating psychotherapy and spiritual traditions, popularized the Enneagram in the professional consulting arena. Naranjo's students, including Ochs, Almaas, and Maitri, spread the Enneagram into Christian communities in the US. Partial validation of the Enneagram has come through experiential and empirical studies since its introduction into psychology. Naranjo's approach to the Enneagram emphasizes the importance of self-awareness and self-transformation. He sees the Enneagram as a tool for understanding the deep-seated psychological and emotional patterns that underlie our behaviors and beliefs.

Naranjo has also written extensively on the Enneagram and its applications in psychotherapy and personal growth. Some of his most influential books include *Character and Neurosis* (1994) and *The Enneagram of Society* (1995).

In the late 1960s, Claudio Naranjo became interested in the Enneagram after meeting Oscar Ichazo and studying with him for a time (Roulo, 2021). Naranjo went on to develop his own understanding of the Enneagram and its application to psychology and psychotherapy. He taught the Enneagram as part of his psychotherapy training programs, and also introduced it to a wider audience through his books and workshops. Naranjo's work with the Enneagram helped to popularize the system in the United States and Europe. He taught the Enneagram at Esalen Institute in California, and later founded the SAT Institute in Chile, which is dedicated to the study of the Enneagram and other spiritual traditions (Roulo, 2021).

Naranjo's approach to the Enneagram emphasizes the importance of self-awareness and self-transformation. He sees the Enneagram as a tool for understanding the deep-seated psychological and emotional patterns that underlie our behaviors and beliefs (Roulo, 2021).

Other influential figures in the development of the Enneagram include Helen Palmer, who popularized the Enneagram in the United States through her books and workshops, and Don Riso and Russ Hudson, who founded the Enneagram Institute and developed their own system of Enneagram typing.

In recent years, the Enneagram has become increasingly popular as a tool for personal growth and development, as well as for understanding and improving relationships. It is used in a variety of settings, including therapy, coaching, leadership development, and spiritual practice.

While the Enneagram has its roots in ancient spiritual traditions and has been adapted and refined over the centuries, its current form as a personality typing system owes much to the work of modern thinkers and practitioners. Despite some controversy and debate over its validity and usefulness, the Enneagram continues to be a popular and widely used tool for self-discovery and personal growth. It has also been integrated into various fields, including business, education, and healthcare.

Some Enneagram enthusiasts have developed their own interpretations and variations of the system, leading to a wide range of Enneagram-related materials and resources available today. This has resulted in some controversy and criticism from those who argue that the Enneagram's original teachings have been distorted and oversimplified.

Despite this, the Enneagram continues to be a popular and widely-used tool for self-discovery and personal growth. Its unique approach to understanding personality types and patterns of behavior has proven useful for many individuals and organizations seeking to improve their relationships, communication, and overall well-being.

THE NINE ENNEAGRAM TYPES

Chapter 4:
Type One–The Perfectionist

Enneagram Type Ones have a strong inclination towards doing things accurately and with high standards. They are known for being meticulous about rules and paying close attention to detail, as well as striving to avoid errors. This often makes them appear to others as perfectionistic, responsible, and demanding individuals (Owens, 2019).

Enneagram Type Ones are often *motivated by a deep desire for perfection* and a belief that the world should adhere to a certain set of standards or principles. They hold themselves to these same high standards, which can lead to self-criticism and a tendency towards being hard on themselves. However, they also have a strong sense of responsibility, and may often take on leadership roles because of their dedication to doing things the "right" way.

Ones can also be *sensitive to criticism or feedback* that challenges their beliefs or methods, as they see it as a personal attack on their integrity. This can lead to rigidity in their thinking and difficulty adapting to change. However, their attention to detail and commitment to doing things correctly can make them valuable assets in many fields, such as law, accounting, or project management.

They are recognized for their *ambitious nature, strong principles, perfectionism, and remarkable self-discipline.* They hold themselves to high standards and constantly aim to enhance their performance, aspiring to reach their full potential.

Key Features in Brief

At the core of Enneagram Type One is a *fear of being flawed, immoral, or corrupt*, while their *ultimate desire is to be virtuous, maintain integrity, and achieve equilibrium.*

Enneagram Type Ones can have a Nine wing or a Two wing. Those with a Nine wing, often referred to as "The Idealist," typically value harmony and inner peace. They seek to create a stable and peaceful environment, often striving to avoid conflict.

Meanwhile, those with a Two wing, known as "The Advocate," have a strong desire to help others and be of service. They believe in being supportive, caring, and generous towards others. They aim to promote positive change in the world, working towards creating a better future for all.

Are You an Enneagram Type One?

If you're uncertain about whether you identify as an Enneagram Type One, there are various online quizzes available. However, if you prefer a quick evaluation, we have one for you. Consider the following 13 statements, which apply to many Type Ones. If at least eight of these statements accurately describe you, it's likely that you're a Type One.

- You're willing to follow instructions, but only if the person giving them is competent.
- You're highly committed to self-improvement and strive to be the best version of yourself.
- You believe that you're usually—or always—right about things.
- You frequently establish goals for yourself and consistently meet them.
- You're willing to sacrifice your own happiness to improve the world around you.
- People have told you that you can come across as critical or condescending.
- You become frustrated when people don't put in enough effort or don't do things correctly.
- You're hard on yourself, even for small errors.
- You seldom lose control of your emotions.
- You've achieved success in your education and/or professional life.
- Merely being happy isn't sufficient; you also need to feel useful.

- You're dependable, and others recognize that they can rely on you.
- Getting affirmation from others is critical to you, even if you don't show it outwardly.

Enneagram Type Ones are often seen as *principled and conscientious individuals who have a strong sense of right and wrong.* They have a natural inclination to live up to their own high standards, which can make them appear rigid or inflexible. However, they are also dedicated and responsible, and are willing to make sacrifices to uphold their values.

Type Ones can be hard on themselves and *may struggle with perfectionism, leading to a tendency towards self-criticism.* They are often high achievers, excelling in their academic or professional pursuits. However, they can also be critical of others when they feel that people are not living up to their own expectations or standards.

Despite their strong sense of duty, Type Ones can also be compassionate and empathetic towards others. They believe that it is their responsibility to make the world a better place and are motivated by a desire to contribute to society. They are also *known for being reliable and dependable,* often taking on leadership roles in their communities or workplaces.

Levels of Development

The Enneagram Type One can experience different levels of development (Type One, n.d.).

Healthy Levels:

1. At their best, Ones become wise and discerning, accepting the world as it is and knowing the best action

to take in each moment. They are compassionate, inspiring, and hopeful, believing that the truth will be heard and that goodness will prevail.

2. Ones at Level Two are conscientious and have a strong sense of personal convictions. They are rational, reasonable, self-disciplined, and moderate in all things. They value morality, personal responsibility, and doing what is right.

3. Ones at Level Three are extremely principled and ethical, always striving to be fair, objective, and just. They have a strong sense of responsibility, personal integrity, and a higher purpose that drives them to become teachers and witnesses to the truth.

Average Levels:

1. At Level Four, Ones become dissatisfied with reality and become high-minded idealists. They believe that it's up to them to improve everything and become advocates and crusaders for causes they believe in. They can be critical of others and explain how things "ought" to be.

2. Ones at Level Five fear making mistakes and strive for consistency with their ideals. They become well-organized, orderly, and often workaholics, while rigidly keeping their feelings and impulses in check. They can be impersonal and puritanical, and their perfectionism can lead to obsession.

3. Ones at Level Six are highly critical of themselves and others, opinionated, and perfectionistic. They often correct people and badger them to do what's right according to their prescriptions. They are impatient,

never satisfied unless things are done according to their standards and can be abrasive, moralizing, and scolding.

<u>Unhealthy Levels:</u>

1. At Level Seven, Ones can become dogmatic, self-righteous, intolerant, and inflexible. They believe they alone know "The Truth," and everyone else is wrong. They can be severe in judgments and rationalize their actions.

2. Ones at Level Eight can become obsessive about the imperfection and wrongdoing of others. They may become hypocritical, doing the opposite of what they preach. They become critical, angry, and punitive, and their perfectionism turns into an obsession.

3. At Level Nine, Ones become condemnatory, cruel, and punitive towards others. They want to rid themselves of wrongdoers, leading to severe depression, nervous breakdowns, and even suicide attempts. They may develop Obsessive-Compulsive and Depressive personality disorders .

Personal Growth Tips For Enneagram Type Ones

Learn to be kind to yourself. Type Ones can have a strong inner critic that can cause them to be hard on themselves, especially during times of stress. However, it is important for Type Ones to be kinder to themselves and to ease up on their inner negative critic. According to Enneagram expert Beatrice Chestnut, Type Ones can benefit from "cultivating an inner voice that is compassionate, encouraging, and supportive." Chestnut suggests that Type Ones can start by imagining how they would speak to a close friend who is going through a difficult time, using the same kind and supportive words with themselves (Chestnut, 2021).

Understand that everyone is following their own journey in life. It is crucial to acknowledge that not everyone is at the same level as you. While Type Ones can be excellent coworkers, mentors, companions, and allies, their strict personal standards may make them appear critical, inflexible, and even difficult to work with to those around them (Brand, 2021). It is essential to develop the ability to appreciate people as they are, and to avoid coming across as preachy or overly concerned with minor details.

Maintain an open perspective. It is important for Type Ones to be open to outside perspectives and understand that people may have different views. While bringing moral clarity and strong principles to work and life is empowering, it is crucial to stay humble and grounded in living those truths, rather than just preaching them. Maintaining an open mind and being receptive to different perspectives can help Type Ones achieve balance in their lives (Brand, 2021).

Manage your self-righteous anger. Your self-righteous anger can be your weakness. You tend to get angry quickly, feeling offended when others do not do things the way you have defined them as right. It is important to step back and understand that your anger can distance people, preventing them from hearing your ideas (Brand, 2021). Moreover, your suppressed anger may lead to health problems like ulcers or high blood pressure, which can lead to more severe health issues in the future.

Embrace your emotions and impulses. To grow and develop, it is crucial for you to acknowledge and embrace your emotions, especially those that stem from your unconscious impulses. You may have a tendency to suppress your feelings and desires, including sexual and aggressive impulses, which are part of being human. Consider keeping a journal or joining a group therapy session to explore and express your emotions in a safe space (Brand, 2021). This can help you realize that you are not alone in your struggles, and others will not judge or condemn you for having human needs and limitations.

Prioritize a healthy work-life balance. While Type Ones' strong work ethic and focus can lead to career success, it's important to prioritize a healthy work-life balance. Type Ones have a tendency to become workaholics, and they may find themselves working late hours at the office, sacrificing time for relationships, family, and self-care. To maintain overall wellness, it's essential to be mindful of the need to balance work and personal life, and to make time for activities outside of work (Brand, 2021). This will not only lead to greater life satisfaction, but it can also prevent burnout and stress-related health issues.

In terms of the specific characteristics of Type One, research has found that individuals who score high on traits associated with conscientiousness—such as organization, self-discipline, and a strong sense of duty—tend to have higher levels of well-being and life satisfaction (Roberts et al., 2014). However, individuals who score very high on conscientiousness can also be prone to anxiety, depression, and perfectionism (Sutin et al., 2010). Overall, while the Enneagram model may not be fully supported by scientific research, there is some evidence to suggest that its types and characteristics may have some validity. Furthermore, the suggested ways of growth for Type Ones align with evidence-based treatments for anxiety, depression, and perfectionism (Type One, n.d.).

Chapter 5:
Type Two—The Helper

According to the Enneagram personality theory, Twos are characterized by their *need for love and a sense of belonging*. They exhibit nurturing, caring and helpful behaviors towards others and are eager to participate in the lives of those around them. They often struggle with saying no when someone asks for their help, as they feel the need to prove their worth by being there for others. Twos fear being alone and unloved, and to cope with this fear, they focus on taking care of others and making themselves central to other people's lives. Their *core motivation is to feel loved and appreciated*, which drives them to express their love towards others through their words and actions (Cain, 2016).

In this chapter, we will explore the core traits, motivations, and fears that define the Type Two personality. We will also discuss common behaviors and tendencies of Twos, including their willingness to assist others, and their struggles with setting boundaries. Through a deeper understanding of this personality type, we can gain insight into our own behavior and that of those around us, ultimately leading to more fulfilling relationships and personal growth.

Key Features in Brief

Enneagram Type Twos are characterized as *empathetic, sincere, and warm-hearted individuals who are inclined to be friendly, generous, and self-sacrificing*. They have a well-intentioned drive to be close to others, but may also engage in people-pleasing behaviors and slip into doing things for others just to feel needed (Schirm, 2022). Their desire to be loved is profound, yet they often struggle with acknowledging their own needs and can become possessive of others.

At their best, Twos are unselfish and altruistic, possessing unconditional love for others. However, their basic fear of being unwanted or unworthy of love can sometimes trigger sentimental or flattering behavior.

Twos with a One wing are known as "Servants," while those with a Three wing are called "The Host/Hostess" (Schirm, 2022).

Key motivations for Type Twos include the desire to be loved, express their feelings for others, be appreciated and needed, and justify their self-image, all of which are intended to elicit a response from others (Don Richard Riso & Hudson, 1999).

Are You an Enneagram Type Two?

To help determine if you might have an Enneagram Type Two personality, take this five-question quiz and answer with a "yes" or "no" to each question:

- Do you enjoy forming close relationships with others?
- Would people describe you as caring?
- Do you find it difficult to say "no" when someone asks you for help?
- Do you engage in acts of service or give back to your community—such as volunteering or donating money—?
- Would you say you are non-judgmental?

If you answered "yes" to most of these questions, there's a good chance you have a Type Two personality. However, keep in mind that the Enneagram is a complex personality system, and taking a deeper dive into all nine types can help provide a more comprehensive understanding of your personality and personal growth opportunities.

Levels of Development

The levels of development for this type are as follows:

Healthy Levels:

1. When someone reaches this level, they become truly selfless, humble, and caring. They possess an altruistic nature, showing unconditional love to both themselves and others. They consider it a privilege to be a part of other people's lives (Type Two, n.d.).

2. At this level, individuals are empathetic and compassionate. They genuinely care about others' needs and show thoughtfulness and warmth. They are forgiving, sincere, and deeply concerned about the well-being of those around them.

3. People at this level are encouraging and appreciative. They have the ability to see the good in others and believe in the importance of service (Type Two, n.d.). While they prioritize taking care of others, they also understand the need to nurture and give to themselves. They embody true love and generosity.

Average Levels:

1. Those at this level yearn for closer connections with others. They tend to engage in people-pleasing behaviors, becoming excessively friendly and emotionally expressive. They have good intentions but may seek approval, flattery, and attention. Love is a central value for them, and they often talk about it (Type Two, n.d.).

2. People at this level become overly intimate and intrusive. They have a strong need to be needed, resulting in their tendency to hover, meddle, and try to control others under the guise of love. They expect something in return for their efforts, leading to mixed messages (Type Two, n.d.). They can become possessive and codependent, going to great lengths to fulfill the needs of others while neglecting their own.

3. At this level, individuals start to feel self-important and self-satisfied. They believe they are indispensable, although they may overestimate their impact on others. They might develop hypochondria and adopt a "martyr"

mindset, sacrificing themselves for the sake of others. They can become overbearing, patronizing, and presumptuous.

<u>Unhealthy Levels:</u>

1. People at this level can be manipulative and self-serving. They use guilt to make others feel indebted to them and often inflict suffering on others. They may turn to food and medication to suppress their emotions and gain sympathy (Type Two, n.d.). They undermine others through belittling and disparaging remarks. They deceive themselves about their motives and display aggressive or selfish behavior.

2. Those at this level become domineering and coercive. They feel entitled to get whatever they want from others, including repayment of old debts, money, or even sexual favors.

3. At this level, individuals excuse and rationalize their actions. They feel abused and victimized by others, which fuels their bitterness, resentment, and anger. They somatize their aggression, resulting in chronic health issues. They "fall apart" and burden others as a way to seek validation. This level is often associated with Histrionic Personality Disorder and Factitious Disorder (Type Two, n.d.).

Personal Growth Tips For Enneagram Type Twos

Practice mindfulness. Enneagram Type Twos can benefit greatly from practicing mindfulness, which involves stepping outside of themselves and observing their personality objectively. By taking a step back, they can observe patterns in their thoughts, feelings, and behaviors, allowing them to gain a deeper understanding of their own needs and desires (Type Two, n.d.). This process can help Twos set healthy boundaries and prioritize self-care, which in turn can lead to personal growth and development. By becoming more self-aware, Twos can break free from their need to be needed by others, and find fulfillment and purpose within themselves.

Embrace self-awareness. Enneagram Type Twos tend to prioritize the emotions and needs of others, often neglecting their own. In order to grow, it's important for Twos to acknowledge and accept their own emotions (Type Two, n.d.). By taking note of their own feelings about things, Twos can better understand their own needs and desires. This process can be aided by activities like journaling, which can help Twos get more in touch with their emotions. By embracing self-awareness and prioritizing their own emotions, Twos can develop a greater sense of self-acceptance, and find more balance in their relationships with others.

Learn to ask and accept "no." As an Enneagram Type Two, you have a natural gift for intuiting the feelings and needs of others. However, it's important to remember that what you think others need may not always align with their actual desires. To cultivate healthy relationships and personal growth, it's crucial to ask others what they need before jumping in to offer assistance (Type Two, n.d.). Effective communication involves clearly communicating your intentions, and being open to the possibility of receiving a "no" in response. It's important for Type Twos to understand that a rejection of their particular offer of help does not equate to a rejection of them as a person. Learning to ask and accept "no" can help Twos develop a more balanced and respectful approach to helping others, while also practicing self-care and boundary-setting.

Practice humility in your good deeds. Instead of seeking recognition and appreciation for your good deeds, practice humility. It's important to remember that helping others should come from a genuine desire to do so, not for the sake of gaining recognition or validation. Avoid drawing attention to your good deeds or reminding others of your past acts of kindness. Instead, focus on helping others without any expectation of recognition or reward. This will not only improve your relationships, but also allow you to experience the joy of helping others for its own sake.

It is important for Type Twos to remember that their desire to help others should come from a place of genuine love and care, rather than a need for validation or a fear of being alone. By learning to set healthy boundaries and practice self-care, Type Twos can continue to express their love and generosity towards others while also taking care of themselves.

Chapter 6:
Type Three–The Achiever

Threes are individuals who are driven to *achieve and stand out from others, as they desire to feel important and valuable.* They may come across as confident, ambitious, and focused on their goals to those around them. However, despite their outward appearance, Threes often struggle with feelings of self-doubt and a lack of intrinsic self-worth, seeking validation through their accomplishments (Enneagram Type 3: The Achiever, 2021). They tend to prioritize their image and how others perceive them, wanting to be seen as successful.

The *biggest fear for Threes is the possibility of being seen as insignificant or failing,* so they strive to excel in all aspects of life as a way to prove their worth (Enneagram Type 3: The Achiever, 2021). Their core motivation stems from a deep-seated need for attention and admiration, which drives them to be successful and significant in order to avoid feeling worthless.

Key Features in Brief

Individuals who identify with the Enneagram Three personality type tend to be *confident, attractive, and charismatic* (Enneagram Type 3: The Achiever, 2021). They possess strong ambition, competence, and energy, and are often driven to advance their status. While diplomatic and poised, they can become overly preoccupied with their image and what others think of them. They may also struggle with workaholism and competitiveness.

At their best, Threes are authentic, self-accepting role models who inspire others.

Threes can become consumed by their pursuit of success and validation, often at the expense of their well-being and relationships (Enneagram Type 3: The Achiever, 2021). Their sense of self-worth is tied to external achievements and recognition, and they may engage in deceitful and manipulative behavior to maintain their image.

Threes have a strong sense of their own identity and are self-accepting. They are able to recognize their strengths and weaknesses without judgment, and can pursue their goals without losing sight of their values and relationships. They are often successful, but they no longer define their worth solely by their achievements.

Threes are *motivated by a fear of worthlessness and a desire to feel valuable and worthwhile*. Depending on their wing type, Threes may be known as "The Charmer"—when they have a Two wing—or "The Professional" when they have a Four wing. Their key motivations include seeking affirmation, attention, admiration, and the desire to distinguish themselves from others by impressing them (Enneagram Type 3: The Achiever, 2021).

Are You an Enneagram Type Three?

If you are curious about whether you might be an Enneagram Type Three, I have created a short quiz consisting of five yes or no questions to help you assess your fit with this personality type. Read the questions below and answer them based on your intuition:

- Do you enjoy being the center of attention?
- Do you typically excel in whatever you do?
- Is it important for you to be perceived as successful?
- Do others often look to you for guidance or leadership?
- Would your friends and family describe you as popular or well-liked?

If you answered "yes" to at least three of these questions, it is possible that you may be a Type Three.

Levels of Development

The levels of development for this type are as follows:

<u>Healthy Levels:</u>

1. At this level, Threes are self-accepting, authentic, and humble. They have a fullness of heart and are benevolent towards others.

2. Threes are self-assured, confident, and charming. They have a high level of self-esteem and adaptability (James, 2021).

3. Threes are ambitious, but not for personal gain. They strive to be outstanding in order to embody widely admired cultural qualities.

Average Levels:

1. At this level, Threes become highly concerned with their performance and achieving their goals. They compare themselves with others and strive for exclusivity and being the "best."

2. Threes become overly concerned with their image and how they are perceived by others. They may lose touch with their own feelings and have problems with intimacy (James, 2021).

3. Threes become narcissistic, exhibiting grandiose notions about themselves and their talents. They become arrogant and contemptuous of others.

Unhealthy Levels:

1. At this level, Threes become exploitative and opportunistic, willing to do whatever it takes to preserve the illusion of their superiority (James, 2021).

2. Threes become devious and deceptive in order to hide their mistakes and wrongdoings. They become malicious and may betray or sabotage others to triumph over them (James, 2021).

3. At the most unhealthy level, Threes become vindictive and seek to destroy others' happiness. They become obsessed with destroying anything that reminds them of

their own shortcomings and failures, exhibiting psychopathic behavior (James, 2021).

Personal Growth Tips For Enneagram Type Threes

Practice truthfulness. To truly develop and grow, Enneagram Type Three individuals must prioritize honesty, both in their relationships with themselves and others. It is crucial to acknowledge and express genuine feelings and needs, rather than suppressing or hiding them in favor of projecting an image of success or importance. The temptation to impress others with exaggerated accomplishments must be resisted, as true authenticity and vulnerability are what truly leave a lasting impression on others.

Learn to slow down. To truly thrive, it's vital for a Type Three to learn how to slow down. When constantly striving for success and recognition, it's easy for them to overlook the present moment or take it for granted. That's why it's crucial for them to pause, relax, and appreciate the here and now. This includes turning off their smartphones and disconnecting from the frenetic pace of life, even if only for a little while. By taking a break from their never-ending to-do list, Threes can recharge and reconnect with themselves, which will ultimately help them achieve their goals with more focus and clarity.

Develop deeper connections through active listening. To cultivate deeper connections with others, it is important for Threes to practice active listening. Often, Threes are so preoccupied with how they are perceived by others that they miss out on opportunities to form meaningful relationships (Cherry, 2019). Active listening involves being fully present in the conversation and giving the speaker your undivided attention. This means putting aside distractions, such as smartphones, and avoiding the urge to steer the conversation back to yourself. By truly hearing what others have to say, Threes can gain a better understanding of those around them and build stronger connections.

Overcome the fear of vulnerability. Threes may find it daunting to embrace vulnerability as it involves revealing their true selves to others, not just the image they want to project. However, personal growth and development require them to confront this fear and become more authentic. By learning to embrace vulnerability, Threes can break down emotional barriers and forge deeper connections with others, ultimately leading to greater personal fulfillment.

Type Three individuals must balance their ambition for success and efficiency with empathy and honesty. They can experience personal growth by releasing the notion that their worth depends on how others perceive them. At times, they may need to take the risk of losing others' approval to follow their genuine desires and live with authenticity. A healthy Three prioritizes sincerity over accomplishments, and understands that their value is not solely based on what they produce or achieve.

Chapter 7: Type Four—The Individualist

According to Ryan Lui, a certified Enneagram practitioner, Fours are commonly referred to as the "individualist" who have a *strong desire for an ideal world*. Their perspective is that of the glass being half-empty, and they yearn for it to be full, with a deep longing for a sense of completeness in life (Regan, 2021).

Enneagram educator Julie Nguyen explains that Fours are *inherently independent and free-spirited individuals*. Their identity is often intertwined with their emotions, leading them to follow what feels right in the moment, which can sometimes result in unfinished projects (Regan, 2021).

Fours desire a *sense of uniqueness, beauty, and completeness in their lives, but they also fear being alone, average, or that their current life is all there is.* They have weaknesses such as being self-centered, envious, and dramatic, but they are also self-aware, passionate, and introspective.

Key Features in Brief

According to Ryan Lui, Fours highly *value individuality, authenticity, and originality, and they also embody these qualities themselves.* They enjoy feeling unique, and want everything in their life to hold meaning and beauty (Regan, 2021).

Lui explains that *Fours are emotional individuals,* which can influence their work and relationships. They have a tendency to get carried away in their daydreams and feelings, which can lead to intense emotions that may sometimes overwhelm others. Enneagram educator Julie Nguyen further states that Fours seek heightened emotional states, which can make them lose touch with reality. Julie Nguyen also states that Fours are romantics who are highly aware of the potential for good in the world. However, this type of mindset can also give birth to negative thinking or depression if they focus too much on what could be, rather than being grateful for what they already have (Regan, 2021).

Fours are *known for their creativity and sensitivity,* which makes them highly reflective and artistically inclined. They have strong self-awareness and can express themselves well. However, this self-awareness can also cause self-centeredness. (Regan, 2021).

Are You an Enneagram Type Four?

Although there are many detailed resources available for exploring your Enneagram type, I can help you get started with a quick five-question quiz just like you did in the previous chapters to determine if you may be a Type Four. By answering these questions with a simple "yes" or "no," you can find out if you fit into this type.

- Do you often feel like your emotions are more intense than those of the people around you?
- Do you enjoy spending time alone to explore your dreams, thoughts, talents, and artistic interests?
- Do you sometimes find yourself indulging in sadness or melancholy?
- Do you ever feel like nobody truly understands you or that your identity is too complex for others to connect with?
- Do you have a tendency to compare yourself to others, sometimes feeling like you fall short?

If you answered "yes" to most of these questions, it's possible that you could be an Enneagram Type Four!

Levels of Development

Just like the previous Enneagram types, Type Fours have their own levels of development that we will explore in this section.

<u>Healthy Levels:</u>

1. Type Fours are deeply creative individuals who express both personal and universal concepts through their work, often creating something that is self-creative, inspired, and regenerative.

2. Type Fours are highly self-aware and introspective, often on a quest for self-discovery, and they are sensitive to their own feelings and those of others. They are gentle, compassionate, and tactful.

3. Type Fours are true to themselves and highly individualistic. They are emotionally honest, self-revealing, and humane (Enneagram Type 4 – the Individualist, 2021). They have an ironic view of self and life, can be both serious and funny, and are emotionally strong and vulnerable at the same time.

Average Levels:

1. Level 4 of the Type Four Enneagram is characterized by an artistic and romantic orientation to life. Individuals at this level seek to create a beautiful and aesthetic environment to cultivate and prolong their personal feelings. They are often highly attuned to beauty and seek to express themselves through art or other creative outlets. They may also have a strong need for authenticity and self-expression, and may resist conforming to societal norms or expectations. While there are many positive aspects to this level, there can also be some negative consequences (Enneagram Type 4 – the Individualist, 2021). They can become self-absorbed, introverted, and overly sensitive, leading to moodiness, shyness, and self-consciousness.

2. Fours tend to internalize everything and take everything personally. They tend to focus on their inner experiences and can become self-indulgent and self-absorbed, which can make it hard for them to connect with others. If Type Fours at this level don't learn to manage their emotions and get out of their heads, they may become stuck in their

patterns of withdrawal and self-absorption, leading to further isolation and unhappiness (Enneagram Type 4 – the Individualist, 2021).

3. Type Fours gradually start to believe that they are different from others and become increasingly disdainful, decadent, sensual, and prone to living in a fantasy world (Enneagram Type 4 – the Individualist, 2021). They may experience self-pity and envy of others, leading to self-indulgence and impracticality.

<u>Unhealthy Levels:</u>

1. This level represents an unhealthy state where a person experiences a deep sense of shame and self-loathing. They become self-inhibiting, angry at themselves, and depressed. They feel alienated from themselves. People at this level may become very critical of themselves, seeing only their flaws and failures. They may also become judgmental of others and feel that they are not understood or appreciated.

2. At this level, individuals may feel tormented by delusional self-contempt, self-hatred, self-reproaches, and morbid thoughts. They may become increasingly isolated and disconnected from others, feeling that they are fundamentally flawed and unworthy of love and acceptance (Enneagram Type 4 – the Individualist, 2021). They may see everything as a source of torment and blame others, driving away anyone who tries to help them.

3. The unhealthy tendencies of Type Four reach their peak. They experience a deep sense of despair and hopelessness, feeling like they have lost all sense of purpose or direction in life. They may become self-

destructive, engaging in reckless behaviors such as substance abuse or self-harm, in an attempt to escape their emotional pain. At this level, individuals with Type Four may also experience thoughts of suicide or engage in suicidal behaviors (Enneagram Type 4 – the Individualist, 2021).

Personal Growth Tips For Enneagram Type Fours

Practice gratitude. In addition to helping with feelings of inadequacy, practicing gratitude can also improve overall well-being and mental health. Research has shown that gratitude practices can increase positive emotions, reduce stress, and improve sleep (Emmons & McCullough, 2003). For Enneagram Type Fours, who may be prone to negative emotions and a focus on what's missing or lacking in their lives, a regular gratitude practice can help shift their perspective towards the positive aspects of their lives and promote greater overall satisfaction.

Separate self from feelings. It is crucial for Enneagram Type Four individuals to understand that their feelings do not define them. They should avoid equating themselves with their emotions as they are not a true source of support. According to "Personality Types" by Don Richard Riso and Russ Hudson, "one of the most important mistakes Fours make is to equate themselves with their feelings." (Don Richard Riso & Hudson, 1999) It's common for Enneagram Type Fours to become deeply attached to their emotions, using them as a primary source of self-understanding. However, this can often lead to a distorted view of the self, and an overemphasis on negative emotions. Therefore, it's essential for Fours to recognize that their feelings are not the ultimate source of support or guidance. Instead, they should strive to understand themselves holistically, considering their thoughts, actions, and experiences in addition to their emotions.

Prioritize consistent productive work. Don't delay taking action until you feel like you are in the "right mood". Enneagram Type Four individuals may have a tendency to wait for inspiration to strike, or to put off tasks until they feel motivated. However, the reality is that they are happiest and most fulfilled when they are working on something productive that aligns with their values and interests (Regan, 2021). Waiting for the perfect mood or inspiration can lead to procrastination and a lack of progress towards their goals.

Embrace constructive feedback to grow. It is crucial for individuals with a type Four Enneagram personality to be receptive to constructive feedback, both positive and negative. It's important to recognize that negative feedback is not an attack on their identity, and positive feedback should not be disregarded or dismissed. Feedback, whether it's criticism or praise, can provide valuable insights and lessons to help them grow and develop. By embracing feedback, Fours can gain a better understanding of themselves and their interactions with others, leading to more fulfilling relationships and a deeper sense of personal growth.

Fours possess a keen sense of appreciation for beauty, intricacy, and uniqueness, and value depth and meaning over superficiality. They are capable of confronting the darker aspects of life without the need to gloss over them. Envy is a major weakness for Fours, as they often compare themselves unfavorably to others who possess qualities they believe they lack (Regan, 2021). It's important for them to remember that every individual has what they need to be themselves, and there's no Enneagram type that's better or worse than others. The strengths and weaknesses of each type manifest differently in every person, depending on their level of maturity. While Fours could benefit from being more selfless and less self-pitying, they are fundamentally independent, creative, and authentic individuals who are in tune with their emotions and desires.

Chapter 8:
Type Five–The Investigator

According to the Enneagram personality system, Fives possess a *cerebral, analytical, and independent nature*. They are driven by a desire to comprehend the world around them, and safeguard their autonomy and privacy to live life on their own terms. Fives tend to examine and dissect information extensively to achieve a thorough understanding before taking any action. While they excel at thinking logically, Fives may *struggle to step outside of their own thoughts and engage with others*. Their inclination to withdraw and keep to themselves can make it challenging for others to understand their inner workings. Fives possess an insatiable curiosity and love to acquire knowledge, which they stockpile like squirrels hoarding nuts for the winter. They prefer to use reason and knowledge as the basis for their decisions, rather than being overwhelmed by emotions. Fives *tend to detach from their feelings and analyze them objectively* (Type Five, n.d.).

Key Features in Brief

Enneagram Five is commonly referred to as The Investigator, owing to their *keen desire to comprehend the underlying mechanisms behind various phenomena*. Fives are highly curious individuals who seek to understand the workings of the world around them, whether it pertains to the natural world, the cosmos, or the inner workings of their own mind. They are *known to approach everything with a critical eye*, frequently challenging accepted beliefs and conducting their own research to test the validity of assumptions. Fives are relentless in their pursuit of knowledge, always seeking to delve deeper and discover new insights.

Fives derive significant benefits from their *ability to concentrate on tasks without being derailed by their emotions*. They are often able to maintain a sense of composure and level-headedness in situations where others may become agitated. However, this strength can also have a downside. Due to their natural inclination towards privacy, Fives may struggle to share personal information with others, preferring to keep their thoughts and feelings to themselves. They may feel that revealing too much about themselves could make them vulnerable to others' demands or expectations. As a result, they may be better at acquiring information than forming intimate connections with others.

When Fives have a Type Four wing, their *emotional expression is enhanced*, allowing them to better communicate and understand their feelings, rather than solely analyzing them. They may become more interested in exploring their creative side and experimenting with new ideas.

On the other hand, when Fives have a Type Six wing, their *observational skills are combined with the foresight of the Six.* They may become more social and better able to contribute to group efforts. Their thinking may shift towards practical problem-solving, and they may develop a stronger, family-oriented social instinct that values stability.

Are You an Enneagram Type Five?

Let's try out the quiz once more. Simply answer with a "yes" or "no" response without overthinking.

- Do you enjoy exploring new concepts, even if they are unfamiliar to you?
- When confronted with a problem, is your initial response to analyze and research it thoroughly before taking action?
- Do you tend to keep your thoughts and emotions private, only sharing with those you trust deeply?
- Do you often misplace objects because you are preoccupied with your thoughts?
- Do you have a tendency to intellectualize your feelings, analyzing them rather than fully experiencing them?

If you have answered at least three or more questions in the affirmative, there's a high chance that you are an Enneagram Type Five.

Levels of Development

Type Five individuals can experience various levels of development, with distinct behaviors and attitudes associated with each level.

<u>Healthy Levels:</u>

1. Type Fives become visionaries, seeing the world from a broad and profound perspective while remaining open-minded. They make groundbreaking discoveries, and innovate new ways of perceiving and doing things (Robledo, 2022).

2. Fives are highly intelligent, curious, and perceptive individuals who possess an unquenchable thirst for knowledge. They are able to concentrate deeply on their interests, anticipate what's coming next, and see patterns and connections where others might miss them. This level of perceptiveness and intelligence makes them valuable in many fields, particularly in science, research, and academia (Robledo, 2022).

3. Enneagram Type Fives reach a high level of competence and expertise in their chosen field of interest. They are driven by their passion for knowledge, and they are excited by the prospect of acquiring new information. They may become pioneers in their field, developing innovative and creative ideas that can be extremely valuable and original. They possess a highly individualistic and idiosyncratic nature, which often leads them to pursue unconventional paths.

<u>Average Levels:</u>

1. Individuals become increasingly focused on conceptualizing and fine-tuning everything before taking

action. They prefer to work things out in their minds, often engaging in model building, preparing, practicing, and gathering more resources. Their approach is studious, and they are continually acquiring new techniques to apply to their interests (Robledo, 2022). At this level, Enneagram Type Fives also become more specialized, and their pursuit of knowledge can sometimes make them seem "intellectual." They often challenge accepted ways of doing things, and seek to discover new and innovative approaches.

2. As they become more detached and preoccupied with their thoughts, Level 5 Fives may retreat from the practical world and become absorbed in offbeat, esoteric subjects.

3. At Level 6 of development, these individuals become increasingly antagonistic towards anything that they perceive as a threat to their inner world and personal vision. They become more provocative and abrasive in their interactions with others, intentionally taking extreme and radical views. This behavior stems from their fear of losing control and feeling overwhelmed by their environment (Robledo, 2022). Type Five individuals at this level may become very cynical and argumentative, engaging in intellectual debates and discussions solely for the sake of proving themselves right and others wrong.

Unhealthy Levels:

1. At this level of development, Enneagram Type Fives become reclusive and isolated from reality. They become eccentric and nihilistic, rejecting and repulsing any social attachments or relationships. They see the world as a

harsh and unforgiving place, and they are convinced that they are too weak to survive in it (Type Five, n.d.).

2. At this level, they become overwhelmed and consumed by their fears and threatening ideas, leading to horrifying delusions and phobias. They begin to see threats everywhere and are often paranoid and suspicious of others' intentions. They may experience panic attacks, nightmares, and other forms of severe anxiety as they struggle to cope with their overwhelming fears (Type Five, n.d.).

3. At this level, the individual seeks oblivion and may resort to self-destructive behavior or even commit suicide. This level of development generally corresponds to the most severe forms of mental illness, including schizophrenia (Type Five, n.d.).

Personal Growth Tips For Enneagram Type Fives

Embrace the idea of seeking help when needed. Enneagram Type Fives have a tendency to desire complete independence and self-sufficiency (Robledo, 2022). However, it's important to recognize that there are people in your life who would be more than willing to lend a hand if you asked. Whenever you find yourself overwhelmed or overloaded, take a moment to consider if there's anyone who can help you with your tasks. Don't be hesitant to seek support when necessary.

Engage in physical activities to promote relaxation. To combat the tendency to overthink and dwell in their thoughts, Enneagram Type Fives can benefit from engaging in physical activities that promote relaxation and mindfulness. Hobbies like running, dancing, yoga, and other activities that involve movement can help Fives get out of their heads and into their bodies, allowing them to unwind and enjoy the present moment. By prioritizing these activities, they can develop a healthy outlet for stress and anxiety, improving their overall well-being.

Embrace the unknown. Instead of fixating on finding all the answers, it can be helpful for Enneagram Type Fives to accept the unknown and embrace ambiguity. It's important to realize that not having all the information or answers doesn't mean failure or inadequacy. Instead, consider taking action based on what you do know, and trust your ability to problem-solve as situations arise. Practicing mindfulness and meditation can also help to reduce the need for constant mental stimulation, and give space to simply be in the present moment.

Recognize distractions and prioritize tasks. Be mindful of when you are investing a lot of time and energy in projects or hobbies that don't align with your goals or improve your self-esteem. While it's okay to explore different interests, they can become distractions from what you really need to do. Taking decisive action towards your priorities can bring more confidence than simply acquiring more knowledge or skills.

Share your knowledge and skills. Instead of hoarding your knowledge and skills like a dragon, sitting on a pile of treasure, share them with others. The world needs what you have to offer, and giving to others will only increase your options in the long run. Holding onto things may make you feel secure, but it can ultimately lead to deprivation. Remember that generosity is key to building lasting connections and increasing opportunities.

Enneagram Type Five individuals often struggle with trusting others, being emotionally vulnerable, and making themselves available in different ways. Unfortunately, their fear of relationship problems can often lead to self-fulfilling prophecies (Robledo, 2022). However, it's crucial to recognize that conflicts in relationships are natural, and it's healthier to work through them than to withdraw into isolation. Remember, building connections with others takes time and effort, but the rewards are worth it.

Chapter 9:
Type Six–The Loyalist

Sixes prioritize stability, striving to mitigate risks and align themselves with dependable authorities and institutions. They *remain watchful and attentive, anticipating potential hazards and taking preemptive measures to avoid them.* Their biggest fear is being caught off guard and incapable of protecting themselves from harm. To manage this fear, they try to prepare for any conceivable circumstance (Type Six: The Loyalist, n.d.).

Sixes *exhibit a steadfast, devoted and dependable nature*, preferring to maintain enduring relationships and ideas that provide a sense of security in an unpredictable world. They are considerate and meticulous, proficient at anticipating and guarding against potential difficulties (Type Six: The Loyalist, n.d.). They approach problem-solving systematically, and are adept at playing the role of a critical evaluator.

Although Sixes *excel at operationalizing and executing projects*, they may become entrenched in a pattern of anticipating worst-case scenarios and fixating on future uncertainties.

Key Features in Brief

Type Sixes are known as Loyalists. This moniker *derives from their reputation for being the most trustworthy, devoted, and faithful personality type.* They are known for their reliability, resolute nature, amiability, and a sharp sense of humor (Type Six: The Loyalist, n.d.). These individuals can be thought of as guardians and cautious skeptics, always anticipating and prepared for what's ahead. They are passionate about the greater good, and are capable of seeing what others may overlook.

Sixes are *highly skilled and proficient individuals* who invest a significant amount of effort in developing their abilities. They work diligently, and are meticulous in their approach. Despite their concerns about potential mishaps, they are *remarkably brave and capable in emergencies*. On the other hand, Sixes have difficulty initially trusting others and tend to overthink, worrying about potential problems that could arise at any moment (Type Six: The Loyalist, n.d.).

During their formative years, Sixes *internalize the notion that the world is perilous and that their authority figures cannot provide them with safety*. Consequently, they develop an acute sensitivity to minor signals that may indicate danger, and safeguard themselves by attempting to anticipate every potential threat and hazard.

Type Sixes with a Five wing exhibit attributes akin to those of Type Fives, displaying a *tendency toward independence and introversion*. They are less inclined to place their trust in others, and prefer to maintain their own counsel.

In contrast, Type Sixes with a Seven wing individuals possess qualities resembling those of Type Sevens, such as being *outgoing and sociable*. They excel at meeting people's needs, and often relish being part of organizations or groups.

Are You an Enneagram Type Six?

Would you like to determine whether you possess the traits of an Enneagram Six personality type? If so, continue reading. In this chapter too, I have crafted a five-question quiz to assist you in making this determination. Simply respond with a "yes" or "no" to the following inquiries:

- Do you frequently advocate for the people in your life?
- Do you have a tendency to worry or feel anxious about potential risks or dangers?
- Do you seek feedback from loved ones before making decisions?
- Do you often question authority figures and challenge the status quo?
- When making decisions, do you take into consideration how your actions may affect others?

If you responded "yes" to the majority of the aforementioned questions, it is highly probable that you possess the traits of a Six.

Levels of Development

Enneagram Type Six can be divided into nine levels of development, ranging from healthy to unhealthy.

<u>Healthy Levels:</u>

1. Enneagram Six individuals are at their healthiest and most developed state. They are confident, self-assured, and able to navigate life's challenges with ease. They are able to balance their independence with their need for connection with others. They are able to form symbiotic, interdependent relationships that are based on mutual trust and support. They are reliable and responsible, and are able to create stability and security in their world (Francis & Singletary, 2022).

2. They have a positive and optimistic outlook, and they are able to inspire and motivate others with their confidence and enthusiasm. They are natural leaders, and their belief in themselves and their abilities leads to true courage, positive thinking, leadership, and rich self-expression. They are able to balance their need for security with their desire for independence, and they are able to maintain healthy relationships based on trust, respect, and mutual support (Francis & Singletary, 2022).

3. They often take on leadership roles and become excellent team players. They are confident in their abilities, and possess a strong sense of purpose. They become community builders, responsible and reliable, and build trust with those around them. They are hardworking, persevering, and often sacrifice their own interests for the greater good (Francis & Singletary, 2022).

<u>Average Levels:</u>

1. Sixes start investing their time and energy into whatever they believe will be safe and stable. However, at this level, their constant search for security can lead to anxiety, and a lack of trust in themselves and others. They may become overly attached to rules, procedures, and structures, and fear change and uncertainty. This can cause them to resist new ideas and challenges, becoming inflexible in their thinking (Francis & Singletary, 2022).

2. Sixes may develop a defensive attitude towards others to avoid being burdened with more responsibilities or demands. This can lead to passive-aggressive behavior, where they become evasive, indecisive, and hesitant in their interactions. They may also become cautious, procrastinate, and show ambivalence towards situations, leading to contradictory and mixed signals. The internal confusion they experience can make them react unpredictably, appearing highly reactive, anxious, and negative towards others (Francis & Singletary, 2022).

3. Sixes tend to compensate for their insecurities by adopting a confrontational and defensive attitude towards others. They become sarcastic and belligerent, blaming others for their problems and taking a tough stance towards those they perceive as "outsiders". Despite their tough exterior, they are actually fearful of authority, and highly suspicious of others. This can lead them to become paranoid and conspiratorial, as they try to silence their own fears. Overall, at this level, Enneagram Six types are trapped in a cycle of fear and defensiveness, which can make it difficult for them to form healthy relationships and achieve their goals (Francis & Singletary, 2022).

<u>Unhealthy Levels:</u>

1. Sixes become highly divisive, disparaging, and berate others who do not share their beliefs. They start to feel like they are in a constant state of crisis, and may become overly reactive to even minor challenges or setbacks.

2. At this level, Sixes' behavior becomes increasingly extreme and fanatical, leading to outbursts of anger and aggression. They may become obsessed with conspiracy theories and alternate realities that reinforce their beliefs of being targeted and under attack (The Enneagram Institute, 2014a).

3. Sixes experience extreme anxiety and a sense of impending doom. They feel like they have ruined their security, and are now defenseless against whatever they perceive as a threat. In extreme cases, Enneagram 6 types at level 9 may exhibit self-destructive and suicidal behavior. They may turn to alcoholism, drug overdoses, or engage in other self-abasing behaviors (The Enneagram Institute, 2014a).

Personal Growth Tips For Enneagram Type Sixes

Overcome self-fulfilling prophecies. When you obsess over a fear or a worry, it can become a self-fulfilling prophecy, leading to unintended consequences. This is especially true for people with the Enneagram type Six personality, who tend to allow their fear to lead to extreme paranoia (Personality Type: Six – the Loyalist or Skeptic, n.d.). To avoid this, it's important for Sixes to recognize when they are over-fixating on their fears and to take steps to calm their anxieties before they spiral out of control.

Challenge catastrophic thinking. Enneagram Type Six personalities are known for their tendency to overthink and imagine worst-case scenarios, leading to anxiety and fear (Personality Type: Six – the Loyalist or Skeptic, n.d.). However, this habit of overthinking can be broken by challenging catastrophic thinking and embracing the present moment. Keeping a journal can be an effective tool in this process as it allows you to reflect on your worries and track how often they materialize in reality.

Recognize pessimism. Enneagram Type Six individuals may struggle with managing their emotions, particularly when upset or angry, and may even turn on others and assign blame for their own mistakes or misfortunes. Additionally, their tendency towards pessimism can lead to dark moods and negative thought patterns that may project onto reality, causing further distress. To overcome these patterns, it's important to recognize the effects of pessimism, and the potential for self-sabotage. One way to break this cycle is to actively challenge negative thought patterns and reframe pessimistic views. This can be done through practices such as cognitive-behavioral therapy or mindfulness techniques.

As Type Six individuals confront their anxieties and recognize that the world is not as perilous as they once believed, they can achieve a state of health and inner peace. This newfound sense of self-esteem enables them to trust their own judgments and opinions, as well as stand up for themselves without submitting blindly to authority or feeling the urge to rebel against it. As a result, they can quietly and confidently make meaningful contributions to their community, demonstrating both serenity and courage.

Chapter 10:
Type Seven–The Enthusiast

Sevens are *driven by their thirst for adventure and their aversion to boredom and pain.* They are known for their vibrant and exuberant demeanor, always eager to try new things and explore the world around them.

Their love for excitement and their desire to live life to the fullest make them appear *lively and fun-loving* to others. They have a reputation for being hedonistic, seeking pleasure and avoiding anything that might cause them discomfort.

Sevens are constantly on the move, hopping from one activity to another in their quest to experience everything life has to offer. Their *busy and active lifestyle* is fueled by their fear of missing out on the good things in life and getting stuck in a monotonous routine (Enneagram Type 7, 2022).

Key Features in Brief

Sevens are *brimming with enthusiasm for life*, eagerly embracing new experiences and opportunities. Their inquisitive nature and positive outlook make them the eternal optimists, always seeing the bright side of any situation. This personality type is appropriately named "The Enthusiast" because Sevens approach life with an *unwavering sense of curiosity and adventure.* They are like children in a candy store, excitedly anticipating all the wonderful things life has to offer (Sarikas, 2020).

Sevens are known for their bold and vivacious personalities, tackling challenges with a cheerful determination. *They possess a unique quality, often described as "chutzpah," a combination of brashness and nerve.* Driven by their fear of missing out and their desire to experience everything life has to offer, Sevens embrace their sense of adventure and embark on new journeys with infectious enthusiasm (Enneagram Type 7, 2022).

Type Sevens with a Six wing exhibits some Six-like traits that set them apart from other Sevens. They tend to be *more skeptical, self-disciplined, and practical, often taking a cautious approach to new experiences (Sarikas, 2020).* In times of crisis, they can be reliable and responsible leaders, valuing loyalty and productivity. This type may find fulfillment in careers that allow them to combine their love for adventure with their desire for structure and responsibility. Examples of such professions include pilot, tour guide, detective, travel agent, and journalist.

On the other hand, Type Sevens with an Eight wing , share qualities with the Type Eight, making them *more assertive, confident, and career-focused than other Sevens* (Sarikas, 2020). They have a fearless attitude and encourage others to pursue their goals with vigor. They may find success in careers that allow them to utilize their natural charisma and leadership abilities, such as law enforcement, motivational speaking, television news, management, and sales.

Are You an Enneagram Type Seven?

If you are confused about your personality type and trying to figure out whether you are an Enneagram Type Seven, then here is a quick quiz for you:

- Do you often find yourself daydreaming about new adventures and experiences?
- Do you tend to avoid situations that could potentially cause discomfort or pain?
- Do you get restless or anxious when you're stuck in the same routine for too long?
- Do you enjoy being the life of the party and making people laugh?
- Do you have a hard time committing to long-term plans or projects because you fear missing out on other opportunities?

If you responded "yes" to the majority of the aforementioned questions, it is highly probable that you possess the traits of a Seven.

Levels of Development

Now, let's discuss the different levels of development for the Type Seven Enneagram personalities.

<u>Healthy Levels:</u>

1. When Type Seven Enneagram individuals are at their best, they have the ability to thoroughly absorb their experiences and cultivate a profound sense of gratitude and appreciation for what they have. They become amazed by the simple pleasures of life and are filled with joy and ecstasy. This heightened state of being also allows them to have glimpses of spiritual reality and recognize the unlimited goodness of life (Mukherjee, 2021).

2. One of the defining characteristics of Type Seven individuals is their ability to find joy and pleasure in even the most mundane aspects of life. They possess an insatiable curiosity and are constantly seeking out new and exciting experiences. They thrive on adventure, variety, and spontaneity and are often drawn to activities that offer a rush of adrenaline or excitement. This makes them very lively and vivacious, as they are quick to express their enthusiasm for anything that captures their attention.

3. Individuals are known for their ability to easily achieve success in a variety of areas. They possess a multitude of talents and are often considered to be generalists who can do many different things well. This makes them highly versatile and adaptable, able to excel in a wide range of environments.

<u>Average Levels:</u>

1. Individuals become increasingly restless and desire more options and choices in their lives. They have a strong need for adventure and new experiences, which often leads them to become "worldly wise" and knowledgeable about a wide range of topics. However, this desire for new experiences can also make them less focused and more easily distracted. Their desire for constant stimulation and novelty can also lead to a sense of emptiness from within or dissatisfaction (Mukherjee, 2021).

2. Type Sevens become increasingly hyperactive and struggle to discriminate what they truly need. They have difficulty saying "no" to themselves, and often throw themselves into a constant state of activity in order to stave off boredom. However, this can lead to a lack of focus and follow-through, as they become involved in too many things at once.

3. Individuals may be addicted to various forms of excess, whether that be material possessions, food, or other indulgences. They may become hardened and insensitive, with a sense of jadedness that prevents them from fully appreciating the pleasures of life (The Enneagram Institute, n.d.-b).

<u>Unhealthy Levels</u>

1. Their desire to escape from their anxieties may lead to impulsive and reckless behavior, as they struggle to control their impulses and may act out in ways that are harmful to themselves and others. They may struggle to know when to stop and may fall into the trap of addiction and excess (Mukherjee, 2021).

2. At this level, individuals may be in flight from themselves, avoiding dealing with anxiety and frustration. They may act out their impulses rather than confronting their issues. They may engage in compulsive behaviors, such as manias or other excessive activities, in an attempt to distract themselves from their internal struggles.

3. Type Seven individuals at Level Nine of the Enneagram are characterized by deep despair and a tendency towards self-destruction. They may feel panic-stricken and claustrophobic, struggling to cope with their internal struggles (The Enneagram Institute, n.d.-b).

Personal Growth Tips For Enneagram Type Sevens

Overcome impulsivity. By resisting the urge to act on every impulse, you can focus your energy on what is truly beneficial for you. This can help you avoid engaging in behaviors that may be harmful or counterproductive in the long run.

Learn to embrace pain. Rather than always seeking out distraction and avoiding discomfort, it can be helpful to pause and check in with yourself when you feel the need to escape from difficult emotions. By acknowledging and accepting painful experiences, you can begin to see the beauty and growth that can come from navigating through challenging times.

Cultivate meaningful connections. While it can be tempting to keep things light and avoid uncomfortable conversations, doing so can prevent you from forming deeper and more meaningful connections with others. By being willing to go below the surface and share your authentic self, you can build trust, intimacy, and understanding with those around you.

Practice delayed gratification. It's easy for Sevens to get caught up in the excitement of the moment and want to have everything immediately. However, it's important to remember that not everything needs to be acquired right away. Take a step back, and assess whether the acquisition is truly necessary or just a temporary desire. By delaying gratification, you may find that you are better able to make decisions that align with your long-term goals and values.

Prioritize quality over quantity in your experiences. Sevens have a tendency to seek out as many new and exciting experiences as possible, but it's important to remember that the quality of an experience is more important than the quantity (Enneagram Type 7 - the Adventurer, n.d.). Focus on being fully present in the moment and giving your full attention to the experience at hand, rather than constantly anticipating the next one. By doing so, you may find that you are able to fully appreciate and enjoy the present experience, leading to greater satisfaction in the long run.

Chapter 11: Type Eight–The Challenger

Eights are characterized by their *strong desire to wield power and control,* while avoiding any hint of vulnerability (Alderson, 2022). They project an assertive, confident, and resolute image to those around them. They may come across as intimidating and argumentative at times, but this behavior stems from their need to stand up for their beliefs and defend the vulnerable.

Individuals who identify as Eights *possess remarkable levels of intensity, energy, and determination.* They exude an aura of power and toughness, and they relish the opportunity to demonstrate their strength in the face of adversity. Eights are known for their willingness to engage in open confrontations and their reluctance to back down from a challenge. Eights have been given the moniker of "The Challenger" due to their propensity for embracing challenges themselves and presenting others with opportunities to push themselves beyond their limits.

Eights are the *epitome of "rugged individualists" within the Enneagram framework.* They value their independence above all else and strive to remain self-sufficient, resisting the notion of being beholden to anyone. Eights often reject societal norms and conventions, and they have the ability to overcome their shame, fears, and concerns about consequences (Alderson, 2022). While they may take into account others' opinions of them, Eights remain steadfast in their own convictions and actions. They approach their endeavors with an unwavering determination that can inspire awe, and sometimes even intimidation in those around them.

Key Features in Brief

Challengers are *driven by their goals and take pride in their self-competence*. They blaze their own trail fearlessly and take great satisfaction in their independence and sharp intellect. Even when they stumble, Challengers hold their heads high and pick themselves back up, emerging stronger than before (Doyle, 2022b).

Eights are *fierce advocates for others*, particularly those who are marginalized, oppressed, or vulnerable. They have a strong sense of justice, and *view the world through a lens of "strong" and "weak" individuals*. They identify themselves as strong, and view it as their responsibility to safeguard those who are not. During childhood, Eights may have been *labeled as "bossy" by their peers*. Many Eights come from environments with high levels of conflict and feel the need to develop a robust personality at an early age to cope and survive (Mukherjee, 2023).

Eights with a Seven wing are *more outgoing and exude vitality* thanks to the influence of the playful, extroverted, and life-affirming Type Seven. These Eights find it easier to enjoy life's pleasures, and they are inclined to channel their energy into initiatives that leave behind a positive impact (Mukherjee, 2023).

Eights with a Nine wing become more approachable and measured. They are *less combative and more open to mediating and negotiating.* These Eights often bring a calm, grounded presence to their confidence, are more oriented towards family and warmth, leading by protecting, rather than intimidating others (Mukherjee, 2023).

Are You an Enneagram Type Eight?

Here are five yes or no questions to determine if someone might have an Enneagram Type Eight personality:

- Do you enjoy being in control and taking charge of situations?
- Are you comfortable with confrontation and open conflict?
- Do you have a strong desire to protect and defend the weak and vulnerable?
- Are you hesitant to show vulnerability or admit weakness?
- Do you consider yourself an independent thinker who doesn't follow social conventions easily?

If you responded "yes" to the majority of the aforementioned questions, it is highly probable that you possess the traits of an Eight.

Levels of Development

Let's briefly discuss the nine levels of development of the Type Eight individuals.

<u>Healthy Levels:</u>

1. At their best, Enneagram Type Eight personalities become self-controlled and generous. They learn to be compassionate, patient, and tolerant by surrendering themselves to a higher authority. They exhibit bravery, even risking their lives to achieve their goals, with a desire to leave a lasting impact on the world. In this state, they may attain true heroism and may even be remembered throughout history for their greatness (Doyle, 2022b).

2. At this level, individuals become self-assured, assertive, and strong. They develop the ability to advocate for their needs and desires confidently. Their "can-do" attitude and strong inner drive make them resourceful and determined. They are able to face challenges head-on and have a firm belief in their ability to overcome any obstacles (Doyle, 2022b).

3. Eights become even more confident and assertive. They have a natural ability to take charge and make things happen, becoming decisive and authoritative leaders that others look up to. Eights in this level champion those around them, acting as providers and protectors who carry others with their strength. They are honorable and

take pride in their ability to use their power and influence for the greater good (Doyle, 2022b).

<u>Average Levels:</u>

1. They may become focused on accumulating wealth, power, and prestige, using their assertiveness and dominance to climb the ladder of success. They place great importance on self-sufficiency and financial independence. At this level, they may deny their own emotional needs and focus solely on acquiring resources and asserting their power (Type Eight: The Challenger, n.d.).

2. At this level, Type Eights become preoccupied with maintaining control and power, and may become confrontational and intimidating to protect their position. Fearful of being vulnerable and losing influence, they may resort to using force or manipulation. They start acting like the "boss" whose word is law (Type Eight: The Challenger, n.d.).

3. At this level, they may become vindictive, seeking revenge on those who have crossed them or threatened their power. These individuals may become paranoid and see enemies everywhere. They also struggle to find inner peace and satisfaction, despite their external success and accomplishments (The Enneagram Institute, n.d.-a).

<u>Unhealthy Levels:</u>

1. At this level, individuals with Enneagram Type Eight may reach a state where they fiercely resist any form of control and become absolutely ruthless, adopting a "might makes right" mentality. This could lead to a

criminal or outlaw-like behavior, where they turn into renegades or con-artists.

2. At this level, Type Eights develop grandiose beliefs about their power, invincibility, and capacity to overcome any obstacle. This leads to megalomania, where they feel all-powerful and invulnerable. They take on too much, often recklessly over-extending themselves beyond their capabilities (Type Eight: The Asserter, n.d.).

3. This level represents the extreme and most unhealthy manifestation of Type Eight. At this level, individuals with this personality type may develop delusions of grandeur and a false sense of invincibility, leading them to recklessly overextend themselves. They may become violent, vengeful, and destructive, exhibiting sociopathic tendencies and a complete disregard for the well-being of others. If they perceive themselves to be in danger, they may resort to brutal and murderous behavior rather than surrendering to anyone else. This level generally corresponds to the Antisocial Personality Disorder (The Enneagram Institute, n.d.-a).

Personal Growth Tips For Enneagram Type Eights

Practice mindful decision-making. As a type that relies on their body and instinct, Eights tend to act impulsively on their emotions, leading to hasty decisions and outbursts. It's important for them to pause and reflect on their thoughts and emotions before taking any action. By practicing mindful decision making, Eights can gain better control over their reactions, and avoid impulsive behavior. Taking time to sort through their thoughts and feelings before reacting can lead to more thoughtful and effective decision-making.

Embrace vulnerability as a strength. It's important to understand that vulnerability is not synonymous with weakness. If you find yourself equating the two, take a moment to explore why that is. Connect with your inner child and recognize that vulnerability takes great courage. Instead of fearing it, embrace it as a strength. This can be challenging, but it's a worthwhile pursuit. Through vulnerability, you can experience deeper levels of intimacy and connection with others.

Learn to yield. As an Eight, it can be challenging to yield to others, even in small situations where little is at stake. However, it's crucial to recognize that constantly desiring to dominate others is a sign of an inflating ego, which can lead to more significant conflicts in the future. Therefore, it's essential to learn to yield occasionally, and allow others to have their way without sacrificing your power or needs.

Challenge your negative beliefs. Despite what you might believe in moments of stress, the world is not always against you. While it can be challenging for Eights to let their guard down and accept support from others, it is essential for their growth and well-being. Challenge your negative beliefs, and recognize that there are people in your life who care about you and want to support you.

Balance your intensity with self-care and respect for others' boundaries. As an Eight, you have a passionate zest for life that can lead to overindulgence and boundary-crossing (Enneagram Type 8 Description, n.d.). It's important to find a balance by practicing self-care and respecting others' boundaries. Don't hesitate to seek the help of a friend or partner to remind you when you're going too far. Remember that moderation can be a life saver, and neglecting your health can have serious consequences. Prioritize your well-being and that of those around you.

Chapter 12:
Type Nine–The Peacemaker

Nines are known for their *peaceful and harmonious nature*, which makes them pleasant companions (The Enneagram Type 9: The Peacemaker, 2022). They prefer to avoid conflicts and emotional turmoil and strive to maintain a serene inner state. However, they can sometimes be firm in their opinions. Despite their tendency to adjust to their environment, they have an aversion to being instructed and might respond in a non-confrontational manner when they sense pressure.

One of the *biggest fears of Nines is being overly dependent on others and potentially alienating them.* To avoid this, they tend to go along with what others want, striving to be accepted and valued by those around them.

The personality type Nine is referred to as The Peacemaker because they are *deeply committed to achieving inner and outer peace,* not just for themselves, but also for those around them (The Enneagram Type 9: The Peacemaker, 2022). Nines are often spiritual seekers with a strong desire to connect with both the universe and others.

Key Features in Brief

Peacemakers *possess a gentle and amiable nature,* making them skilled at mediating and counseling within a group of friends or colleagues. They put in a lot of effort behind the scenes to ensure that the group's harmony remains steady and undisturbed. Since childhood, Peacemakers have been adept at getting along with their classmates, and they make valuable contributions to group projects. They have a knack for viewing a situation from multiple perspectives, and refrain from hastily drawing conclusions (Wagner, 1980).

Nines are *unassuming and modest individuals* who prioritize maintaining stability. They appreciate and value the small things in life and take pleasure in the simple joys. Nines are widely admired by almost everyone for their inclusive and considerate nature, providing a safe environment for people to express themselves freely. However, they *tend to suppress their own opinions and desires*, often saying yes to others before considering their own needs. They tend to avoid conflict, even when it may be beneficial for their personal growth (Wagner, 1980).

When a Nine has an Eight wing , they receive several characteristics of the assertive nature associated with the type Eight personality. Nines with an Eight wing tend to be *more*

energetic, self-assured, and pragmatic. They also have a greater ability to tap into their anger and are more willing to confront conflicts.

When a Nine has a One wing, the Type One personality influences them to *become more disciplined, organized, and self-assured.* Having a strong One wing can greatly assist Nines in discovering their own unique voice, as they tend to hold themselves to a higher standard of morality and may be more inclined to express their viewpoints to others.

Are You an Enneagram Type Nine?

Here's a yes or no personality quiz for Type Nine:

- Do you value inner peace and harmony in your relationships and surroundings?
- Do you sometimes struggle to express your own opinions and desires in order to keep the peace with others?
- Do you have a tendency to procrastinate or delay making decisions?
- Do you feel a strong connection to spirituality or a higher power?
- Are you usually easy-going and agreeable in group settings?

If you responded "yes" to the majority of the aforementioned questions, it is highly probable that you possess the traits of a Nine.

Levels of Development

Let's explore the nine levels of development of the Type Nine Enneagram:

<u>Healthy Levels:</u>

1. Type Nines become self-assured and experience a deep sense of fulfillment, achieving a state of contentment and equanimity because they are present and fully engaged with themselves. They possess a paradoxical quality of being at one with themselves, which allows them to form more profound relationships with others. They feel intensely alive and are fully connected to themselves and those around them (Hook et al., 2020).

2. Nines have a heightened appreciation for the beauty of everyday life and take pleasure in the simple things. They are patient, unpretentious, and good-natured, embodying a genuine kindness that stems from their desire to create a harmonious environment. They are not motivated by material wealth or social status, but rather by the desire to live a peaceful and fulfilling life (Hook et al., 2020).

3. Nines possess a keen ability to see the bigger picture and understand the perspectives of others. They are adept at finding common ground and creating a peaceful resolution to conflicts. They have a talent for synthesizing different opinions and ideas, creating a unified vision that everyone can agree on.

<u>Average Levels:</u>

1. Nines tend to fall into conventional roles and expectations, not asserting their own individuality and creativity. They become passive, allowing others to make decisions for them, and go along with the status quo without questioning it. They may use philosophies and stock sayings to deflect others and avoid confronting their own issues.

2. Nines become more disengaged from reality and become increasingly complacent. They tend to become mentally hazy and start indulging in comforting fantasies to distract themselves from reality. They become indifferent to the world around them, unwilling to exert themselves or make any significant effort (Hook et al., 2020).

3. Type Nine individuals become increasingly focused on maintaining peace and avoiding conflict, even at the cost of their own needs and desires. They may become stubborn and fatalistic, feeling as though they have no control over their circumstances or the people around them. They may avoid taking action to address problems, preferring to minimize them or to simply hope that they will go away on their own.

Unhealthy levels:

1. Type Nines may neglect their responsibilities and become a danger to themselves and others. They may feel powerless, helpless, and trapped in their own world, unable to see a way out. Others may become frustrated and angry by their lack of action and disconnection from reality.

2. Type Nines experience pathological dissociation, in which they attempt to block out anything that could potentially affect them, leading to a complete loss of connection with reality (The Enneagram Institute, 2021). They become depersonalized, numb, and lose the ability to function in their daily lives. In this state, Nines may feel as if they are in a dreamlike state or watching themselves from afar. They may struggle to remember things or have difficulty focusing, making it hard to carry out even basic tasks.

3. The Type Nine individual has completely abandoned themselves and their desires, becoming a shattered shell of a person. They may have extreme difficulty making decisions or taking any action, and may rely heavily on others to make decisions for them. They may also experience hallucinations or delusions, and have a distorted sense of reality (The Enneagram Institute, 2021).

Personal Growth Tips For Enneagram Type Nines

Acknowledge your own desires. Nines tend to prioritize the needs and desires of others, often neglecting their own (Doyle, 2022c). They may feel that their own wants and needs are not as important as those of others, and they fear that asserting themselves will lead to conflict. However, this habit of neglecting themselves can limit their potential for personal growth and fulfillment. To break this habit, Nines need to pay attention to their own wants and needs. This means taking the time to reflect on their thoughts and feelings without any external influence. They can start by asking themselves questions like, "what do I want?" and "what do I need?". They can also try journaling or meditating to connect with their inner selves and gain a deeper understanding of their own desires.

Shift your perspective on conflict. Instead of immediately avoiding any kind of conflict, try to reframe your thinking about it. What might seem like a major disagreement to you might actually be a minor issue to the other person. Before disengaging from the situation, take a moment to remind yourself that the stakes are often lower than you initially perceive them to be.

Build assertiveness. If you find it challenging to be direct and assertive in conversations, start practicing with the people you feel most comfortable with. Gradually, work your way up to communicating more assertively in everyday situations. This will help you build the confidence to speak up for yourself when you need to. Remember, being assertive is not the same as being aggressive. Assertiveness involves expressing your thoughts and feelings in a clear and respectful manner, while still being open to listening to others. It allows you to set healthy boundaries and take control of your life. So, don't be afraid to start small, working your way up to more challenging situations. The more you practice being assertive, the more natural and effortless it will become.

Embrace discomfort as a path to growth. Instead of avoiding challenging situations, try staying with them and seeing them through to the other side. Remember that growth often comes from discomfort, and that facing difficult situations can help you become a stronger and more resilient person. Focus on the positive outcomes that can come from staying with something difficult, rather than on the discomfort in the moment. With practice, you can learn to embrace discomfort as a path to growth and transformation.

When you encounter a decision that feels overwhelming, resist the urge to seek advice from others right away. Instead, take some time to reflect on your own thoughts and feelings. What do you truly want in this situation? What are your personal values and priorities? Trust yourself to make the decision that aligns with your own desires and needs. Remember, it's okay to make mistakes and learn from them. Taking ownership of your decisions can lead to a stronger sense of self-confidence and self-reliance.

ENNEAGRAM AND PERSONAL DEVELOPMENT

Chapter 13:
Using the Enneagram for Self-Discovery

The idea of self-discovery may conjure up images of meditating while burning incense, but in reality, it's a practical, ongoing journey that ebbs and flows with the ups and downs of life. There are times, like this past month, when I naturally feel more introspective and reflective. While I need daily moments of quiet reflection, these more intense periods prompt a deeper search for self and my place in relation to the divine.

The diversity of human experience fascinates me. We can be in the same moment, yet perceive it differently based on our unique perspectives and temperaments. My life experiences have heightened my awareness of the importance of understanding my own lens, and that of those I care for. It's a beautiful journey, though I acknowledge that uncovering the truth about myself can be bitter at times, as it brings to light my hidden fears, shame, and anger. However, this is where I've found the deepest healing and self-compassion.

Our personal outlook on life shapes our preferences and actions, from our taste in food to how we spend our leisure time. Though our individual perspectives define us, they can also limit our ability to appreciate alternative viewpoints, hindering our personal growth and development.

Why is Self-Discovery Important?

Self-discovery can have several benefits, including enhancing one's self-awareness and intuition, as well as increasing self-worth and the ability to stand up for oneself (Carroll & Ivanoff, 2016). Additionally, self-discovery can help individuals identify and name their emotions, understand their sources, and reframe negative self-talk into positive self-talk. This process can also help people set boundaries in relationships by understanding their values and what they are willing to tolerate. Moreover, self-discovery can help individuals identify their fears and work towards overcoming them, as well as diagnose and work on bad habits while building better ones. Finally, self-discovery can help people set more meaningful goals by gaining a better understanding of their desires and aspirations (McLeod, 2022).

Let's Start the Inner Work

The Enneagram is a powerful tool for self-discovery that can help individuals understand their unconscious patterns and motivations. However, the Enneagram is not just a personality typing system; it is also a tool for inner work and personal growth. The Enneagram can assist individuals in identifying their fears, desires, and automatic responses, which can be challenging but can also lead to personal transformation.

The inner work with the Enneagram involves becoming aware of one's habitual patterns, emotional triggers, and automatic responses. By recognizing these patterns, individuals can begin to understand the root causes of their behaviors, and how they relate to their Enneagram type. This self-awareness can lead to a greater sense of empathy and compassion towards oneself and others.

Furthermore, the Enneagram offers a unique approach to personal growth by emphasizing the integration of all nine types. Individuals can learn from the strengths and weaknesses of each type and incorporate them into their personal development. For example, an individual who identifies as a Type Five can learn from the Type Two by exploring the importance of relationships and connection in their lives.

The Enneagram also highlights the importance of practices such as mindfulness, self-compassion, and self-reflection in personal growth. These practices can help individuals become more present and aware of their thoughts, emotions, and behaviors, and can also aid in breaking free from limiting beliefs and patterns.

In conclusion, the Enneagram can be a powerful tool for individuals looking to embark on a journey of self-discovery and personal growth. The inner work with the Enneagram involves becoming aware of one's habitual patterns, emotional triggers, and automatic responses, and utilizing this knowledge to develop greater self-awareness, empathy, and compassion. By integrating the strengths and weaknesses of all nine types and engaging in mindfulness, self-compassion, and self-reflection practices, individuals can unlock their full potential and transform their lives.

Potential Challenges and Pitfalls of Using Enneagram for Self-Discovery

While the Enneagram can be a powerful tool for self-discovery and personal growth, there are also potential challenges and pitfalls that individuals may encounter when using this system.

One of the main challenges is the risk of mistyping. Identifying one's Enneagram type can be a complex and nuanced process that involves self-reflection, self-awareness, and sometimes the guidance of a trained professional. However, there is a risk of individuals mistyping themselves or others, which can lead to inaccurate information and hinder personal growth (Belle, 2020).

Another potential challenge is the risk of becoming overly identified with one's Enneagram type (The Enneagram Model Explained and Why It Isn't Always a Good Idea, n.d.). While understanding one's Enneagram type can provide valuable insights into one's patterns and behaviors, it is important to remember that the Enneagram is not meant to define individuals as static or limited beings. Instead, it is a tool for self-awareness and personal growth, and individuals should strive to cultivate a sense of openness and flexibility in their approach.

Additionally, the Enneagram can be a deeply personal and emotional journey, and it may bring up difficult or uncomfortable feelings for individuals. It is important to approach this process with self-compassion, and a willingness to explore and work through these feelings.

Another pitfall of using the Enneagram for self-discovery is the temptation to use it to justify or reinforce negative patterns or behaviors (The Enneagram Model Explained and Why It Isn't Always a Good Idea, n.d.). For example, an individual who identifies as a Type Eight may use their Enneagram type to justify aggressive or confrontational behavior, rather than using it as a tool for understanding and transforming those patterns.

Finally, it is important to remember that the Enneagram is just one tool for self-discovery and personal growth. It is not a substitute for professional therapy or other forms of support, and individuals should seek out additional resources as needed (Belle, 2020).

All in all, while the Enneagram can be a valuable tool for self-discovery and personal growth, it is important to approach it with mindfulness, self-awareness, and a willingness to work through potential challenges and pitfalls. By staying open to the process and seeking out additional support as needed, individuals can use the Enneagram to unlock their full potential and transform their lives.

Chapter 14:
Understanding Your
Strengths and Weaknesses

The Enneagram is not just about identifying your type, but also about understanding the interconnectedness of all the types. Each type has a unique perspective and gifts to offer, and by recognizing and appreciating these differences, you can build stronger and more diverse relationships. It isn't just about putting a label on your personality; it's about discovering your unique strengths and weaknesses. It requires being honest with yourself about areas where you struggle, as well as areas where you shine. Remember, it's totally okay not to be perfect all the time, or to fit perfectly into one Enneagram type. Your instincts may lead you in that direction, but the more you learn about yourself, the more control you can exercise over your choices. So, don't worry if you don't always excel—that's all part of the journey!

How Does the Enneagram Help You Understand Your Strengths and Weaknesses?

Have you ever wondered what drives your behavior and thought patterns, or what areas you need to work on to improve yourself? The Enneagram is a powerful tool that can help you gain self-awareness and understand your strengths and weaknesses. But, you have already learned this in the previous chapters.

By identifying your Enneagram type, you can gain a deeper understanding of your core motivations and behaviors. This can help you identify areas where you need to focus your personal development efforts, such as improving your communication skills or emotional intelligence.

Research has shown that the Enneagram can be a valuable tool for self-development and personal growth (Lapid-Bogda, 2004). One study found that individuals who used the Enneagram as part of their personal development process reported significant improvements in their emotional intelligence, communication skills, and ability to work effectively with others (Ritz & Seville, 2016).

Each of the nine Enneagram types has a distinct set of core motivations and behaviors, which can help you understand why you think and act the way you do. For example, if you identify as an Enneagram Type One, also known as the Perfectionist, you may have a strong desire to do things right and a tendency to be critical of yourself and others. By understanding these traits, you can work on developing self-compassion, and learn to focus on progress, rather than perfection (Doyle, 2022a).

If you identify as an Enneagram Type Two, also known as the Helper, you may have a strong desire to help others and be liked by them. With this knowledge, you can work on setting healthy boundaries and taking care of your own needs (Doyle, 2022a).

Tips to Work On Your Strengths

One approach is to focus on developing your *"growth points,"* which are the aspects of your Enneagram type that are less developed or underutilized (Don Richard Riso & Hudson, 1999). By focusing on these growth points, you can expand your range of behavior and develop new skills and strengths.

For example, if you are an Enneagram Type Five, also known as the Investigator, you may tend to withdraw from others and focus on your own thoughts and ideas. Your growth point may be to develop more connection with others, and to learn to express your ideas and feelings more openly. By intentionally working on these areas, you can become more well-rounded and effective in your personal and professional life.

Another approach is to focus on developing your "*wings*," which are the adjacent Enneagram types that influence your behavior (Don Richard Riso & Hudson, 1999). For example, if you are an Enneagram Type Two, also known as the Helper, your wings are either Type One, the Perfectionist, or Type Three, the Achiever. By focusing on the positive traits of your wings, such as the Perfectionist's attention to detail, or the Achiever's drive and ambition, you can develop new strengths and expand your range of behavior.

Research has shown that using the Enneagram in this way can lead to significant improvements in personal growth and well-being (Ritz & Seville, 2016). By focusing on your growth points and wings and intentionally working on developing your strengths, you can become more self-aware and effective in your personal and professional life.

Tips to Overcome Your Weaknesses

In addition to developing your strengths, the Enneagram can also be used to identify and overcome your weaknesses. By gaining a deeper understanding of your Enneagram type and the patterns of behavior that result from it, you can work to overcome negative behaviors and improve your overall well-being.

One way to do this is to focus on your "*stress point*," which is the Enneagram type that you tend to adopt when you are under stress (Don Richard Riso & Hudson, 1999). When you are in a state of stress, you may exhibit behaviors that are unhealthy or counterproductive. By identifying your stress point and learning to recognize when you are in a state of stress, you can work to overcome these negative behaviors and return to a more healthy state.

For example, if you are an Enneagram Type One, also known as the Perfectionist, your stress point may be Type Four, the Individualist. When you are under stress, you may become more emotional, withdrawing from others. By learning to recognize when you are in a state of stress and focusing on healthy coping mechanisms, such as exercise or meditation, you can overcome these negative behaviors, and return to a more balanced state.

Another approach is to focus on your "*blind spot*," which is the aspect of your personality that you may be unaware of, or may not fully understand (Don Richard Riso & Hudson, 1999). By identifying your blind spot and working to become more aware of it, you can overcome negative behaviors and become more well-rounded.

For example, if you are an Enneagram Type Seven, also known as the Enthusiast, your blind spot may be the negative impact that your impulsivity and restlessness can have on others. By working to become more aware of these negative behaviors, and developing strategies to control them, you can become more effective in your personal and professional relationships.

Research has shown that using the Enneagram in this way can lead to significant improvements in personal growth and well-being (Grahek, 2018). By focusing on your stress point and blind spot and intentionally working on overcoming your weaknesses, you can become more self-aware and effective in your personal and professional life.

One of the *key benefits of the Enneagram is that it promotes self-acceptance and self-compassion.* By recognizing that each Enneagram type has its own unique strengths and challenges, you can begin to embrace your own personality and stop comparing yourself to others. Instead of feeling shame or guilt about your weaknesses, you can view them as opportunities for growth and learning.

Another benefit of the Enneagram is that it *promotes empathy and understanding towards others.* By gaining a deeper understanding of the motivations and behaviors of people with different Enneagram types, you can become more effective in your personal and professional relationships. You can learn to communicate more effectively, collaborate more productively, and resolve conflicts more peacefully.

Finally, it's worth noting that *the Enneagram is not a magic solution to all of life's problems.* While it can be a powerful tool, it's important to remember that each individual is unique and complex, and that no personality system can fully capture the complexity of human nature. However, the Enneagram can help you identify patterns of behavior that may be holding you back, and provide a roadmap for personal transformation. By recognizing your patterns and working to break free from them, you can experience greater freedom and fulfillment in your life.

Chapter 15: Using the Enneagram for Personal Growth and Development

By discovering your Enneagram type and unpacking its implications, we can gain insight into ourselves and others, cultivate self-awareness, and develop healthier relationships. This chapter will guide you through the process of using the Enneagram for personal growth and development. Whether you're new to the Enneagram, or have been studying it for years, you'll find practical tips, exercises, and insights that can help you on your journey. *Throughout this chapter, we'll emphasize that the Enneagram is not a one-size-fits-all solution*, but rather a dynamic framework that can be adapted to your unique needs and goals.

Start With Understanding Your Personality Type

Investigate your core traits and tendencies. Now that you have reached this portion of the book, I am assuming that you know which Enneagram type you fall into. So, once you have identified that, it's crucial that you figure out the underlying behaviors and motivations that shape your personality.

Examine the wings and variations. You are already aware of the fact that every Enneagram type has its own set of distinctive traits, but each type has a certain degree of variability within it too. For example, in the previous chapters, you learned about "wings", adjacent Enneagram types that modify and influence your dominant type. Then there are also subtypes, or "instinctual variants", that reflect different expressions of your Enneagram type based on your primary survival strategy. By now you should be researching these aspects of your personality to get a better grasp of what your Enneagram means.

Recognize your levels of development. The Enneagram is not just a static system of nine types, but a dynamic model that accounts for different levels of psychological health and growth. In the previous chapters, I have covered the levels of development in great detail and how each type can manifest at different stages of your life under different circumstances. Your task is to understand these different levels of development, so that you can understand your own patterns of behavior, and identify the areas in your life that qualify for personal growth.

Explore your integration and disintegration points. Each Enneagram type has two other types that it connects to through its "integration" and "disintegration" points. These points reveal the ways in which your type can expand or contract under stress or in times of growth. You need to understand how you can access the positive qualities of your integration point and avoid the pitfalls of your disintegration point, thus enhancing your personal development.

Embrace your unique path. Finally, it's important to remember that the Enneagram is a tool for self-discovery, not a prescriptive formula for personal growth. Hence, your personality type is only one facet of your identity. By integrating your Enneagram insights with other practices and perspectives, you can create a holistic approach to personal growth and development.

Identify Your Triggers and Patterns

One of the most powerful aspects of the Enneagram is its ability to help us recognize our unconscious patterns of behavior, including the triggers that set off our automatic reactions. By becoming more aware of our triggers and patterns, we can start to take more intentional and conscious actions, rather than simply reacting from a place of habit. For instance, if you're a Type Two, you might have a tendency to overextend yourself to help others, which can lead to burnout and resentment if you're not careful (Chestnut, 2013).

To recognize your triggers and patterns, it can be helpful to reflect on your past experiences, and identify recurring themes or situations that trigger strong emotional reactions or unhelpful behaviors. You might also pay attention to your physical sensations, such as tension in your body or racing thoughts, as these can be indicators of an impending trigger or pattern. Once you've identified your triggers and patterns, you can start to explore healthier responses and strategies for managing them.

One useful tool for recognizing triggers and patterns is the Enneagram's concept of the "holy ideas" and "virtues" associated with each type. These qualities represent the positive aspects of each type's underlying motivations and can serve as a guide for healthier behavior. For instance, if you're a Type Four, your holy idea is that you are inherently connected to all things, while your virtue is equanimity. By focusing on these qualities, you can shift your attention away from your triggers and towards more constructive and empowering behaviors (Don Richard Riso & Hudson, 1999).

In addition, working with a therapist or coach who is trained in the Enneagram can be a helpful way to deepen your understanding of your triggers and patterns and develop personalized strategies for growth.

Address Your Desires and Core Fears

At the heart of the Enneagram system are the core fears and desires that drive each type's behavior. By understanding these underlying motivations, you can gain insight into why you think, feel, and act the way you do. For instance, if you're a Type Five, you might have a deep fear of being overwhelmed or depleted, which can lead you to hoard resources and withdraw from social situations (Palmer, 1991).

To address your core fears and desires, it can be helpful to reflect on how they show up in your life and relationships. You might ask yourself questions like: What situations trigger my fear? What activities or experiences bring me a sense of satisfaction or fulfillment? By exploring these questions, you can start to develop a deeper awareness of your underlying motivations and how they impact your behavior.

One helpful tool for addressing core fears and desires is the Enneagram's concept of the "passions" and "fixations" associated with each type. These qualities represent the negative aspects of each type's underlying motivations and can help you recognize when you're getting caught up in unhelpful patterns of thought or behavior. For instance, if you're a Type Nine, your passion is sloth, which can manifest as a tendency to avoid conflict or prioritize others' needs over your own. By recognizing when you're slipping into a state of sloth, you can take steps to become more proactive and assertive in your life (Don Richard Riso & Hudson, 1999).

Develop Healthy Coping Mechanisms

One of the benefits of using the Enneagram for personal growth and development is that it can help you identify and develop healthier coping mechanisms. Each Enneagram type has its own set of strengths and weaknesses, and by recognizing these patterns, you can start to build more effective ways of coping with stress and adversity.

For instance, if you're a Type Three, you might have a tendency to push yourself to achieve at all costs, which can lead to burnout and a sense of disconnection from your true self (Chestnut, 2013). To develop healthier coping mechanisms, you might explore practices like mindfulness meditation, which can help you tune into your inner experience, and build resilience in the face of stress.

Another helpful tool for developing healthy coping mechanisms is the Enneagram's concept of the "wings" associated with each type. These qualities represent the traits that are adjacent to your core type and can serve as a source of support and balance. For instance, if you're a Type Six with a Five wing, you might lean on your analytical and problem-solving skills to navigate difficult situations (Don Richard Riso & Hudson, 1999).

In addition, working with a therapist or coach who is trained in the Enneagram can be a powerful way to develop healthier coping mechanisms. By exploring your type's unique strengths and challenges, you can identify concrete steps towards building resilience, improving your relationships, and achieving your goals. Therapists and coaches who use the Enneagram may also incorporate other evidence-based practices, such as cognitive-behavioral therapy or mindfulness-based stress reduction, to help you build a well-rounded toolkit for coping with life's challenges.

Continue Your Enneagram Journey

Continuing your Enneagram journey involves ongoing self-awareness and growth. Here are some ways to continue your Enneagram journey:

- Attend workshops and seminars: There are many workshops and seminars available that delve deeper into Enneagram theory and offer guidance on how to apply it to your personal growth and development. These events can help you gain a better understanding of your type and how to navigate your inner world.
- Read books: There are many books available on the Enneagram that offer insight into each type and how to work with the challenges and strengths associated with each. Reading Enneagram books can also help you deepen your understanding of the Enneagram system as a whole.
- Work with a coach or therapist: Working with a certified Enneagram coach or therapist can provide personalized

guidance and support as you navigate your Enneagram journey. They can help you identify patterns and work through challenges, as well as offer tools and resources to help you continue your personal growth.

- Join a community: Joining an Enneagram community can provide support and encouragement as you continue your journey. Whether it's attending a local Enneagram meetup group or joining an online community, connecting with others who share your interest in the Enneagram can help you feel more connected and supported in your journey.

Developing new behaviors to replace old, unhelpful habits is key to finding personal freedom. While this process may take time, and there is no quick fix, the Enneagram can be a valuable tool for transformation. However, it is important to approach this process without judgment, recognizing that it may be challenging to let go of ingrained habits that have been developed over years. With patience and commitment, it is possible to create healthier habits and live a more fulfilling life.

ENNEAGRAM AND RELATIONSHIPS

Chapter 16:
Understanding and Relating to Others

As you already know, the Enneagram is a model of human personality that describes nine interconnected types, each with its own set of core motivations, fears, and desires. It is used not only as a tool for personal growth and self-awareness, but also as a means of understanding and relating to others.

The system is based on the idea that *each person has a dominant personality type* that influences their thoughts, feelings, and behaviors. This type is shaped by a combination of genetic, environmental, and cultural factors, and reflects the unique ways in which a person navigates the world around them.

Understanding the Enneagram can be helpful in relating to others because it provides a framework for understanding the underlying motivations and fears that drive people's behavior. By recognizing the different Enneagram types, we can gain insight into *why people act the way they do, and develop greater empathy and compassion for their struggles and challenges.*

One study found that individuals who completed an Enneagram-based training program reported increased self-awareness and a greater ability to understand and communicate with others (Abdel-Khalek, 2013). Another study found that the Enneagram was helpful in improving communication and teamwork in the workplace (Vidal & Gómez, 2016).

Overall, the Enneagram can be a useful tool for individuals and organizations seeking to improve interpersonal relationships, communication, and collaboration. By understanding and relating to others through the lens of the Enneagram, we can build stronger, more fulfilling connections with the people around us.

Developing Empathy and Compassion

The Enneagram provides a valuable tool for understanding behaviors that may irritate or frustrate us. For example, we may find it difficult to get along with overly competitive people, or those who dominate conversations. The Enneagram can help us understand the deeper motivations behind these behaviors, leading to greater compassion and mercy towards others. Rather than avoiding these behaviors, we can look at them with understanding and empathy.

As an example, I once worked with a colleague who constantly corrected others in front of clients. Initially, I assumed the person was simply trying to compete for their position. However, after learning their Enneagram type, which was Type One, I realized that the corrections were motivated by a desire for correctness, rather than malice or ambition. Understanding this helped me become more patient and sympathetic towards them.

The Enneagram is particularly useful for developing empathy towards others. I prefer to believe that empathy is the Enneagram's greatest feature. In addition to understanding others, the Enneagram can also help individuals understand themselves. By identifying the core motivations behind their behaviors, individuals can gain insight into their deepest desires and sins. This can help them address the root causes of their struggles, and seek growth, as you read in the previous chapters of this book.

Some people believe that Enneagram-type tests have drawbacks because of the potential to excuse behavior as "just how you are." I acknowledge that there is a tendency to utilize its behavioral explanations to avoid altering. A person of type 7 may utilize the Enneagram as a justification for reckless and shallow behavior. If someone points out the destructive potential of their habits, they may invoke their "enthusiast" label and dismiss legitimate warnings.

However, recognizing your greatest vulnerability can also be your greatest advantage. Type Nines are considered the Peacemaker. The downside of their personality type is avoiding conflict in order to have a perceived peaceful environment. However, when Type Nines recognize this tendency, they can serve as an important component in the community's healing.

At its most developed, the Nine can perceive tension, they also have the ability to assist people in addressing issues in a productive manner.

Learning to Integrate Enneagram in Your Interpersonal Interactions

Recognize the Enneagram type that others have. Recognizing Enneagram types in others can be a powerful tool for building stronger relationships and improving communication. By understanding someone's Enneagram type, you can tailor your communication style to better suit their needs, avoid misunderstandings, and build trust and empathy. One way to begin identifying someone's Enneagram type is to pay attention to their behavior patterns. Each type has its own set of behaviors that are associated with their core motivation (Brown, 2023). For example, a Type One is often perfectionistic and detail-oriented, while a Type Two is often focused on pleasing others and meeting their needs.

Another way to identify someone's Enneagram type is to listen to the language they use to describe themselves and others (Lee, 2015). Each type has its own language and way of seeing the world. For example, a Type Four may use phrases like "I feel so misunderstood" or "no one truly gets me," while a Type Eight may use language that is more forceful and direct. By paying attention to the language someone uses, you can get a better sense of their Enneagram type.

It is important to note that identifying someone's Enneagram type should not be used as a way to label or stereotype them. Rather, it should be used as a tool to deepen your understanding of them and their behavior (Lee, 2015).

Manage conflicts with understanding of the Enneagram. Managing conflict can be tough—and I can't agree more with you on that—but having an understanding of the Enneagram can help to navigate difficult situations with more empathy and understanding. Here are some ways to use the Enneagram to manage conflict:

- When conflict arises, take a step back and try to identify the other person's Enneagram type. This can help you understand their perspective and motivations, which can help to defuse the situation.

- Each Enneagram type has their own communication style, and understanding this can help you communicate more effectively during conflict. For example, Type Nines tend to avoid conflict, while Type Eights are more confrontational.

- Conflict often arises due to underlying issues that have not been addressed. By understanding each person's Enneagram type, you can better understand what these underlying issues might be. For example, a Type One may be driven by a desire for perfection, while a Type Four may struggle with feelings of inadequacy.

Using Enneagram understanding in daily life involves applying the insights gained from knowing one's own and other's Enneagram types to improve personal and interpersonal relationships. This can include paying attention to one's own patterns of behavior and identifying how they relate to one's Enneagram type, as well as recognizing the Enneagram types of others in order to understand and empathize with their motivations and actions, all of which you have already learned in this chapter and now, you need to start applying them in your own life.

Chapter 17:
Understanding the Enneagram in Teams and Organizations

Understanding the Enneagram in teams and organizations can be a game-changer when it comes to *building successful and harmonious work environments*. The Enneagram is a powerful personality typing tool that can help individuals gain a deeper understanding of themselves, and their colleagues. It provides a framework for identifying and working with personality traits that can enhance or hinder individual and team performance.

In this chapter, we will explore the Enneagram system and its applications in the context of teams and organizations. By the end of this chapter, you will have a solid understanding of how the Enneagram can be used to enhance team dynamics, foster communication, and improve performance in the workplace. You will also gain insight into strategies of successful Enneagram implementations and understand how to avoid common misconceptions that can undermine its effectiveness.

Benefits of Enneagram in the Workplace Setting

The Enneagram offers numerous benefits to teams and organizations when used as a tool for understanding individual and team dynamics.

- The Enneagram provides a common language for discussing personality types and traits, allowing team members to communicate more effectively and work together more cohesively. According to a study by Palmer, the Enneagram can help team members develop greater self-awareness and empathy for others, leading to improved communication and collaboration (Palmer, 1991).
- The Enneagram can enhance individual and team performance by providing insights into motivation, decision-making, and behavior patterns. In a study by Kark, Shamir, and Chen, the Enneagram was found to be a useful tool for leadership development, providing leaders with a greater understanding of their own strengths and weaknesses, and how to better manage their teams (Kark et al., 2003).
- The Enneagram can be used to create more effective teams by balancing individual strengths and weaknesses.

As noted by Lapid-Bogda, the Enneagram can help teams identify gaps in skills and knowledge, allowing for the creation of more well-rounded teams (Lapid-Bogda, 2004). By leveraging the unique strengths of each team member, the Enneagram can lead to higher levels of team performance.

- The Enneagram can facilitate personal and professional growth by providing a roadmap for self-improvement. By understanding their Enneagram type and corresponding strengths and weaknesses, team members can identify areas for personal and professional development. This can lead to greater job satisfaction, higher levels of engagement, and improved performance (Rickerd, 2019).

Thus, by leveraging the insights provided by the Enneagram, teams and organizations can build stronger, more cohesive teams and create a more positive and productive work environment.

Implementation Strategies

Implementing the Enneagram in teams and organizations requires careful planning and consideration. Here are some strategies for successfully integrating the Enneagram into your team or organizational culture:

Define the purpose and goals. Before implementing the Enneagram, it's important to clearly define the purpose and goals of using it in your organization. This could include improving communication, building stronger teams, or developing leadership skills. Defining the purpose and goals will help ensure that everyone involved is aligned and working towards a common objective.

Educate your team. Introducing the Enneagram to your team requires education and training. Consider offering workshops or training sessions to help team members understand the Enneagram system and their own Enneagram type. This will help create a shared language and understanding of the Enneagram within your organization.

Encourage self-discovery. Encourage team members to explore and discover their own Enneagram type through self-reflection and assessment tools. This can be done individually, or as a team-building activity. Encouraging self-discovery will help team members develop greater self-awareness and empathy for others.

Create a safe and supportive environment. Implementing the Enneagram can be a sensitive and personal topic. Creating a safe and supportive environment where team members feel comfortable discussing their Enneagram type and related issues is crucial to success. Consider setting ground rules for discussions, such as confidentiality and respect.

Address resistance and misconceptions. Some team members may be resistant or skeptical about the Enneagram. Addressing misconceptions and concerns upfront can help mitigate resistance and build buy-in. Consider addressing common misconceptions, such as the Enneagram being a personality test, and clarify that it is a tool for self-discovery and personal growth.

Enhance team dynamics. Once team members have a better understanding of the Enneagram system, use it to enhance team dynamics. For example, identify each team member's Enneagram type and corresponding strengths and weaknesses, and use this knowledge to build more effective teams, delegate tasks, and provide feedback.

Make the Enneagram part of your organizational culture. Finally, to maximize the benefits of the Enneagram, make it part of your organizational culture. This can include incorporating the Enneagram into performance evaluations, leadership development programs, and team-building activities.

Learn to Avoid the Pitfalls

While the Enneagram can be a powerful tool for improving team dynamics and organizational culture, there are also some common pitfalls and misconceptions to be aware of. In this section, we'll explore these pitfalls and offer some friendly advice on how to avoid them.

Pitfall 1: Enneagram Typing Stereotypes

One common pitfall is falling into the trap of Enneagram typing stereotypes. It's important to remember that the Enneagram is a tool for self-discovery, not a rigid categorization system. Avoid making assumptions about team members based on their Enneagram type, and instead use it as a starting point for understanding their unique strengths and weaknesses.

Friendly Advice: Encourage team members to embrace their Enneagram type as a way to better understand themselves and their colleagues. Remind them that the Enneagram is just one aspect of their personality, and that everyone is unique.

Pitfall 2: Lack of Enneagram Education and Training

Another pitfall is not providing adequate education and training on the Enneagram. Without proper understanding and training, team members may misinterpret or misuse the Enneagram, leading to confusion and potential conflict.

Friendly Advice: Offer Enneagram education and training to team members to ensure they have a solid understanding of the system and how to use it effectively. Encourage open communication and questions to clarify any misunderstandings.

Pitfall 3: Enneagram Used as a Weapon

Another pitfall is using the Enneagram as a weapon, such as using it to criticize or judge team members. This can lead to hurt feelings and damaged relationships.

Friendly Advice: Remind team members that the Enneagram is a tool for understanding and empathy, not criticism or judgment. Encourage them to use the Enneagram to better understand and appreciate the unique strengths and perspectives of their colleagues.

Tips For Incorporating Enneagram Training and Development

Here are some tips for incorporating Enneagram training and development into your team or organization:

- Customize training: Enneagram training should be customized to your team or organization's unique needs and goals. Consider incorporating real-life examples and exercises to make the training more engaging and relevant.

- Provide ongoing support: Enneagram development is an ongoing process, and team members may need ongoing support to fully integrate the Enneagram into their work and personal lives. Consider providing ongoing coaching or follow-up training sessions to reinforce the Enneagram principles.

- Encourage open communication: Enneagram development requires open and honest communication. Encourage team members to be open and honest about their Enneagram types, and how they impact their work and relationships.

- Lead by example: Enneagram training starts at the top. Encourage leaders to model Enneagram principles in their work and relationships, and to actively encourage their team members to embrace the Enneagram as a tool for growth and development.

- Use Enneagram typing as a starting point, not a label: Enneagram typing should be used as a starting point for self-awareness and growth, not as a label that defines a person. Encourage team members to embrace their Enneagram type as a tool for growth and development, rather than as a fixed characteristic.

- Integrate Enneagram development into performance management: Consider integrating Enneagram development into performance management processes, such as goal-setting and performance reviews. This can help team members apply Enneagram principles to their work and track their progress over time.

- Consider Enneagram diversity: While Enneagram development can offer many benefits, it's important to recognize that individuals may have different levels of comfort with the Enneagram, or may not find it relevant to their work. Be mindful of Enneagram diversity, and ensure that training and development opportunities are inclusive and respectful of all team members.

- Encourage collaboration and feedback: Encourage team members to collaborate and provide feedback to one another as they apply Enneagram principles to their work and relationships. This can help team members learn from one another and deepen their understanding of the Enneagram.

In conclusion, while the Enneagram can be a valuable tool for teams and organizations, it's important to be aware of the potential pitfalls and misconceptions. By avoiding Enneagram typing stereotypes, providing adequate education and training, viewing the Enneagram as a tool for growth rather than a label, and using it to promote empathy rather than criticism, teams and organizations can maximize the benefits of the Enneagram and achieve greater success.

Chapter 18:
Using the Enneagram in Relationships and Communication

Are you hearing the word 'Enneagram' too much nowadays? Well, that's probably because it has gained quite the popularity in recent years as a tool for personal growth and self-awareness. However, the Enneagram can also be a valuable resource for enhancing our relationships with others, both in romantic and family settings. In this chapter, we will explore how the Enneagram can be used to improve relationships and communication.

Using the Enneagram to Improve Communication in Relationships

Have you ever felt like you just can't seem to get through to your partner or loved one, no matter how hard you try? Maybe you feel like you're speaking a different language, or that they're just not getting what you're trying to say. Well, you're not alone! Communication can be tricky, and sometimes it feels like we're not speaking the same language as the people closest to us.

That's where the Enneagram comes in. The Enneagram is a powerful tool that can help us better understand ourselves and others. You have already learned about each type in depth in the previous part of this book, but let's take a look at how each Enneagram type communicates and some tips for how to communicate with them effectively:

Type One—The Perfectionist: Ones tend to communicate with clarity and precision, but they can also come across as critical and judgmental. To communicate effectively with a One, try to focus on the positive, and be specific with your feedback (Rimland, 2019).

Type Two—The Helper: Twos are warm, empathetic, and great listeners, but they can also be prone to people-pleasing and neglecting their own needs. To communicate effectively with a Two, make sure to express your appreciation for their efforts, and encourage them to take care of themselves too (Yuan, 2019).

Type Three—The Achiever: Threes are confident, goal-oriented, and great at multitasking, but they can also be competitive and overly focused on success. To communicate effectively with a Three, be direct and concise, and make sure to acknowledge their hard work (Rimland, 2019).

Type Four—The Individualist: Fours are creative, introspective, and value authenticity, but they can also be moody and overly focused on their emotions. To communicate effectively with a Four, be empathetic, and show interest in their feelings and experiences (Yuan, 2019).

Type Five—The Investigator: Fives are analytical, insightful, and value privacy, but they can also be withdrawn and emotionally detached. To communicate effectively with a Five, be patient, give them space when they need it, and ask for their input and expertise (Christian, 2020).

Type Six—The Loyalist: Sixes are loyal, responsible, and great at anticipating potential problems, but they can also be anxious and prone to self-doubt. To communicate effectively with a Six, be supportive and offer reassurance when they need it, and be clear and direct in your communication (Rimland, 2019).

Type Seven—The Enthusiast: Sevens are optimistic, adventurous, and love to have fun, but they can also be impulsive and distractible. To communicate effectively with a Seven, keep things light and positive, and allow them room to explore new ideas and experiences (Yuan, 2019).

Type Eight—The Challenger: Eights are confident, assertive, and value strength and control, but they can also be confrontational and intimidating. To communicate effectively with an Eight, be honest and direct, but also show respect for their boundaries and opinions (Christian, 2020).

Type Nine—The Peacemaker: Nines are easygoing, diplomatic, and great at finding common ground, but they can also be passive and indecisive. To communicate effectively with a Nine, be patient, avoid putting pressure on them, and make sure to listen actively to their perspective (Rimland, 2019).

By understanding each Enneagram type's communication style and adapting our approach accordingly, we can improve our communication and build stronger relationships.

The Enneagram and Love Languages

Love is a universal language, but did you know that each person has their own unique way of expressing and receiving love? These love languages were first introduced by Dr. Gary Chapman and include acts of service, quality time, words of affirmation, physical touch, and receiving gifts. Knowing your partner's love language can be a game-changer in your relationship, and when combined with the Enneagram, it can be a powerful tool for enhancing your connection and communication.

Let's take a look at how each Enneagram type's love language tends to manifest, and how you can speak your partner's love language more effectively:

Type One—The Perfectionist: Ones tend to express love through acts of service, such as doing chores, or running errands for their partner. If your partner is a One, try to show your appreciation for their efforts and help out, either around the house or with tasks they find important (Strong, 2020).

Type Two—The Helper: Twos express love through spending quality time, such as doing things together or supporting their partner's goals. If your partner is a Two, make sure to give them your undivided attention, and offer your support and encouragement (The Enneagram and Love Languages, 2022).

Type Three—The Achiever: Threes express love through quality time and words of affirmation, such as praise and recognition for their achievements. If your partner is a Three, make sure to acknowledge their hard work, and make time for shared activities and experiences (Shatto, 2020).

Type Four—The Individualist: Fours express love by doing things such as sharing deep conversations or expressing their emotions. If your partner is a Four, some things that you can do are making sure to validate their feelings and showing interest in their unique perspective (The Enneagram and Love Languages, 2022).

Type Five—The Investigator: Fives show their love by sharing their knowledge or doing things together. If your partner is a Five, make sure to respect their need for solitude and give them space when they need it, but also show appreciation for their contributions (Strong, 2020).

Type Six—The Loyalist: Sixes express love through acts of service and words of affirmation, such as providing support and reassurance. If your partner is a Six, make sure to show your commitment and dependability, and provide a sense of safety and security (Shatto, 2020).

Type Seven—The Enthusiast: Sevens express love through quality time and physical touch, such as shared adventures and playful affection. If your partner is a Seven, make sure to join them in their fun, and show your love through playful gestures and physical affection (The Enneagram and Love Languages, 2022).

Type Eight—The Challenger: Eights show their love through acts like protective gestures and taking care of their partner's needs. If your partner is an Eight, make sure to show your support and appreciation for their strength and protectiveness (Strong, 2020).

Type Nine—The Peacemaker: Last but definitely not the least, Nines express love through shared experiences and providing a sense of peace and stability. If your partner is a Nine, make sure to show your interest and attention, and help them feel heard and understood (Shatto, 2020).

With the Enneagram and love languages as your guide, you can build a stronger, more loving relationship.

Overcoming Relationship Challenges With the Enneagram

Every relationship goes through its own share of ups and downs. Here are some common relationship challenges, and how the Enneagram can help you overcome them:

Communication breakdown. Misunderstandings and communication breakdowns can happen in any relationship. I can't stress this enough, but by understanding your own and your partner's Enneagram type, you can identify your communication style, and adapt it to better communicate with each other. For example, if you're a Type One, and your partner is a Type Eight, you may need to be more direct and assertive in your communication style, while your partner may need to work on listening more actively.

Different perspectives. Each Enneagram type has its own unique perspective on the world, which can sometimes clash with your partner's. By understanding your partner's perspective and learning to appreciate their unique strengths and challenges, you can build greater empathy and understanding in your relationship. This can help you overcome differences and find common ground.

Emotional triggers. Every Enneagram type has its own set of emotional triggers and patterns of behavior. By recognizing your own and your partner's triggers, you can avoid getting caught up in reactive patterns, and instead work together to address underlying issues. For example, if you're a Type Four, and your partner is a Type Nine, you may need to be more aware of your tendency to withdraw or become moody, while your partner may need to work on expressing their needs more assertively.

Different needs and expectations. Each Enneagram type has its own set of needs and expectations in a relationship. By understanding your own and your partner's needs, you can work together to create a more fulfilling and satisfying relationship. For example, if you're a Type Two, and your partner is a Type Five, you may need to communicate your need for emotional connection and support, while your partner may need to express their need for space and independence.

Remember that when it comes to relationship challenges, the Enneagram is definitely not a one-size-fits-all solution. But, what it can do is that it can help you start communicating in a more open and honest manner.

Can the Enneagram Help Strengthen Parent-Child Relationships Too?

It's true that parenting is one of the most rewarding phases in life, but, at the same time, it can be one of the most challenging ones too. Here are some ways the Enneagram can help you strengthen your parent-child relationship:

Understanding your child's perspective. Each Enneagram type has its own unique perspective on the world, and by understanding your child's type, you can gain insight into their needs, strengths, and challenges. This understanding can help you connect with your child on a deeper level and be more empathetic and supportive of their growth and development.

Tailoring your parenting style. Each Enneagram type has its own set of needs and expectations, and by understanding your own type and your child's type, you can tailor your parenting style to better meet their needs. For example, if you're a Type One, and your child is a Type Seven, you may need to work on being more flexible and spontaneous to meet your child's need for excitement and variety.

Recognizing triggers and patterns. Every Enneagram type has its own set of triggers and patterns of behavior, and by recognizing these patterns in yourself and your child, you can avoid reactive patterns, instead working together to address underlying issues. For example, if you're a Type Eight, and your child is a Type Four, you may need to be aware of your tendency to be more forceful and direct, while your child may need more space and sensitivity to express their emotions.

Building communication. Effective communication is essential to building a strong parent-child relationship, and the Enneagram can help you understand your communication style and adapt it to better connect with your child. By speaking your child's Enneagram language, you can help them feel understood and valued, which can lead to a more positive and supportive relationship.

In conclusion, the Enneagram is a valuable tool for building stronger and more fulfilling relationships, whether with romantic partners, family members, or children.

Conclusion

In conclusion, the Enneagram provides a unique approach to understanding personality types, not only focusing on how each type behaves when healthy and balanced, but also on how they can return to a state of ascendance when they become unbalanced. By recognizing that all people have the components of every type within them, the Enneagram offers a path towards greater self-awareness and personal growth. This growth involves returning to emotional, physical, and intellectual balance, and learning how to navigate conflict in a more balanced and appropriate way. The key to ascendance lies in acknowledging our strengths, as well as our weaknesses, and learning how to overcome them. Whether you're overly assertive, compliant, or withdrawn, the Enneagram offers practical tools and exercises to help you become more balanced, and live a more fulfilling life.

Furthermore, the Enneagram offers a powerful tool for personal and spiritual growth by revealing our unconscious patterns and the motivations behind our behavior. By understanding these patterns and motivations, we can break free from our limited perspectives, and transform our lives. The Enneagram helps us to understand our deepest fears, desires, and motivations, and how they influence our thoughts, emotions, and actions. This knowledge allows us to cultivate greater self-awareness, compassion, and acceptance, and to develop more fulfilling and harmonious relationships with ourselves and others. The Enneagram is not just a personality typing system, but a holistic approach to self-discovery and personal development that can lead to greater happiness, fulfillment, and inner peace.

If you are someone who identifies as a Type One, you might often struggle with perfectionism, and can become overly critical of myself and others. However, you will see that when you are in a healthy and balanced state, you can use your attention to detail and high standards to make positive changes in your life and the world around you.

On the other hand, when you are in an unhealthy state, you may become rigid and inflexible, causing you to miss out on opportunities for growth and connection. By recognizing your tendencies and working to stay balanced, you can use your strengths to your advantage while avoiding the pitfalls of your weaknesses.

Similarly, a friend of mine who identifies as a Type Nine often struggles with assertiveness and standing up for themselves.

However, they've learned that when they're in a healthy and balanced state, they can use their gift for empathy and understanding to create harmony and bring people together.

But when they're in an unhealthy state, they may become complacent and avoid conflict, causing them to miss out on important opportunities for growth and not standing up for what they believe in. By recognizing their tendencies and working to stay balanced, they can use their strengths to build connections while still advocating for themselves and others when necessary.

Figuring out your Enneagram type can be a little tricky, but don't worry, I've got some tips to help you out. It's important to approach the process in the right way. Rather than focusing on your strengths, or what you aspire to be, try to identify the type that you would be most embarrassed to admit you are. It can be tough to confront your flaws, but it's the first step in repairing them and living a more authentic life.

The Enneagram is a powerful tool for understanding how your life experiences have shaped you and identifying areas for growth. While it may be tempting to look at your behaviors and try to decide your type based on those, it's important to consider the motivations and experiences behind those actions. Remember that some behaviors may have been learned from other types or from your environment, so they may not be an accurate reflection of your type.

It's also important to be aware of the possibility of confusing your direction of integration with your actual type. To avoid this, think about what your best self looks like, and what your worst self looks like. Your best self should align with your type or the direction of integration from your type, while your worst self will align with your type or the direction of disintegration.

So, don't get discouraged if identifying your type feels challenging at first. With a little reflection and honesty, you'll be able to unlock a wealth of insights about yourself and move towards a more fulfilling life.

While some may turn to tests to identify their Enneagram type, I have found them to be less accurate than a thorough reading of all the type descriptions. By focusing on the flaws within each type, you can better identify which one resonates with your own personal demons and learn how to banish them. Even if you think you already know your type, it is worth learning about all the types and their best and worst qualities, as these aspects are present in all of us to some extent. Ultimately, expanding your knowledge of the Enneagram can provide valuable insights into the motivations of others and help foster greater understanding and compassion.

References

Abdel-Khalek, A. M. (2013). The Enneagram of personality: A validity study in an Arabic-speaking sample. *Psychological Reports, 112*(2), 397–414. https://doi.org/10.2466/02.09.PR0.112.2.397-414

Alderson, J. (2022, July 26). *Enneagram type 8: So assertive.* So Syncd. https://www.sosyncd.com/enneagram-type-8/

Alexander, M., & Schnipke, B. (2020). The Enneagram: A primer for psychiatry residents. *American Journal of Psychiatry Residents' Journal, 15*(3), 2–5. https://doi.org/10.1176/appi.ajp-rj.2020.150301

Bayside Church. (2016, December 30). *How to change your life using the Enneagram — Part 1: The nine types and deadly passions.* Medium. https://medium.com/@BaysideChurch/how-to-use-the-enneagram-find-your-number-and-transform-your-life-c7dc3649b897

Belle, E. (2020, June 30). *How does the Enneagram work and how useful is it?* Healthline. https://www.healthline.com/health/mental-health/how-does-the-enneagram-work

Bernes, M. (n.d.). *What are the nine Enneagram types? How to interpret them?* www.makipeople.com. Retrieved May 17, 2023, from https://www.makipeople.com/resources/how-to-interpret-nine-enneagram-types

Booth, J. (2022, April 29). *The 9 Enneagram personality types: Strengths, weaknesses and more.* Forbes Health. https://www.forbes.com/health/mind/enneagram-types/

Brand, S. (2021, February 20). *An Enneagram guide for self-care: Type 1.* Heights Family Counseling. https://heightsfamilycounseling.com/blog/2021/2/20/an-enneagram-guide-for-self-care-type-1

Brown, S. (2023). Studying communication competence level and the Enneagram type. *Journal of Student Research at Indiana University East, 5*(1).

https://scholarworks.iu.edu/journals/index.php/jsriue/article/view/357
44

Cain, S. (2016). *Quiet power : the secret strengths of introverted kids*. New York
Puffin Books United States Dial Books For Young Readers.

Carroll, J. S., & Ivanoff, S. D. (2016). Increasing self-awareness through
self-discovery: A grounded theory study of women leaders. *Journal of
Leadership Education, 15*(2), 139–151.
https://doi.org/10.12806/V15/I2/R6

Cherry, K. (2019, July). *What is the Enneagram of personality?* Verywell Mind.
https://www.verywellmind.com/the-enneagram-of-personality-4691757

Chestnut, B. (2013). *The complete Enneagram*. She Writes Press.

Chestnut, B. (2021). *The Enneagram*. Beatrice Chestnut.
https://www.beatricechestnut.com/enneagram

Christian, K. (2020, January 29). *How to cultivate healthier relationships based
on your Enneagram type*. The Good Trade.
https://www.thegoodtrade.com/features/enneagram-in-relationships/

Christian, K. (2021, January 8). *What are Enneagram types?* The Good
Trade. https://www.thegoodtrade.com/features/what-are-enneagram-
types/

Cloete, D. (2010). *Origins and history of the Enneagram*. Integrative9.com.
https://www.integrative9.com/enneagram/history/

Cloete, D. (2022, April 6). *Nine holy ideas of the Enneagram*. Integrative9.
https://www.integrative9.com/media/articles/51/The-Enneagram-of-
Holy-Ideas

Don Richard Riso, & Hudson, R. (1999). *Wisdom of the Enneagram: The
complete guide to psychological and spiritual growth for the nine personality types*.
Bantam.

Doyle, E. (2022a, April 30). *A helpful guide to the Enneagram motivations of all
9 types*. Enneagram Gift. https://enneagramgift.com/enneagram-
motivations/

Doyle, E. (2022b, June 1). *Enneagram type 8 identity + notorious traits of the
Challenger*. Enneagram Gifts. https://enneagramgift.com/enneagram-
type-8/

Doyle, E. (2022c, November 14). *Enneagram 9: The Peacemaker.* Cloverleaf. https://cloverleaf.me/blog/enneagram-type-9-the-peacemaker/

Emmons, R. A., & McCullough, M. E. (2003). Counting blessings versus burdens: An experimental investigation of gratitude and subjective well-being in daily life. *Journal of Personality and Social Psychology, 84*(2), 377–389. https://doi.org/10.1037/0022-3514.84.2.377

Enneagram centers of intelligence. (2020, January 21). Enneagram Explained. https://enneagramexplained.com/enneagram-centers-of-intelligence/

Enneagram type 3: The Achiever. (2021, July 20). Enneagram Explained. https://enneagramexplained.com/enneagram-3-the-achiever/

Enneagram type 4 – The Individualist. (2021, October 28). Enneagramuniverse.com. https://enneagramuniverse.com/enneagram/learn/enneagram-types/enneagram-type-4-the-individualist/

Enneagram type 7. (2022, October 21). Www.personalitydata.org. https://www.personalitydata.org/enneagram/type-7

Enneagram type 7 - The Adventurer. (n.d.). Www.crystalknows.com. https://www.crystalknows.com/enneagram/type-7

Enneagram type 8 description. (n.d.). David N. Daniels, M.D. Retrieved May 17, 2023, from https://drdaviddaniels.com/type-8/

Francis, A., & Singletary, J. (2022). *The Enneagram and communication styles.* https://baylor-ir.tdl.org/bitstream/handle/2104/11826/alex_francis1_honorsthesis%20.pdf?sequence=1

Grahek, M. (2018). The Enneagram: An empirical study of its factor structure. *Journal of Adult Development, 25*(3), 153–161. https://doi.org/10.1007/s10804-018-9287-6

Hook, J. N., Hall, T. W., Davis, D. E., Van Tongeren, D. R., & Conner, M. (2020). The Enneagram: A systematic review of the literature and directions for future research. *Journal of Clinical Psychology, 77*(4), 865–883. https://doi.org/10.1002/jclp.23097

How the Enneagram system works. (2014). The Enneagram Institute. https://www.enneagraminstitute.com/how-the-enneagram-system-works

James, J. (2021, November 7). *The existential emptiness of the Enneagram type 3. The 3 in* Me. https://medium.com/the-3-in-me/the-existential-emptiness-of-the-enneagram-type-3-ee84a9c50c49

Kark, R., Shamir, B., & Chen, G. (2003). The two faces of transformational leadership: Empowerment and dependency. *Journal of Applied Psychology, 88*(2), 246–255. https://doi.org/10.1037/0021-9010.88.2.246

Lapid-Bogda, G. (2004). *Bringing out the best in yourself at work.* McGraw Hill Professional.

Lee, M.-R. (2015). A study on the effects of Enneagram group counseling on nursing students. *International Journal of Bio-Science and Bio-Technology, 7*(5), 235–246. https://doi.org/10.14257/ijbsbt.2015.7.5.22

Maitri, S. (2000). *The spiritual dimension of the Enneagram.* Penguin.

McLeod, S. (2022). *Maslow's hierarchy of needs.* Simply Psychology. https://www.simplypsychology.org/maslow.html

Mukherjee, C. (2021, November 12). *All about enneagram 7 personality types – the Enthusiast.* ThePleasantPersonality. https://thepleasantpersonality.com/enneagram-type-7/

Mukherjee, C. (2023, March 2). *Enneagram 8 personality description – an energetic challenger.* ThePleasantPersonality. https://thepleasantpersonality.com/enneagram-8-personality-description/

Owens, M. (2019, August 8). *Enneagram type 1: The perfectionist.* Truity. https://www.truity.com/enneagram/personality-type-1-perfectionist

Palmer, H. (1991). *The Enneagram : understanding yourself and the others in your life.* HarperOne.

Personality type: Six – the Loyalist or Skeptic. (n.d.). Www.theworldcounts.com. Retrieved May 17, 2023, from https://www.theworldcounts.com/purpose/enneagram-number-6-personality-type-six-loyalist

Regan, S. (2021, July 8). *Are you an enneagram type4? Here's everything you should know.* Mindbodygreen. https://www.mindbodygreen.com/articles/enneagram-type-4-traits-strengths-compatibility-and-more

Rickerd, G. (2019, November 23). *Enneagram in the workplace: Using your type to your advantage.* Atomic Spin. https://spin.atomicobject.com/2019/11/23/enneagram-in-the-workplace/

Rimland, A. (2019, September 12). *How the Enneagram can improve your relationships.* Thrive Couple & Family Counseling Services. https://thrivefamilyservices.com/enneagram-improve-relationships/

Ritz, E. M., & Seville, C. (2016). The Enneagram: A model for enhancing teamwork in the workplace. *Journal of Management Development, 35*(2), 217–228. https://doi.org/10.1108/JMD-08-2014-0113

Roberts, B. W., Lejuez, C., Krueger, R. F., Richards, J. M., & Hill, P. L. (2014). What is conscientiousness and how can it be assessed? *Developmental Psychology, 50*(5), 1315–1330. https://doi.org/10.1037/a0031109

Robledo, I. (2022, March 16). *Enneagram 5 in stress & growth* . Making Mindfulness Fun. https://www.makingmindfulnessfun.com/enneagram-5-stress-growth/

Roulo, L. (2021, January 28). *Modern twists to the ancient Enneagram: How the personality system has changed over the last 20 years.* Truity. https://www.truity.com/blog/modern-twists-ancient-enneagram-how-personality-system-has-changed-over-last-20-years

Sarikas, C. (2020, December 23). *Enneagram type 7: The Enthusiast.* Blog.prepscholar.com. https://blog.prepscholar.com/enneagram-type-7-careers-relationships

Schirm, A. (2022, November 22). *Enneagram Two health tips - the ultimate guide.* The Living Well. https://thelivingwell.com/enneagram-two-health-tips-the-ultimate-guide/

Shatto, R. (2020, October 8). *Here's what your Enneagram type says about your love language.* Elite Daily. https://www.elitedaily.com/p/heres-what-your-enneagram-type-says-about-your-love-language-37937360

Storm, S. (2020, August 6). *Integration, disintegration and your Enneagram type.* Psychology Junkie. https://www.psychologyjunkie.com/enneagram-integration-disintegration/

Strong, R. (2020, August 5). *Here's what your Enneagram type says about your love language.* Elite Daily. https://www.elitedaily.com/p/your-enneagram-type-love-language-probably-are-in-sync-32180244

Sutin, A. R., Costa, P. T., Wethington, E., & Eaton, W. (2010). Turning points and lessons learned: Stressful life events and personality trait development across middle adulthood. *Psychology and Aging, 25*(3), 524–533. https://doi.org/10.1037/a0018751

The Enneagram and love languages. (2022, April 8). Enneagram Explained. https://enneagramexplained.com/the-enneagram-and-love-languages/

The Enneagram Institute. (n.d.-a). *Type Eight.* The Enneagram Institute. https://www.enneagraminstitute.com/type-8

The Enneagram Institute. (n.d.-b). *Type Seven.* The Enneagram Institute. https://www.enneagraminstitute.com/type-7

The Enneagram Institute. (2014a). *Type Six.* The Enneagram Institute. https://www.enneagraminstitute.com/type-6

The Enneagram Institute. (2014b). *Traditional Enneagram (History).* The Enneagram Institute. https://www.enneagraminstitute.com/the-traditional-enneagram

The Enneagram Institute. (2021). *Type Nine.* The Enneagram Institute. https://www.enneagraminstitute.com/type-9

The Enneagram model explained and why it isn't always a good idea. (n.d.). Www.bestenneagramtest.com. Retrieved May 14, 2023, from https://www.bestenneagramtest.com/blog/the-enneagram-model-explained-and-why-it-isn-t-always-a-good-idea-to-take-it

The Enneagram type 9: The Peacemaker. (2022, September 8). Www.traitlab.com. https://www.traitlab.com/blog/enneagram-type-9

The nine Enneagram types [Complete Descriptions]. (n.d.). Personalitypath.com. https://personalitypath.com/enneagram/9-personality-types/

Type Eight: The Asserter. (n.d.). Leadership Greater Hartford. Retrieved May 17, 2023, from https://leadershipgh.org/enneagramprofiler/type-eight-the-asserter/

Type Eight: The Challenger. (n.d.). Enneagram Today. Retrieved May 17, 2023, from https://enneagramtoday.com/what-is-the-enneagram/type-8/

Type Five. (n.d.). The Enneagram Institute. https://www.enneagraminstitute.com/type-5

Type One. (n.d.). The Enneagram Institute. https://www.enneagraminstitute.com/type-1

Type Six: The Loyalist. (n.d.). Enneagram Academy. https://enneagramacademy.com/enneagram-types/type-six-the-loyalist

Type Two. (n.d.). The Enneagram Institute. https://www.enneagraminstitute.com/type-2

Vidal, M. A., & Gómez, J. (2016). Improving teamwork through the Enneagram. *Team Performance Management, 22*(1/2), 38–53. https://doi.org/10.1108/TPM-09-2014-0040

Wagner, J. (1980). A descriptive, reliability, and validity study of the Enneagram personality typology. *Dissertations.* https://ecommons.luc.edu/luc_diss/2109

Wagner, J. (2010, December 30). *History of the Enneagram.* The Enneagram Spectrum of Personality Styles. http://enneagramspectrum.com/173/history-of-the-enneagram/

Yuan, L. (2019, September 10). *Here's how you communicate, based on your Enneagram type.* Psychology Junkie. https://www.psychologyjunkie.com/heres-how-you-communicate-based-on-your-enneagram-type/

HEALING YOUR INNER CHILD

Release Emotional Blocks, Overcome Trauma, Build Self-Love, and Live a Life of Authentic Happiness

Sofia Visconti

TABLE OF CONTENTS

Introduction

Have you ever sat down at night, struggling to sleep, wondering about the same questions over and over again? Why do I keep repeating the same relationship patterns? Why do I keep attracting the same type of people? Why am I so afraid of life? Why is it so hard for me to be my authentic self? Why do I self-sabotage and play small? Where is my voice? Why am I so afraid to express myself? Where do all my feelings of insistent stress and anxiety come from? Why do I feel so drained? Why do I feel disconnected from my emotions? Why do I feel like a spectator in my own life? Is it even possible to be free from all my fears? Will I ever be comfortable in my skin and know who I really am? When is all this going to stop? How do I stop this vicious cycle of repeating negative experiences?

If such questions and more like these haunts you repeatedly, please do know that you aren't alone. We live in a broken world where certain unhealthy and abnormal patterns are normalized. We live in a world where many people find it easier to hate or hurt others while loving and being kind to the other person almost feels like a foreign concept. It's sad. When you grow up dehumanized, neglected, abused, bullied, belittled, and treated like you aren't worthy of love, care, and respect, all that becomes all you know. Unless someone ventures on a serious journey of healing and personal growth, they will repeat the same unkind things to their loved ones and children. Indeed, it is true that "hurt people really do hurt other people."

When we think of childhood trauma, it's easy to fall into the trap of blaming our parents or caregivers for not giving us the love and care we deeply need. However, things aren't always as simple as that. While it's true that other people knowingly just mistreat others, it's also true that sometimes the way parents bring up their children is merely a by-product or replication of how they were brought up. So, if they are not treated well, their emotions are invalidated constantly, and their needs are ignored, they are likely also to use the same parenting strategies on their children unless they are self-aware and developed.

Them hurting their children just because they possibly didn't know better doesn't negate how hurtful it is to raise one's child in a toxic way. Thus, all the feelings of children who grow up abused or mistreated are supposed to be validated no matter what. Even more, when they become adults, it's important to recognize that the pain of childhood trauma is deep and doesn't just go away simply because now you've aged. That pain continues to stay in our minds, hearts, and bodies until we fully do the inner child healing work. Unfortunately, it's impossible to stop attracting more pain and toxic experiences unless the work is done.

It's true that for many people, it wasn't their fault for experiencing the trauma or abuse they faced. However, what's important is to recognize that it's your responsibility to heal and break your connection to every negative cycle or pattern. You might feel like it's impossible to ever be okay again, but nothing could be any further from the truth. Change is possible! Human beings are designed with the unique ability to adapt and grow. Every day, thousands of cells in your body are working full time to replace dead cells with new cells and keep the healthy cells active and in good condition. Every time you learn something new or practice repeatedly new hobbies, your brain develops neural connections and gets reprogrammed through a process called neuroplasticity. No matter what happened in your past, change is inevitable if you make up your mind to reclaim your true identity and life. Our past can only haunt and control us for as long as we allow it to. Once you decide that enough is enough, there is no limit to the amount of greatness that awaits you.

When you were young, your spirit was trampled upon and hurt multiple times. That child's soul may have been crushed and their voice silenced. In a bid to try to survive and not be cut off or abandoned by their caregivers, that child probably shed off parts of themselves and developed people-pleasing habits or coping mechanisms. All such survival strategies robbed the child of healthily living their life and developing a healthy relationship with themselves. It's hard to love yourself when your environment keeps echoing to you the message that you aren't good enough unless you wear the masks people would rather see. It's hard to create healthy relationships with others when your self-worth is low. People can feel how we feel about ourselves. If someone detects that you don't love or value yourself, they are likely to poke at those insecurities and treat you poorly unless they are mature. This phenomenon explains why people who have unhealed childhood trauma often attract toxic relationships. Thus, if you have ever experienced toxic relationships, don't ever believe that that's all you are worthy of having. You deserve so much more. You are more than what your adverse childhood experiences forced you to believe about yourself.

When you experience trauma, your self-concept and self-worth are not the only things that change. Your brain also changes. That's why transformation has to also include the healing and growth of your brain. Your mind might have trained you to believe that there is danger and then feel afraid and want to run; that's where you now have to retrain the brain to teach it to see opportunities instead of threats everywhere. When you are an adult, you are no longer a helpless, dependent child who can't take responsibility for themself. Thus, it might have been understandable to have adopted certain coping mechanisms when you were a child, but once you grow older, you no longer need those things to protect you. There are many healthy ways you can protect and care for yourself. That's what this book is going to help you master. You will be equipped with tools to help you function at your best in your life. You will be able to learn to love yourself and others fearlessly and authentically.

Trauma changes the way you view yourself, others, and life. Through the lessons in this book, you will master how to regulate, think, behave, and perceive things correctly. Here are some myriad problems associated with experiencing childhood trauma (Aletheia, 2023):

- Struggling to set and maintain healthy boundaries.
- Being confused or unsure about your identity.
- A tendency to be a people-pleaser is seen as constantly abandoning your needs while catering to others.
- Being stagnant and unable to achieve your potential.
- Negative self-talk and being overly critical of oneself and others.
- Inability to regulate your emotions healthily. For example, often experience bouts of anger or suppress your emotions due to fear of rejection.
- Challenges with growing healthy and lasting relationships.
- Self-sabotage across every domain of your life. For example, in relationships, your health, or your health.
- Impulsive reactions.
- Disassociation or frequently checking out. Finding it hard to be present and grounded in reality.
- Low self-worth, self-esteem, self-confidence and often feeling inept.
- Have flashbacks or nightmares of the abuse, distress, or neglect you went through.
- Deteriorating physical health. For example, having insistent migraines and autoimmune diseases.
- Insecure attachment styles like dismissive-avoidant, fearful-avoidant, and anxious attachment.

This book will give you practical guidelines and tips on ways to make amends with the past and heal. You will finally be able to resolve your childhood trauma and be a healthy, securely attached individual. You will learn therapeutic techniques to resolve the trauma. These also include emotional regulation tools and cognitive behavioral therapy strategies. The inability to effectively communicate and set boundaries is a severe weakness that often leads to repeated cycles of toxic relationships. Hence, you will also be equipped with tools to reframe your self-image, build healthy self-esteem, and establish firm boundaries.

There is no way things will continue to be the same if you start to do things differently. Sometimes, when things don't go well, we may tend to focus on waiting for others to change, especially the people who hurt us. However, this is often futile since people only change when they want, not because you want them to. However, what you have control over is yourself. You can work on yourself and become who you have always wanted to be. This, in turn, inevitably allows you to attract a different reality that matches your frequency, vibration, and who you would have evolved to become.

Your inner child is more than just a common metaphor used in psychology. It represents you and the experiences you went through. Your inner child is the key to understanding who you are as an adult and why certain things often transpire the way they do, specifically in your life. This book offers you a holistic approach to healing, manifesting a fulfilling life full of abandonment and positive experiences. Your mental health deserves your love and care. You deserve to be who you were meant to be and achieve the life of your dreams. You are more than enough and worthy of happiness and freedom from your pain. Are you ready to get started? Let's dive in!

Chapter 1:
Recognizing and Understanding
the Wounded Inner Child in You

Being a parent does not only entail physically looking after your child. It also involves being there for them psychologically, emotionally, mentally, and spiritually. It's understanding and accepting that a child is helpless at a certain stage. They wholly depend on you to keep them holistically safe in a world that's all new to them. Sadly, this is not always something every parent understands before they start a family. Therefore, what ends up taking place is the child growing up in a dysfunctional and unsafe environment. They cry and signal for help, but those bids for attention are ignored or outrightly dismissed. The child learns that they can't rely on their caregivers for support. As a result, many problems start to unfold as the child tries to adapt to different coping mechanisms to survive. This is what gives rise to childhood trauma and wounds.

Although the adults meant to look after children should ideally fulfill their role well, it's also important to make room for empathy and understand why some caregivers might struggle to fulfill their responsibilities. The pain inflicted on the child is usually, in most cases, unintentional. Most times the caregivers might actually be oblivious to what's happening and the impact of their parenting style on the child's overall development. Some adults just continue to generational traumas by treating their children the same way they were treated. This often happens if the parents came from an unsafe background and didn't end up taking responsibility for their healing when they grew up. As a result, how they treat their children is all that they know. That's the only way they know how to love and care for others. That's the blueprint their caregivers passed on to them. Unless they are open to change and growth, they, too, become limited to what's familiar to them, even though it might be toxic parenting styles.

Having reviewed these possible reasons why caregivers treat children the way they do, it's important to consider forgiving them for their inability to give you what you need. For most people, if they had known better, they probably would have treated you better and given you a healthy childhood experience. When we don't look at things this way, we run the risk of living the rest of our lives bitter and in victim mode, always blaming others for what they didn't give us instead of taking control and being responsible for our healing now that we are grown.

Now, let's revisit the past. Childhood wounds start to appear when a child feels endangered. These wounds are deep-seated and emotional. They affect the child's psyche and even impair their brain development. The child starts to grow up seeing the world from a very different outlook. Instead of life and the world being an exciting adventure to explore and enjoy, almost everything feels frightening and dangerous. The child starts to grow up with a heightened fight and flee-activated nervous system. Instead of being relaxed and having a positive view of themselves, they grow up and start to live on edge and feel defective.

The underlying core belief most people who have Childhood trauma have is that "There is something wrong with me; that's why people don't love me or care about my needs and feelings." This core belief is what breaks down the child's self-worth and self-esteem and shatters their confidence. It makes the child fearful of social interactions or relationships. They start to believe that since their closest people abandoned them, they will never be lovable and accepted by anyone else. To learn more about the effects of childhood trauma and how to identify the wounds or recognize the impact of it, let's move on to the next section.

How an Unhealed Inner Child Feels

Your inner child is a part of who you are, the child you are that lives inside your psyche. No matter how much we age, our inner child never dies. That child represents how you felt or saw the world when you were young. That child carries the memories of all that happened to you in your past. That child might either be happy, sad, or numb. The well-being of that child will determine your well-being and overall happiness. If that child still has unresolved wounds and pain, they won't stop hurting until that pain is addressed. Whenever that child is hurting, you are also hurting. Whenever that child is healed, you are also healed, and the outcome of your life experiences gives a testament to what's going on within you. People who are hurting or tend to hurt others signify that they have an unhealed inner child that's crying out for comfort, love, safety, and healing. Unless that child is healed, there is no end to the cycle of problems that will keep coming because of unresolved past trauma.

We must stay connected to our inner child because they are part of who we are. When we numb that child's feelings and silence their voice, pain is inevitable. It's important to know the primary condition of your inner child. For adults who grew up with childhood trauma, that inner child probably feels this way most of the time:

- Very afraid of the world and people.
- Plagued with insistent feelings of inadequacy and worthlessness.
- Strongly believe they are unlovable.
- Struggles to trust people.
- Has constant negative self-talk.
- May think positively of others but negatively of oneself.
- Feels like a burden to others and may want to isolate or be hyper-independent as a result of this belief.
- Thinks they are not smart or gifted.
- Feels ashamed of who they are.
- Believes they are defective and not worthy of love, care, and respect.
- Struggles with self-doubt.
- Has low self-esteem.
- Feels insecure and often self-conscious.

- Believes they deserve to be punished or ill-treated.
- Believes they are not a good person.
- Always self-critical.
- Doesn't feel safe.
- Undermines their strengths and overinflates their weaknesses.

This is not even an exhaustive list. All these feelings are pervasive no matter where you go or what age you are unless healing takes place. When your inner child still feels this way, it means that's how you feel about yourself at the core of your being. Your life becomes a reflection of these ingrained beliefs and feelings. The question is, what really causes this painful and harmful way of viewing yourself and others? Let's find out the answers in the next section.

Things That Caused You to Feel Unsafe in Your Childhood

Do you recall how your caregivers responded to you when you were young? When you expressed distress and reached out for help, what were the typical responses you would get? Below are common patterns you would notice from a child who was raised without adequate emotional attunement and experienced neglect on different levels (Merck, 2018):

- Having your ideas or opinions was shunned. You were forced to only go along with what was presented to you. This leads you to lose confidence in your thoughts or capabilities.
- When you express yourself authentically, you would either be punished or scolded.

- Being spontaneous and free was discouraged. You had to follow rigid rules and ways to live or do things.
- Spending time with friends, exploring your interests, or just doing what you wanted was not allowed.
- Showing negative feelings or emotions was not allowed. If you tried to express your discomfort or hurt, you would be accused of being ungrateful or selfish.
- You would be laughed at, humiliated, looked down upon, and shamed for who you are by your family members.
- Thoughtless words were often hurled at you, and you were expected to just take it. It became "normal" to accept verbal and emotional abuse.
- You were violated physically either by being beaten down or screamed at, pushed around, or your physical possessions like clothes or toys taken without your permission.
- Your caregivers made you feel responsible for their needs and happiness. They blamed you for their problems and made it an expectation for you to do something about it.
- You weren't allowed to focus on your needs. Doing this would lead to being accused of being selfish or bad.
- Physical affection or words of affirmation were rare. You would constantly be criticized, and almost all the good things you did would be downplayed.
- People would lie about you to always get you in trouble and find justifications for scapegoating you.
- It was rare to experience any form of emotional attunement or support. You had to learn to soothe yourself and be self-reliant.
- You were left to figure out life or deal with your pain alone.

- When people were nice to you, it was usually only when you took on the people-pleasing role. Unconditional love was almost nonexistent. Love was almost like a transaction you had to complete. If your parents are nice to you, then it would mean you had to either abandon yourself and focus on doing whatever they wanted or suffer the consequences of negligence if you didn't comply.

Constantly going through such experiences was probably what you went through for most of your childhood. This would mean that your inner child largely felt alone, misunderstood, unloved, unaccepted, judged, criticized, engulfed, and neglected for the most part.

Signs You Might Still Have a Wounded Inner Child as an Adult

We don't just simply get over our past just because we want to. The pain of what happened had to be processed first. Suppressing those memories and emotions only prolongs the suffering. One way or the other, the wounded child will still leave a trail of tears across every aspect of your life until that child's pain is validated, and they are given a chance to experience what they always needed. This means that in our adult lives, or even as you were growing up, chances are that you started experiencing the aftereffects of having a broken childhood. Let's now review what some signs of a wounded inner child are that you might experience:

- You feel like you must always be responsible for other people's problems and happiness, especially those close to you or family members.
- You often deny your authentic reality and operate in "people-pleaser mode."
- You are an error hoarder. You don't easily let go, express your hurt, and forgive. You internalize your hurt instead of acting out in passive-aggressive ways.
- You can stand up for others but find it hard to stand up for yourself. People often walk over you and see you as weak.
- You struggle to be assertive, articulate yourself, or think on the spot. When someone attacks you, instead of thinking on your feet an assertive response to give them, you either freeze or just let them treat you anyhow.
- You always feel inadequate and not good enough. This makes you downplay your abilities and settle for less.

- You often find yourself in relationships with toxic or abusive patterns.
- You believe that you are, deep down, a really bad person. No matter what you do, you feel like everyone can still see how defective or bad you are.
- You feel like people are ashamed of associating with you, so at times, or most times, you isolate yourself due to this belief.
- You often feel uncomfortable in your own skin and appear rigid to others.
- You are very hard on yourself and expect perfection. This attitude may also spill onto others as you tend to reject them when they are imperfect, just like how you were rejected as a child for not being perfect.
- You lack confidence and self-efficacy. As a result, you have trouble getting certain things done from start to finish. You tend to easily write yourself off.
- You over-give and over-function in relationships. This may be due to the belief that you are not worthy of love for just who you are.
- You might have a type A personality or show signs of being an overachiever. This comes from an unhealthy place whereby you believe that anything less than perfect will cause you to not be loved or accepted by others. So, you don't take failure very well.
- You have trouble having a growth mindset. You tend to be fixed and set in your ways because you don't easily believe in your ability to change. You also fear trying new things due to the fear of failure and rejection.
- You feel like you don't belong.

- You often find yourself feeling misunderstood by others and in constant fights.
- You struggle with so much anxiety.
- You desire love, connection, and intimacy but can sometimes push away people when they come too close. This happens because subconsciously, you have learned to associate "love" with pain since your caregivers who were meant to love you caused you so much pain and suffering.
- You don't trust anyone, including yourself.
- You feel very isolated in your life. Most of your relationships tend to be surface-level.
- You often find yourself chasing people to love you or having unrequited love instead of mutual love and respect.
- You have an intense fear of people and tend to avoid social interactions as much as possible.
- You might have some form of addiction that you use to numb your pain or run away from it. This could be being a workaholic, alcoholic, drug addict, sex addict, binge eater, or tending to watch pornography a lot.
- You struggle to be interdependent; you are either hyper-independent or too dependent on others.
- You might have anger management issues or passive-aggressive behavior.
- You tend to attract unhealthy partners like users, abusers, narcissists, or other people with insecure attachment styles.
- You might have a pattern of mistreating the people close to you. Without realizing it, the way you were treated by

your caregivers might be the same way you start to treat others.

- You might be codependent and struggle with self-love deficiency.
- You often neglect yourself. Self-care and meeting your needs might be difficult for you. You may even feel bad for doing something nice for yourself.
- You might have an urge to rebel or retaliate in some way. In extreme cases, you might find yourself indulging in criminal activities and detached from other people's feelings.
- You may struggle to have empathy for others since you never got to experience empathy in your childhood.
- You struggle to understand yourself. Self-reflection might not always be an easy thing for you to do. Since you already believe that you are a bad person, the last thing you may want is to always have that thrown in your face or think about it. This is also why you may have a habit of avoiding difficult conversations and being defensive.
- You feel safe alone. Even though you crave connection, you may also have a strong desire to be left alone most times due to your alone time feeling like that's the only time you will ever be safe from the "harsh world out there."
- You struggle to know who you really are. Identity crisis is a common theme in your life.
- You often look for external validation to feel good about yourself.

The Science of Trauma: How Childhood Trauma Affects Your Brain and Behavior

Experiencing an adverse childhood doesn't only hurt the child's emotions. It also causes serious damage to their brain and negatively affects their personality development.

Below are some examples of how childhood trauma causes severe brain damage.

Heightened Stress Hormone Levels

Cortisol and adrenaline are stress hormones often released whenever there is any sort of perceived or real threats and danger. However, when these hormones are released and prompt you to take action, they cause your blood to flow to different parts of your body except the "thinking part" of the brain. This basically means that when your stress hormone levels are high, you switch to survival mode, and reason and rationality often get thrown out the window.

For example, if you think that someone wants to hurt you, you may not have the capacity to even question the rationality of your thought and just quickly act in a way to protect yourself from that person. As a result, if that person wanted to be your friend but you interpreted their closeness as a threat, you end up pushing them away one way or the other.

Bear in mind that all this may just be in your head. Reality might be totally different. They just wanted to be your friend, but because your stress hormone levels are often high, you just end up acting out of fear and being prone to negative bias. When such experiences get repeated over someone's social experiences, it can lead to *social thinning*. This is whereby people also start to reject or walk away from you since you reject or think the worst of them. Experiencing this outcome also ends up leading to more repeated traumatic events as you start to feel like people always reject you and assume that it's really because you are defective or unlovable. It's highly unlikely that you will realize that your outlook on life and response to things is what's actually causing the negative cycles to repeat themselves. This correct perception of reality can only come a little through self-awareness and healing work.

It's unhealthy for the body to keep operating under high-stress levels. Physically, if it continues, you may begin to be at risk for struggling with high blood pressure and high blood glucose levels—which may result in type diabetes later on in life, abdominal obesity, development of lupus, poor immune system, osteoporosis, and a myriad of mental health problems such as depression (Merck, 2018).

When hormone levels change in irregular and radical ways, it eventually affects the overall infrastructure of the brain and possibly causes lifelong health problems.

Epigenetics

Have you ever heard of the phrase "gene modification?" This is basically when your genes change or get turned off or on depending on your life experiences and the environment you live in. The study of how genes alter is called epigenetics. For instance, you may have grown up being multi-talented, but due to being talked down or mistreated, you might end up being able to do only a few things, which might not be even a quarter of your true innate potential. Or if you were born with the capacity to be free-spirited and fearless, abuse and childhood trauma can instill fear in you to the point where it becomes who you are.

Trauma causes gene modification. It can stifle your growth and abilities and even affect your physical features. Have you ever noticed people who used to look very different from how they ended up looking when their lives changed for the better? Maybe they didn't have outstanding physical features deemed by society as being "good-looking." But suddenly, the moment poverty and hardship go out the window, they evolve and look like a totally different person, stunning from head to toe. That's the bright side of epigenetics! The sad part is that child abuse and trauma can make someone's physical features not very pleasant or make them have stunted growth.

Impact on the Immune System

Your brain also controls the immune system. Your immune system is inevitably affected if your brain isn't healthy. Your immune system is a network of cells, nerves, organs, and tissues all working together to protect your body and serve you. You are shielded from diseases, and your cells renew and grow because of your immune system.

When someone experiences trauma, their immunity is impaired or compromised due to irregular and abnormal hormonal level fluctuations. You are also likely to experience inflammation very easily and take longer to heal from diseases compared to a healthy person with a normal upbringing.

Examples of diseases associated with having impaired immunity include asthma, allergies, anxiety, cardiovascular disease, depression, and being at risk of getting cancer too.

Neurological Alterations

Our brains are made up of billions of neurons that control our ability to learn, see, hear, reason, and form neural pathways for the habits we have.

When those neurons are exposed to high levels of stress hormones, it can weaken them and prevent them from being able to do their job well. This means that you may end up growing up with memory retention problems, learning disorders, difficulty coping with stress, and overall restrained cognitive ability. If that child had the potential to be an A student at school, they might end up just scoring average or even worse marks due to how their brain was affected adversely.

They might also become so used to the negative habits they adopted as a way to survive, such as being alone most of the time and having extreme social anxiety due to the way their neural pathways developed to reinforce those new coping mechanisms. For instance, you might have an avoidant attachment style and assume that that's just how you are; you prefer to be a loner. However, that might not actually be a true reflection of how you originally would have been if you weren't exposed to childhood trauma. Your personality might just be what your brain adjusted to thinking, and that's how it can protect you from "danger."

Personal Narratives: Developing Insecure Attachment Styles

Most people who have childhood trauma end up with an insecure attachment style. However, this can be changed, and someone can become securely attached once they heal. The attachment theory was developed by a psychologist called John Bowlby in the 1950s. This was after he experimented and observed how babies reacted to their mothers under different conditions.

Your attachment style is how you relate and bond to people based on your perception of social interactions or people. This style is formed during childhood based on how your caregivers respond to your needs.

There are three insecure attachment styles, namely (Moore, 2022):

- Anxious-preoccupied
- Avoidant-dismissive
- Disorganized (fearful-avoidant)

A child who has healthy development ends up growing up with a secure attachment style. This happens when the caregivers are responsive to their child's needs, loving, and emotionally attuned, not only sporadically but consistently.

This makes the child grow up trusting people and feeling worthy of love and care. They also become brave enough to explore the world, try new things, and play because they know that if they cry out for help, their caregivers will show up. This becomes the blueprint for their relationships growing up. Let's explore insecure attachment styles more.

Anxious-Preoccupied

This insecure attachment style usually develops within the first 18 months of a child's life. During this formative stage, the child gets inconsistent attention and attunement from their caregivers. One moment they might be loving and present; the next, they are distant or just negligent.

The child may start to interpret that inconsistency very negatively and feel like their caregiver is unpredictable and unreliable. So even when the caregiver is there, the child might still be on edge and untrusting because they think they will be left in no time again. The child grows up longing for love and always feeling like they have to please their parents just to avoid abandonment. This can also go on in adult relationships where you see anxiously attached people always chasing love, abandoning their needs while pleasing their partners just to get their validation, presence, and love.

Dismissive-Avoidant

This style develops when the caregivers are very emotionally neglectful and insensitive to the child's needs. The child might have gone to the parent expressing discomfort or crying and then forced to be quiet or not show any negative emotion. This would then force the child to always resort to self-soothing strategies and grow up hyper-independent.

In adult relationships, dismissive avoidants continue the same pattern of being overly self-reliant, dismissing their emotions and other people's emotions, or believing that they are defective. This comes from interpreting their rejection in childhood as a sign of disapproval or that something is wrong with them. So, they grow up with shame and fear of intimacy even though they need it the most. They avoid people or maintain surface-level relationships because they fear that if people get close, they will see how defective they are and leave them.

Disorganized (Fearful-Avoidant)

Children who experience child abuse or grow up in bizarre and dysfunctional families often end up developing this attachment style. The caregivers raise the child in unpredictable ways. One moment, they are loving, and the next, they are being aggressive or outright abusive to the child.

A child might be punished for something, and then rewarded for the same thing at other times. So, the child ends up confused and fearful in their relationships. They form the belief that people close to you are not always safe. Hence, they often tend to run away from people and also come back because they know the flip side of how someone can be.

Fearful-avoidant adults can end up being in relationships where the same childhood trauma they experienced is replicated. If unhealed, they can unfortunately and unintentionally also treat their children the same way. Hence perpetuating the cycle of generational trauma and abuse.

The good news in all this is that even though you might have grown up experiencing adverse and traumatic things, it's possible to heal and develop a secure attachment style. That's the beauty of the journey you are on now. The more you learn new ways of seeing yourself and the world, the better you become equipped to free yourself from past hurts and heal your inner child.

This chapter has explored the problem of childhood trauma and how its effects show up as time goes on. Let's move on to the next chapter, where we will explore techniques for healing and recreating healthy new beginnings.

Chapter 2:
Methods and Techniques for Healing

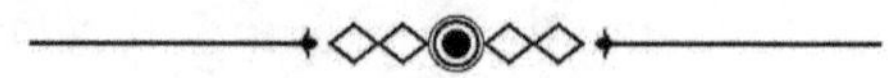

When we undergo childhood trauma, a lot of painful emotions are generated. Often, the child fails to have the support needed to process that trauma. Their caregivers might be distant and unable to attune to the child's emotional needs. This leaves the child feeling neglected and having to deal with heavy emotions that they don't even understand well. The easiest yet hurtful option to survive would be to either numb and suppress those emotions or just enmesh and morph yourself into whatever people want you to be like.

However, doing this doesn't make the trauma go away. Ignoring emotions doesn't make them disappear. They remain stored up as energy in our minds and bodies. Those emotions start to manifest in our lives either through passive-aggressive ways or addictive behaviors such as overreliance on drugs, substances, food, sex, and even being a workaholic and perfectionist. Your personality becomes largely influenced by your coping mechanisms. You lose the essence of who you truly are. You can even spend years of your life struggling with identity crises and the inability to connect deeply with others. Healing means taking time to address all that pain, process the emotions that weren't dealt with, and reframe your mindset so that you adopt the correct beliefs and thoughts about yourself and others.

True healing is a journey where you commit to connecting to the authentic version of who you are. You learn to embrace your emotions, be present for yourself and others, and meet your needs without feeling guilty for doing so.

Since most intense emotions like anger or sadness are often shamed or socially unacceptable, you might struggle to face them and even feel like what's the point. However, you now have to give yourself the attunement and presence you always longed to receive from your caregivers. Refusal to accept the difficult emotions within you only makes healing impossible because you would be disassociating from your pain.

Perhaps you might have grown up being scolded whenever you showed pain or cried. Your parents might have said to you, "Stop crying," and dismissed your pain when you needed their empathy and understanding the most. This may make you grow up believing that it's wrong to feel your emotions. However, nothing could be any further from the truth. Once emotions are felt and processed, they pass away like clouds fade away. However, not dealing with them is similar to clouds getting bigger and heavier and yet not raining. Feeling and processing your emotions is like seeing clouds finally release the rain. It will only rain for a few hours, days, weeks, or months, but the rain will gradually stop. Similarly, healing will be difficult, and you will feel those emotions for a while, but eventually, things will clear up. You inevitably reach a place of emotional and mental clarity. This frees you to invest more of your energy in building your life instead of worrying about unresolved hurt.

Before we dive into the methods of healing, let's unpack examples of the painful incidents that you might have gone through. Those experiences might include:

- Losing a loved one and not knowing how to process the grief.
- Being exposed to domestic violence.

- Going through emotional, verbal, sexual, or physical abuse.
- Experiencing racism.
- Lack of physical and emotional care. Not being given basic needs such as adequate food, a safe shelter, or clothing.
- Having your emotions constantly dismissed or shamed.
- Being bullied at school.
- Transactional love. You only got treated kindly whenever you did something for your caregivers, like tending to their needs or acting the way they wanted you to.
- Being left to care for yourself when you were sick.
- Frequently being passed around relatives and changing homes due to not having a stable long-term caregiver.
- Seeing adults under the influence of drugs and alcohol.
- Witnessing a parent being abused by their partner.
- Being forced to raise other children while you were also a child.
- Not being allowed to chase your dreams or have friends. Your life had to revolve around being available to do whatever your caregivers wanted.

Practical Exercises to Heal From Childhood Trauma

One of the biggest motivators for healing from childhood trauma is looking into the horizon and seeing how your future can turn out to be once you free yourself. Think about it: Up until now, most of your relationships and life choices might have been deeply damaged by the wounds you incurred from your past. You might have had a pattern of pushing away people, downplaying yourself, self-sabotaging, moving with low confidence, distrusting others, avoiding social interactions, self-inflicting pain on yourself, attracting toxic relationships, and so on. All of that can now become a thing of the past once you dive into the healing work. The main objective of healing from childhood trauma is to accept what happened and grow from it. It's to allow yourself to use your hardships as fuel for unleashing the best version of yourself instead of letting what happened consume and break you down. Ready to get started? Let's begin.

Become Grounded

Our minds are always racing to many places and filled with thoughts of the past, present, or future. To interrupt that pattern, take some time to become grounded in the present. Bring your full attention to the "now." Feel your spirit and soul reside inside your body. Be present inside your body. You can take time to feel the tension and weight your body is carrying. Massage yourself gently while you still train yourself to be fully in the moment.

Travel Back to Your Past

Once you have practiced being fully present with yourself, try your best to recall what usually triggers you. What are the things people say, do, think, or don't do that set you off? Which incidents triggered you the most? Why do you think they did? What do you think could be the underlying problem or pain point? Can you think of something in your past that created the wound you noticed? For example, if you have a pattern of easily giving up relationships or instantly blocking someone you feel violated your trust, could there possibly be someone in your past who did the same thing to you? Write down everything that comes to mind. Recall as much as you can and record everything that comes to your mind. Bear in mind that revisiting your past might evoke dormant emotions in you to hit you very hard. If this happens, don't run away. Continue to allow yourself to feel the pain and keep looking deeper into what happened.

Pay Attention to the Physical Sensations Arising

Once you start diving into the past, your mind might not be able to recognize that you are safe and not in danger like how you were when the events that hurt you happened. So, your fight-and-flee response is likely to be activated. This is your body also showing you how you probably felt when the traumatic events happened. You might sense tightness, notice your heart race more, and even start to sweat or feel lightheaded. All this is happening because your emotions are percolating. Take your time to explore all the sensations you are getting and label them as much as you can; for example, "I feel terrified and unsafe."

Be Emotionally Present for Yourself and Name Every Emotion You Sense

Printing a list of different names for emotions beforehand can help correctly identify and understand each emotion you notice. Try your best not to block out uncomfortable emotions. Instead, allow yourself to feel them and label each of them using "I" statements. For example, "I am deeply hurt and feel worthless." "I don't feel lovable because my parents always wanted me to be someone I'm not and didn't compliment who I am. I am angry at them for that."

Compassionately Acknowledge Your Emotions

For most of your life, your emotions might have been vilified and despised. Now it's time to acknowledge and compassionately accept them as part of who you are. Accept them as your loving messengers sent to inform you about your truth. Without them, you would be disconnected from the reality of the impact of what happened to you. Your emotions were there to advocate for you and be your voice. Start loving them more than ever before, all of them; this includes anger, bitterness, anything and everything! This exercise helps you to no longer be at war with yourself but learn to fight the real enemy—the injustice that happened to you.

Get in Touch With Your Core Needs That Were Unmet

Being in touch with your emotions, listening to them, feeling the pain, and processing everything helps you to notice what caused all the pain. You will start to have ideas of what you needed that you were deprived of. Write down everything that comes to mind. Be very clear about your needs, because, to this day, you are still craving to have those needs met. Tell yourself that you deserve to have your needs met and begin to acknowledge each one of them instead of living in disassociation.

Let It All Out

Writing is a great way to give your emotions a voice. Let it all out. Share everything you recall. If you wish to speak to someone, you can do so. Let them know that you don't need advice or anything; you just want them to be present with you in your experiences. Also, write down all the counterproductive coping mechanisms you adopted in a bid to survive. Then, write how you would respond differently to those situations now that you know better and can protect yourself.

Let the Pain Go

After processing everything, it's now time to return to your body in the present and move forward on a clean slate. If there is someone you want to express your resentment or anger to, you can write a letter to that person, read it out loud, and burn it once you are done. Visualize all the energy and pain that was stored up inside you. If you get triggered again and experience a relapse, don't be hard on yourself. It just means that some wounds might need more time before you can fully be healed from their impact. You can repeat this process when necessary until you feel fully liberated from your past.

Techniques for Healing Trauma

When working with a therapist or someone else who can support your healing journey, these techniques can be very helpful in your path to overcoming past trauma.

Eye Movement Desensitization and Reprocessing (EMDR)

This is a psychotherapy approach to helping reduce the effects of trauma. It can lessen the intensity of memories you have of what happened before. It works by moving your eyes from side to side while also harnessing talk therapy to explore and reframe negative beliefs, thoughts, and emotions that were repressed in you. You can make use of affirmations to silence negative self-talk and reprogram your mind for healing and health.

Cognitive Processing Therapy (CPT)

This is an action-focused approach to healing the effects of childhood trauma. You do this by examining your life and taking note of negative cycles and patterns that resulted from the unhealthy beliefs and thoughts you adopted from experiencing trauma. You learn to adapt to new ways of approaching things. You start to practice thinking, talking, and acting differently. All this allows you to no longer be a victim of your past. It can also help you start to perform very well in your endeavors due to no longer having negative voices and the wrong outlook on life holding you back.

Art or Music Therapy

Sometimes, you might find it hard to express yourself through words. In such situations, using art and singing can help you to express yourself. You can use images and colors or the emotions in certain parts of your songs to tell your story.

Exposure Therapy

This is a very effective way to heal from the effects of trauma. Trauma makes us avoid things we are afraid of. For example, you might avoid socializing, confrontations, conflict, getting close to people, or being emotionally expressive. The only way you can heal from this is by doing the very thing you avoid. You can only heal from this by doing the very thing you avoid. This allows you to confront your fears and no longer allow them to run your life.

Breaking Habit Loops

If you've observed your habits closely before doing anything, there is always a loop that you follow. This loop is comprised of three components that trigger you to action out something. Let's review what those components are.

A Cue

Before doing something you often do, a cue or trigger usually makes you participate in your habits. This cue could be a specific place, time, emotional state, what you watch, or being around certain people. For example, if you lay on your bed during the day, you will likely take a nap or watch Netflix. In this case, being in bed is the cue that triggers the habit of napping or Netflix and chilling.

Your Routine

We all follow some pattern every day. Maybe you always wake up at 6:00 a.m. Or perhaps you enjoy snacking just before bedtime. You are likely to repeat most habits mainly because your mind has been programmed to repeat them at certain times.

Rewards

You will most likely repeat habits that you feel have the most benefits for you. For example, if you feel that sleeping helps you feel better, you will likely repeat that habit consistently. You would be less motivated to repeat habits that aren't pleasurable to you.

You can break your habit loop by identifying the habits that are pulling you back. So check your routine and decide to replace that time with a new habit that will yield better results for you. Be mindful of your triggers. Try to avoid places or things that make it hard for you to resist bad habits. For example, if you keep going to fast-food restaurants when yet you want to eat healthy, it might make that goal almost impossible to achieve. Another way to kick start new habits is to use your guilty pleasures as your reward. If you attach something exciting to look forward to once you finish a habit you find boring or addictive, you can have enough motivation to get it done.

Finally, the key to creating new habits is to consistently keep doing them until new neural pathways are formed in your brain that allow those habits to be repeated almost automatically or naturally without you having to force yourself so much. The same goes for overcoming bad behaviors we might have adopted due to childhood traumas. For instance, if you always keep people at arm's length, you can practice being more open to deep conversations and sharing your life with others. Don't isolate yourself. The more you keep at it, the less social anxiety you will have.

Embracing Self-Love and Self-Compassion

One of the biggest core wounds resulting from childhood trauma is self-love deficiency. Learning how to develop this love for ourselves is important instead of always looking for it outside us. No measure of love we get outside ourselves will ever be enough to quench the thirst our soul has for self-love.

Below are some helpful tips to help you cultivate deep-seated compassion for yourself and lasting self-love:

- **Permit yourself to make mistakes:** You probably recall being hurt and rejected for making mistakes and consequently terrified of failure. However, life gives you countless growth opportunities where you won't always have answers to everything. Only leaping when you are sure you won't fail may stifle your growth and make it hard for you to feel self-actualized. Therefore, start to commit to being a risk taker. Remember that there is no such thing as failure if you try to improve yourself. Remember that no matter what happens, you will always be there to cheer for yourself. Embrace the growth mindset and remember that making mistakes is human!

- **Love yourself the way you would love someone you deeply care about:** It's often very easy to love others. We are, at times, willing to sacrifice so much for those we love and yet give ourselves breadcrumbs. Create a blueprint of how you would love someone you care about. Start doing all those things for you. Be emotionally available for yourself and start being sensitive and responsive to your needs.

- **Maintain healthy boundaries:** Before, you might have let others walk all over you. However, now it's time to learn to say no and only do what you deem best. It's okay to say no to your loved ones if they expect too much from you. It's okay to avoid toxic relationships and call out unacceptable behaviors. Start standing your ground and learning how to be more assertive.

- **Use affirmations to reframe your mindset:** Traumatic experiences can incite a pattern of constant negative self-talk. You might have believed very negative things about yourself and others. Start to detox all that poison and replace unhealthy thoughts with empowering and positive affirmations. Connect to your true worth and practice showing up as the person you have always wanted to be.

- **Never compromise your self-care:** Take some time each day to look after your body, soul, and mind. Nourish your mind with books that grow your confidence and self-esteem. Take some time to exercise each day. Eat healthy. Sleep well. Make some time to connect with others and enjoy relationships. Continue to unleash your full potential.

- **Journal:** Write your thoughts and progress daily. Set goals and have clear action plans on what you will do to create the life of your dreams. Ask for help where need be. Nourish your connections and leverage your support network to help to improve.

- **Build your self-trust:** Develop a healthy relationship with yourself by committing to always keep your word. Once you set your mind on something, do it. The more you accomplish your goals and get things done, the more your self-efficacy will grow. Your self-trust will improve, and this will give you momentum to keep taking on bigger challenges in life. Be clear about your purpose, and never stop at anything until you achieve it.

- **Forgive those who hurt you:** Holding on to resentment is like drinking poison and expecting people who hurt you to suffer. It's not worth it. It only makes you miserable and prevents you from being your best self to others. Begin to let go of all past hurts. If there are conversations you feel need to be had for you to have closure, reach out to the people and speak about it respectfully. Doing this can be the beginning of new, beautiful relationships with people who hurt you. Speak your truth and live your truth no matter what; authenticity is gold.

Now that we have covered methods you can employ to begin your healing journey let's move forward to unpacking more on what you can do to recreate the life you wish to see. The next chapter will explore ways to set effective boundaries, enhance emotional intelligence, and cultivate authentic relationships.

Chapter 3:
Processing the Pain and Finding Peace

One of the most frustrating things is to know that something is not okay, but you just can't put a finger on it. We see ourselves repeating the same cycles of failed relationships, living with the same fears, sabotaging our success, and living way below our potential. Even though it can be evident that there is a huge problem that needs to be resolved, not knowing what that problem is exactly can make us postpone working on solving things. We start to give in to distractions and even lie to ourselves that we are happy.

However, the heart always knows its own pain and bitterness. While we are in our own company, our lives flash before us, and we get the same reminders that things are not okay. Sadness starts to sink into our hearts. Contentment and lasting joy become rare. No matter how much we achieve today, our unhealed past still haunts us until we gather the courage to face it. Not doing so means living the rest of our lives, lacking peace of mind, and settling for mediocrity. This chapter is meant to help you travel back to your past and make sense of it.

What really happened? Why did you end up having the personality you have now? Where does your deep-rooted sadness come from? Where do all your fears come from? Why do they have such a strong hold on you? Who is the real you? If it wasn't forgo-getters all the adverse childhood experiences you had, who would you have evolved to be? Do you remember who originally hurt you? What were the needs you had when you were a child that were either violated or neglected? What happened? Can you travel back with me now? You don't have to do it alone.

Understanding the Link Between Your Past and Present Life

At this stage, you have to get ready to face your past in its entirety. Get ready to sit in the true reality of what happened to you. It's the only way you can be emotionally detoxed and set free from the pain from your past that has been driving most of your decisions about how you choose to live.

Writing is one of the best ways to give yourself a safe outlet to pour out your heart. Find a quiet place without distractions where you can have a meditative state and listen to all the pain that you have been repressing for long. It's now time to give your inner child a voice. Let that child speak their truth and express everything. Do you notice how that child has been trying their best to be heard throughout your life up until now?

That child is the one who tells you that they don't feel safe in certain situations, and it would manifest as you choose to either isolate yourself from certain people and environments or just keep others at arm's length. That child still cries out for intimacy, though. This manifests in your chasing after love and affection from others because connection is a human need we all can't live without. As soon as that child feels frightened by the people it's trying to get affection from, the child withdraws again. You see this through you having a cycle of unstable relationships where, at times, you are hot and other times cold. This child speaks in many other ways. Maybe the child fears humiliation and failure due to thinking by not doing well. It means rejection is coming. As a result, the child in you makes you avoid taking worthwhile risks by all means possible.

You stay for years in your comfort zone. Trying to be safe and free from ridicule or criticism. But that still doesn't spare the child from hurting. The comfort zone doesn't feel right. The child wants to soar and do well. So, you feel that conundrum from within you as you longingly look at your peers who seem to just be go-getters. They take risks; they progress in life. They push themselves and grow career-wise. Their whole lives seem to be progressive. You take a look at your life and realize that there isn't much progress. Your life is hardly a reflection of your true potential. But why? Who is stopping you from growing? It might seem like it's external resources outside your control, like not having enough resources or other people getting in your way. But if we deeply look at the matter, the truth is that no one and nothing can hold you back unless you let it. This means you have been the one getting in the way of your success. You didn't do this intentionally, of course. All you were trying to do was protect the child in you from being hurt again. However, playing it safe has undoubtedly proved to be an unwise survival strategy. It's kept you in your comfort zone. It's boxed you and stopped you from living your life to the fullest.

Upon realizing how much you have been blocking your own progress by playing it safe one way or the other, you may feel very angry at yourself. Before you sink into that dark place, consider this perspective. Do you realize that all you have been doing up until now were things to protect the wounded inner child in you? You didn't want that child to hurt again. To be subjected to the same pain as what happened in the past. So, you did what you knew was best for you up until now. Even though some of the ways you tried to cope were unhealthy and counterproductive, it doesn't change the fact that you have been fighting all your life to protect that vulnerable child whose pain you so vividly recall. It might not have been the best strategy to protect the child that you adopted, but what matters most is that you did something! You have been fighting the good fight.

You might have felt alone numerous times. Perhaps you no longer have a companion you could just trust with that inner child. However, it was hard for you to trust others. Even those who wanted to get close to you. You still looked at them with suspicion as you recalled how people who were meant to protect and love you in your childhood days neglected you when you needed them.

Your understanding of people close to you became that even they might not be reliable at all. So, trust was broken even before you got to give people a chance to show up for you in your present life. Before someone got close to you, you would already believe the story in your head that they are not trustworthy or reliable.

All this can explain why relationships seem to just fail in your life. It's because of the story you learned to believe about yourself and others. You told yourself that story over and over again countless times throughout your life until it became a self-fulfilling prophecy. As you saw people walk away, maybe you didn't stop and critically think why that's happening. As you felt like the same relationship dynamics you experienced when you were a child were repeating themselves in your present life, maybe you didn't open your mind to seeing things from a different perspective. Since chances are that you only trusted yourself, hearing other perspectives that could have been true might have been almost impossible.

Thankfully, reading this book is a sign that you have matured to a point where you realized that to heal and create a new life, maybe it's wise to open your heart to wisdom and learn from others. I would like to commend you for that courage and express my gratitude to you. Thank you for loving yourself enough to never give up. Now, it's time for you to get answers. You might feel like no one ever went through the same experiences you did or would ever understand you. But that's far from reality. The truth is that many people go through similar adverse experiences and childhood traumas. As we explore the topic of attachment styles in this chapter, you will notice that you are not alone at all.

The great news is that once you make sense of your past, healing becomes a lot easier and very much achievable. Another who had childhood wounds and insecure attachment styles can heal and develop a secure attachment style. You can be free from your fears and pain that used to run your life and hold you back. After this chapter, you will be ready to dive fully into your healing and redesign the great life you were always meant to live. It's never too late! The past was just a fraction of your life. Now you have the rest of eternity to step into your authentic self and live a life you will be genuinely happy.

Understanding Different Attachment Styles and How They Develop

Children are born completely dependent on their parents for survival. Any distance from their parents can be distressing, especially in the early days. They form their attachment to their caregiver in the early years of their lives. This entails the kind of emotional bond developed. John Bowlby, a British psychologist, developed the attachment theory in the late 1960s. It was after he carried out an experiment and saw how newborn babies reacted to their mothers after minutes of being separated. Four distinct attachment styles were observed (Mandriota, 2021):

- Anxious Preoccupied
- Dismissive Avoidant
- Disorganized Fearful Avoidant
- Secure

Babies that showed an anxious attachment style had inconsistent attunement from their mothers. Their needs were met, and then the mother would sometimes leave unexpectedly, and this would make the child very dysregulated. They would also struggle to feel secure even after the parent was back because of worrying that the parent would leave again. Anxiously attached children grow up having low self-worth and viewing others as being better than them. They interpret inconsistent parenting as a sign that they are not worthy of love. Hence, they end up looking outside themselves for love and validation because they inwardly don't believe they are worthy of love. This creates a toxic dynamic where Anxiously attached people always seem to chase people for love and end up being disappointed because no one's love can be a good substitute for self-love. They also tend to abandon themselves in their pursuit of winning other people's validation.

Children who showed the avoidant attachment style lacked emotional attunement. Either they cried or showed discomfort and didn't receive a response at all. Maybe the parent would show up way later after the child was already exhausted and despondent. Instead of welcoming the parent with joy, the avoidant child starts to avoid their parent due to no longer trusting them. Children who grow up avoidant end up developing hyper-independence, and they also struggle to maintain emotional intimacy due to fearing being abandoned and engulfed.

The fear of being engulfed in relationships comes from situations where the child growing up is forced to look after the parent or feel responsible for their happiness to the point where they can't attend to their needs. Consequently, it makes them grow up feeling very uncomfortable when people are too close to them because they subconsciously worry that the same unhealthy dynamics will repeat themselves. They end up pulling people whenever they crave intimacy and also pushing them away once their fears get activated. Dismissive avoidants end up abandoning other partner or others in relationships due to their extreme need to self-preserve and avoid feeling controlled.

Babies who develop the disorganized fearful avoidant attachment style typically have a parent who is usually chaotic, abusive, and also affectionate sometimes. So they grow up very afraid of people in relationships, and as a result, they can push away others too when their fears activate. However, the moment they sense distance, they start trying to get close to you again due to the confusing conundrum they find themselves in, where they know that they can also get affection from the same person who abuses or treats them poorly.

As people grow up, these attachment styles continue to show their pretty or ugly faces in relationships. All insecure attachment styles cause a lot of heartache in relationships. The bond is often not strong and healthy. There is a lot of emotional volatility, which a secure person can find to be very destabilizing and unbearable. If someone with an insecure attachment style pairs up with someone who is securely attached, their negative outlook on life and attachment style can end up causing the securely attached person to either be avoidant, anxious, or also have a disorganized attachment style depending on how they were treated.

This shows that when trauma isn't healed, it makes you suffer, and other people you come across end up suffering from your wounds, too. The cycle repeats itself over and over again until someone courageous puts in the work and raises children who are securely attached.

Babies that develop a secure attachment style feel safe and well-attuned to their parents. They would cry or show discomfort, and their needs would be met. This would subconsciously teach them that the world is a safe place and that they are worthy of having their needs met including receiving love.

It would also make them feel safe about being independent and exploring their world more because they would know that if anything happens and they cry out, they are likely to get a response. Ultimately, their early experiences make them grow up as self-assured, expressive, emotionally mature, and healthy people. They trust people and tend to enjoy interdependence in their relationships.

Without emotional awareness, it's impossible to notice and understand how children's trauma related to how your caregivers treated you might still be negatively impacting your relationships. You are likely to repeat the same survival strategies in your relationships and suffer from the same wound unless you amass the courage to face your past and work on developing a secure attachment.

Most people who are insecurely attached tend to be very unaware of the toxic habits they use to try to protect themselves from their fears. This makes them attract the same relationship and have history repeat itself in their current lives. To short-circuit that cycle and put an end to the childhood trauma and pain caused by adverse childhood experiences, let's now dive into exploring ways you can heal. Healing means learning to be true to yourself and no longer leaving out of fear. It's having emotional clarity and learning to express and stand up for your needs while also showing up for others in a balanced way. It means learning to develop sincere, quality connections with others and, most importantly, with yourself.

How to Heal and Develop a Secure Attachment Style

It's definitely possible to heal from any unhealthy attachment style. What's important is remembering that your attachment style was your way of adapting to the unsafe feelings you had. You did what you knew best then to protect yourself. However, those coping mechanisms don't have to continue to define you or influence your behaviors. When you were a child, it was understandable that you ended up acting in those ways and couldn't do anything more because you were still a dependent.

For example, if you are an avoidant, you might have learned to shut down your emotions just so that you won't be judged, dismissed, or abandoned. If you were anxiously attached, you might have felt the need to be a people-pleaser just so you could get the reassurance and love you desperately needed.

Nevertheless, now that you are an adult, you cannot continue to think in ways that jeopardize your freedom. Unlike a helpless child, you now can meet your needs in healthy ways. You no longer have to employ maladaptive strategies to survive. Recognize and acknowledge that there are better ways to do things. Prepare your mind and heart to face the truth and no longer live in the imagined fear of abandonment.

The first step in healing from insecure attachment styles is to develop holistic self-awareness. You have to know yourself for who you really are. You can also start to identify your emotions and make an effort to understand them.

Notice your behavioral patterns and start questioning why you act that way. Keep asking yourself why until you get to the underlying root core beliefs you developed about yourself and others, which drive your thoughts and actions. Some of those core beliefs may be true.

However, most core beliefs people develop after experiencing trauma tend to be quite warped and irrational. For instance, you might develop a belief that people generally don't like you and that you are defective. We all have flaws, but to see yourself as damaged good isn't a healthy thing to be okay with accepting. That belief can drive you into settling for the bare minimum in relationships and not attracting any abundance in your life. It can fuel learned helplessness, leading to you living way below your potential and still being unaffected as much by it because of believing that you can't do any better.

To help you fully identify and understand the key characteristics of each attachment style, here is a summary (Cherry, 2023b):

Signs of Anxiously Preoccupied Attachment Style:

- tend to be codependent
- fear abandonment more than anything
- overly dependent on external validation
- struggle to self-soothe and tend to overly rely on others for their emotional regulation
- extremely afraid of rejection
- usually clingy in relationships
- feel very unworthy of love
- struggle with low self-esteem
- due to their fragile sense of self-worth, they tend to be very sensitive to criticism

- don't easily trust
- always craving for approval or compliments from others
- can at times have jealous tendencies

Signs of Dismissive Avoidant Attachment Style:

- have a background of being left to look after themselves
- might have been reprimanded or humiliated for being dependent or asking for their needs to be met
- may have been mistreated whenever they tried to express their needs
- having caregivers who were very slow to attend to their needs
- grow up believing they don't need others and can make it on their own
- usually alone
- don't feel comfortable with people getting too close to them even though they do desire intimacy
- tend to push away people and dismiss their needs and emotions
- don't trust people easily
- tend to pride themselves on being independent but secretly also feel empty and sad that they live isolated lives
- struggle to compromise; they feel like people force them to sacrifice what matters to them
- afraid of vulnerability due to having painful memories of being mistreated whenever they expressed vulnerability in their early years
- avoid intimacy, especially emotional

- have a hard time understanding their emotions or being emotionally available to others
- sensitive to criticism
- often self-absorbed, people feel alone in relationships with them
- can ghost or abandon people from nowhere whenever their fears get activated

Signs of Disorganized Fearful Avoidant Attachment Style:

- grew up with caregivers who were sources of your comfort and pain
- extreme fear of rejection
- acting every hot and cold, confused love
- having a hard time trusting people
- feeling very afraid of people you love
- often show traits of both anxious and dismissive, avoidant attachment style
- have a hard time regulating your emotions
- can end up acting abusive, like how your caregivers used to abuse or mistreat you
- poor boundaries
- low self-esteem
- inability to form secure attachments, often inconsistent

Signs of Secure Attachment Style:

- have great interpersonal skills
- self-awareness
- interdependent
- comfortable being vulnerable and intimate

- healthy self-esteem
- emotionally available for themselves and others
- possess great self-regulation skills
- good at receiving constructive feedback and self-reflecting
- effectively manage conflicts
- usually in their true frame
- okay with being alone
- comfortable asking for help when necessary

Healing Strategies

Before treating any ailment, the first step is to always correctly diagnose what's wrong. Once you know what your attachment style is and what caused it, it's easier to start implementing healing techniques to help you overcome your past trauma.

Having insecure attachment styles is a sign that your childhood was traumatic, and that's why you ended up attaching to people the way you do. As shared previously, the great news is that you can certainly change your behavioral and thought patterns. Your mindset doesn't have to continue to be an extension of your childhood trauma anymore.

Below are suggested strategies to help you develop a secure attachment style.

Step 1: Acceptance

Accepting that something is wrong is what's needed to unfold the healing process. The more you continue to be defensive or pretend to be happy with the way you handle things, the further you will be from healing and becoming the best version of yourself. Acceptance means having the courage to face all of who you really are.

Trauma makes us take on a "false self." We hide behind the new maladaptive personalities we created to survive. Remember that what makes it hard to love yourself and have healthy relationships is that who you act like is not even a true representation of the real you. So that's why you feel disconnected from yourself and find it hard to have fulfilling relationships that feel safe. You probably worry that people will find out who you really are and all your insecurities, and hence why you play hot and cold games or settle for shallow relationships where you don't allow anyone to truly see you. Begin to accept all your wounds and remember that they don't make you any less valuable or worthy of love. When you start accepting yourself for where you are now, you short-circuit the cycle of attracting rejection. When we reject ourselves, whether subconsciously or overtly, we also attract people who reject us. Conversely, when you start accepting and no longer harshly judging yourself, you will also attract more acceptance and compassion from others.

Step 2: Forgiveness

This is a huge step. It's not something you should force yourself to do overnight. What matters is getting the process started so that you can let go of the bitterness and resentment possibly stored in your heart. You probably feel angry and hurt that your caregivers didn't love and treat you the way you deserved. You may feel like they messed you up and robbed you of a great life you could have had. You might be blaming and accusing them a lot for what they did. This mentality makes it hard for you to operate on a good and high frequency. You become sour, and that hurt can seep into many of your relationships as you unknowingly also perpetuate the unhealthy cycles of hurting others.

Unforgiveness prolongs the loneliness and abandonment you feel. Therefore, it's important to remember that for you to have the love and security of healthy relationships, you always longed for, you have to let go of unforgiveness since it blocks intimacy and causes you to ignore many opportunities for rebuilding healthy relationships.

What's even more important is remembering that unforgiveness frees you from the bondage of living in resentment. Sadness and stress never leave people who hold on to unforgiveness. To set yourself free and find your lasting joy again, practice letting go.

To ensure that forgiveness takes place sincerely and from the heart, you have to give your pain a voice. There are many things you wished to say that you might have lived in fear of expressing. To truly be free from that pain, you have to pour your heart into your loved ones and anyone who hurt you. Even if they don't respond well, that's not what should matter. What's most important is that you get to exercise showing up for that inner wounded child inside you who was so afraid to speak up or who got dismissed. As you share your story, don't expect people to validate your pain; you validate your own pain by sharing it.

You can also start by writing down your story and reading it out loud to yourself. Become the parent who gets to safely take care of the inner child hurting inside you.

Once you have expressed your hurt, get ready for the next step: repairing the relationship you have with yourself and others.

Step 3: Visualize Your New Life

Now that you have unearthed your past pain, stood up for yourself, and made amends with the past, it's time to look forward and no longer live your life facing the rearview mirror. Wherever your focus goes, energy will always flow in that direction. The point of this step is to stop allowing any of your focus and energy to be pumped in the wrong direction anymore. You may not have had control over your past, but now you have full control of your present and future, and it's up to you to recreate the life of your dreams. The power and responsibility of helping lie in your hands, meaning you have full control of what your life story will now become.

This step is about strategizing how you will now treat yourself well so that you can develop a secure attachment style because of the way you represent yourself. Remember, previously, we learned that babies that develop a secure attachment style end up being that way because of how their parents loved them. Now, you get the chance to be your caregiver. Now, you can give your inner child a chance to receive the unconditional and consistent love, respect, care, attention, and affection they always longed to have. Imagine how exciting that is! You can give yourself the limitless love that will help you to feel self-assured and have healthy relationships with others.

Start creating routines and plans for how you will take care of yourself. What are the daily activities you will do to meet your needs moving forward? What are your needs? What are the values and principles you would like to live by moving forward? What are your boundaries, and how will you communicate them to others and maintain them? What are your dreams and purpose? What do you enjoy doing? What do you dislike? What would you like to explore about yourself? What have you always to be and do? What's stopping you? What can you do to make a way to achieve your goals and dreams? What are you afraid of? How will you face those fears?

This is the part where you have to put in a lot of work to redesign your life and write down a blueprint of the life you want to create for yourself. Take some time to meditate and think deeply about this, and keep updating your vision as more answers keep coming to you. Use the above questions as guidelines to help you envision and redesign your life.

Step 4: Action Out Your Plan

The next step is to implement your plans. All your goals have to be time-bound. You can set short- and long-term goals of what you would like to accomplish. Every area of your life needs to be well-balanced; there shouldn't be negligence in any aspect of your life. The key is to now practice living a life where you are truly attuned and connected with your needs. Every dismissed need or emotion will only hurt you even more.

Make sure that your health, relationships, recreational life, career, family, dreams, spiritual life, and mental health are well catered for. Conduct weekly evaluation sessions where you assess how things are going and adjust what needs to be adjusted accordingly.

This stage is the habit formation stage. It's the time when you have to let go of old habits and press forward to create new ones. It takes time, about three weeks on average, for the brain to get used to new habits and form established neural pathways that will reinforce those new habits. Your goal should be to never give up within those first weeks. It only gets easier with time. Even if you do falter here and there, don't be hard on yourself. Keep trying; as long as you don't give up, you are still going to be on the winning path.

Our brains are built very uniquely with special abilities to adapt and change. As you form new habits, your brain will be engraving them into your new being through the process called neuroplasticity. Simply put the brain changes based on how you train it (through adopting new habits).

You can also journal your process and take some time to celebrate your small wins along the way. Don't wait for perfection to come before you can start being proud of yourself. There is no such thing! The whole excitement and fun lies in making the most of your journey and enjoying every step along the way.

Yes, you will have times when you might relapse and return to old habits, but just keep going. You will learn what works better and what doesn't through trial and error. Always exercise self-compassion and be your biggest cheerleader.

Think about how a loving parent would treat their child who is learning new things for the first time; that parent won't reprimand or reject the child for making mistakes. The parent just wants what's best for the child and offers all the necessary support and encouragement. The child also doesn't take to heart their mistakes. They just keep going until they master whatever new skill they are trying to acquire.

Children also learn a lot from observation. You can also adopt the same strategy and try your best to emulate people who model the behaviors and mindsets you wish to have. Become that loving and encouraging parent to your inner child who only cheers them on. This will silence any previous patterns of negative self-talk and create a new, loving way for you to communicate with yourself.

Examples of habits you can practice to heal your inner child include:

- Practicing saying "no" if you don't want to do something or agree with it.
- Speaking your truth always, even if you are worried it might offend someone.
- Being intentional about creating deep bonds with others, making the first move.
- Taking time to understand and process your emotions instead of shutting them down.
- Create a well-balanced life, and don't forget to have fun.
- Practice healthy self-regulation strategies like taking nature walks, listening to music, and asking to confide in a trusted friend.
- Speak well of people who hurt you, and let go of the old story.

- Give what you want to receive from others.
- Practice being fully present with yourself and others.
- Become a great listener; start by listening to yourself well.
- Create a routine and be disciplined to stick to it.
- Delay gratification, do things the right way.
- Avoid using unhealthy coping mechanisms to deal with your emotional pain, e.g., isolating yourself, pretending you are okay, people-pleasing.
- Set and enforce your boundaries assertively.
- Focus on learning how to love and validate yourself instead of expecting others to do it for you.
- Explore the world, and try new things.
- Practice communicating your needs effectively.
- Do things that challenge your fears.
- Ask for help when you need it.
- Use affirmations to plant new healthy beliefs and thoughts in your mind.
- Eat well.
- Exercise regularly.
- Get adequate sleep.
- Spoil yourself from time to time.
- Respect your time, and avoid procrastinating.
- Let go of negative self-talk and ruminate on what happened to you in your childhood.

Step 5: Develop and Nurture a Strong Support Network

You can go far by trying to do things alone, but you will go even way further if you open your heart to allowing others to be there for you too. Start to create and nourish new relationships with friends and family members who care about you. Invest your time and energy into building those connections so that there is mutual respect and reciprocal support. Practice giving and receiving love in those relationships. Being in actual relationships with different people gives us the real-life training and experience we need to overcome our bad habits and become better people.

Be open to receiving feedback from others. Self-reflect and always find ways to better yourself. Share your struggles with others and ensure that you are not hyper-independent or too dependent in the relationships. Practice balanced self-regulation and mutual healthy dependency.

When your fears are activated, instead of leaving into your old coping mechanisms and catering to those fears, be vulnerable and share with your loved ones about your struggle so that they can support you and also not take your behavior personally.

Consider also working closely with a professional such as a counselor, mentor, or therapist to help you heal even faster and gain perspective. They, too, can be a part of your support network.

Step 6: Practice Mindful Living

Our traumas cause us to live most of our lives looking behind us or worrying too much about the uncertain future such that we can forget to be fully present in the "now." This can create a cycle of always feeling like you are behind in your own life and unable to keep pace and manage your daily responsibilities.

Mindfulness is the practice of focusing on the present and living with intention. Instead of allowing your mind to wander in all sorts of places, start taking control. Practice Being in your true frame and being fully present. If you feel distracted, take a break and empty your mind through the process of meditation, writing, or talking about what's bothering you.

Focus on winning each day at a time. Don't live your life always being plagued with worries and anxieties about what happened before or what you don't have control over. Your gift is today; make it count.

If you live this way, you will look back one day and be astounded at the enormous progress you made by just living one day at a time and training your mind to focus on "today." That mentally frees you from being controlled by your past or future.

Step 7: Let Go of All Limitations

Growing up, you probably gave yourself labels of who you are and what you can do. Other people might also have told you what you can and cannot do. They may have given you labels like, "You aren't good at sport" or "You are a shy person."

These are the kinds of labels you now have to question and challenge.

This stage is an ongoing stage where you now have to live the rest of your life detoxing from any unhealthy and unnecessary limitations in your life. Unplugging yourself from wrong core beliefs, thoughts, habits, words, and company should be your lifetime practice. Just as we all have to clean our homes every day and throw away any waste, you too have to clean up your mind and life every day by letting go of anything that doesn't serve you.

Step 8: Enjoy Your New Life and Be Grateful

Realize how you are no longer a victim of your past. Isn't it wonderful to look back at your journey and see how much growth you have experienced and will continue to? Now it's time to fall in love with everything about your life and who you are. Replace complaints and grumbling with gratitude. Always find things to be grateful for and kill the negative bias that might lure you to focus on negative things.

Life will always be full of challenges, but if you have the right mindset, you can always use those challenges as stepping stones to a more meaningful life.

Begin to serve and help others heal from their pain, too. Giving people what you always wanted to have brings deeper levels of healing and satisfaction in your soul, too.

Now that we have unpacked how you can dive deeply into your healing process, it's time to grow even more. The next chapters will help you how to master important strengths, such as knowing how to love yourself and be your most authentic and confident self. Ready to get started? Let's go!

Chapter 4:
Living Mindfully and Learning
to Love Yourself Fully

The life you used to live before facing the pain of your hurting inner child was probably a life of merely trying to survive instead of thriving. It's hard and almost impossible to love yourself when your inner child's feelings and needs are exiled or suppressed.

You lived a life mainly led by your fears instead of healthy beliefs. Navigating your new life as the mature and more healed version of you will require you to re-assess your core beliefs and form new habits that will help your inner child feel safe and learn to trust you as their new capable and adult protector.

You might have gotten so accustomed to minimizing yourself, allowing people to walk over you, not having clear boundaries, and living a people-pleasing life in an attempt to protect your ego and gain validation. This pattern disconnects you from the true desires and feelings of your heart. You become your own bully in your own life. When people see you treating yourself that way, it also teaches them how to treat you. You will likely have a hard time attracting love and respect if you don't give love and respect to yourself first. You are bound to be dismissed and undermined in your personal and professional life if you have made it a habit to downplay yourself and dismiss your strengths.

Thus, your life becomes a mirror of how you treat yourself. At face value, it might have looked like it was other people's fault why you weren't happy or making it as far as you could. However, in hindsight, you can notice the link between what you accept for yourself and what ends up being the reality of your life. If you settle for the bare minimum in your relationships, that's all that most people in your life are likely to sow into you. However, if you make it clear that you deserve more and sow the seeds to reap more in every domain of your life, there is no way that a harvest of abundance won't come your way.

This chapter will teach you lessons to help you take radical responsibility for your life. It will inspire you to create the change you desire to see in every aspect of your life. It all starts with learning to heal the relationship you have with yourself. Once you build a healthy relationship with yourself, that relationship will become a blueprint or standard of how all your other relationships are meant to be. The idea that we attract what we are is no myth. We can only invite the love, stability, peace, respect, happiness, and harmony we long for into our lives when we first learn to gift ourselves those attributes before anyone else can.

Having said that, are you now ready to get started with making over your life such that it will be a true reflection of your worth and myriad talents and gifts? Let's get started.

Developing Emotional Awareness

Our emotions are beautiful, and important messages are gifted to us to help us stay connected to our needs. They remind us how we feel when our needs are being violated or respected or when our values are being dismissed.

Childhood neglect causes many of us to disconnect from our true emotions. This makes it hard for you to know what you need and even who you are. You end up lying to yourself or forcing yourself to fit in just to feel needed or loved. However, living this way does not create a healthy foundation for developing a great relationship with yourself and others. How can people love and respect you if you are disconnected from your true self? How can others trust you if you change and easily morph yourself into anything or anyone just to avoid rejection? Disconnecting with our emotions makes us lose credibility and a sense of groundedness. We become like dry leaves being tossed about by the wind in any direction and at any time.

The first step in developing emotional awareness is to practice being true to yourself. Let's review the steps below to learn how to connect with your true feelings and develop better self-awareness.

Acknowledging Your Inner Child Feelings

Think about what it takes to know how someone feels. You make time to listen to them attentively. This gives you the chance to read their verbal and non-verbal communication to fully understand what they are going through. Similarly, for you to connect with your true feelings, you have to give your inner child quality time and just listen to them. Your emotions are stored in your inner child's consciousness.

You can give your inner child a platform to speak by writing a letter to your adult self on their behalf. In that letter, allow your inner child to tell you their raw emotions, what they want, what makes them happy, what upsets them, their dreams, and so on. Let that inner child express their frustrations to your adult self because, chances are, your inner child probably had a hard time trusting you and feels neglected up until now. To build a trusting relationship between you and your inner child, they first have to know that you will hear them out and no longer dismiss their needs. Listen without interrupting or imposing your adult opinions on the inner child. Just let them be and listen to their untold story.

Keep in mind that your inner child may have different emotional states. Sometimes, they might sound upset, other times playful, and other times, maybe even sassy. Just listen to them with an open and compassionate heart. Immerse yourself in your inner child's feelings and remember those raw feelings you often hide from people. That letter from your inner child to your adult self now can sound something like this:

Dear Adult Self,

It must have taken you a lot of courage to finally open and listen to me,

What took you so long? I felt so suffocated and unloved every time you ignored me.

I tried to tell you that dismissing me would never make you happy, but you're so stubborn and full of fear that you chose to live an inauthentic life.

Why do you doubt yourself so much? Remember all my strengths. You hardly ever used any of them to create the life we deserve.

Did you know that I was the coolest kid and also the smartest at school? You probably forgot because you chose to listen to naysayers and haters instead of following your heart and truth. Now look, we have been reduced to living an average, boring, isolated, and painful life.

You spend most of your time chasing love and pleasing people who don't even care about you. Why do you do that? I care about you, but you ignore me and make me feel like I'm not good enough for you. You would rather be loved by others than focus on learning to love yourself.

How does that make any sense, though? You expect people to love you when you don't love yourself. I am you! The way you treat me is exactly how you treat yourself.

Can you please also stop using all sorts of external achievements to mask your miserable life? There's no amount of money or fake relationships that can give us the happiness we need when we are just free to be ourselves.

Who you are is beautiful. Please believe in me. I need you to stop mistreating me. If you don't stop, I will scream out loud in many ways until I get your attention. That can look like you end up being sick or mentally ill. I don't want that for you because I am you. It will just hurt me to see you keep on suffering. But something has to be done to get you to listen to me.

Can we just be friends and embrace this gift of life together? I would like to join you as your partner, not an angry self, protesting against your choices.

I hope to hear from you soon. Please take action before it's too late. I love you. Hope you believe me.

With love,

Your inner child.

Wouldn't reading that letter make you tear up? This is an example of allowing your inner child to express their feelings. All you have to do after reading their letter is to acknowledge their feelings. Apologize where you have to. Respond with empathy. Assure your inner child that you will protect and not neglect them again. Words matter, but what will truly make your inner child feel validated is when you consistently prove through your thoughtful actions that you are now there for them.

Meditate and Journaling

Carve out time each day to talk to your inner child. Make it part of your daily routine. Do emotional check-in sessions with them. This is when you get to tap into your raw feelings and listen intently to what your inner child is telling you. Remember, your inner child is a true representation of who you are. That person wants to be seen, heard, and loved. Furthermore, your inner child wants to explore life adventures and work alongside you. Integrating your inner child into who you are now will help you feel truly connected to yourself. Once you reach this point, you begin to love yourself because you are being truly connected to the real you.

Meditation means being still and concentrating your thoughts on specific subjects or a certain thought or memory. You can plan your meditation sessions, for example:

- **Monday's topic**: Remembering games I enjoyed playing when I was young.
- **Tuesday's topic:** Unearthing and examining my core beliefs.
- **Wednesday's topic:** Creating new healthy core beliefs and writing affirmations to help me reinforce them.
- **Thursday's topic:** Unplugging from all the negative words I was told that are still attached to my soul.
- **Friday's topic:** Reviewing my self-talk and using positive affirmations to replace unkind words I say to myself.
- **Saturday's topic:** Coming up with a comprehensive list of new adventures I must explore.
- **Sunday's topic:** Tapping into my anger and bitterness. Letting go of past hurt and forgiving those who wounded me.

Sounds great, right? You can switch up the topics as you see fit. The more you listen to your inner child, the more you will know what that child needs you to address. You can add the topic they tell you about to your meditation schedule. It doesn't have to take long. Ideally, 30 minutes of spending quality time with yourself, meditating, and journaling would be best. However, you can still do it for a shorter time frame. Play calm, soothing music as you meditate to help you sink deep into your memories and thoughts and tap into your creativity.

Inject Playfulness Into Your Life

Your inner child wants to have fun. Most adults can end up making themselves live miserable lives because they block the playful side of themselves. Who wrote a rule that being an adult means you can't have fun? If you are following that invisible rule, maybe consider changing your ways.

Part of the suppressed emotions of your inner child is the need to be carefree and play. Remember how children tend to just get along with anyone. They can make friends easily and also get over other people's mistakes easily. Return to that enjoyable and adventure-filled way of being. Practice making friends with others and letting go of offenses instead of harboring bitterness. That will restore to your soul that essence of purity and being adorable, which we love about children.

Don't hide behind chores and work and use that as an excuse for not making time to play. Practice effective time management skills to create a work-life balance and carve out time for fun activities.

Learn About Emotional Intelligence

One of the best ways to build a healthy relationship with yourself and others is to develop your emotional intelligence (EQ). This refers to your ability to deeply understand and appropriately respond to your emotions and those of others.

Five key components of emotional intelligence include being self-aware, having the ability to self-regulate effectively, having interpersonal skills, having empathy, and being self-motivated.

- **Self-awareness:** This refers to your knowledge of your true emotions, feelings, thoughts, values, standards, flaws, weaknesses, strengths, and so on. Self-awareness comes in two forms: public and private self-awareness. To develop healthy relationships with others, you have to know how people perceive you; that's public self-awareness. On the other hand, private self-awareness is being in touch with how you feel inside. Other people may be clueless about your internal state. An example of private self-awareness is knowing that you are scared of losing your partner in a relationship. Your partner might not know that you have that fear, but only you might know it. Listening to trustworthy feedback and pondering on your habits and emotions can help you develop a good idea of who you holistically are. Doing inner child healing work like you are now also helping to grow your self-awareness.

- **Self-regulation:** We all have to take responsibility for our emotions. Self-regulation is coming up with practices or things to do to help you effectively manage your emotions. This means instead of just yelling at people or acting moody all day when you are upset; you resort to healthy practices to self-soothe. Examples are doing breathing exercises, meditating, exercising, journaling, listening to calming music, making your favorite meal, or talking to a trusted friend who can help you feel better. Self-regulation doesn't mean that you always have to do it alone. You can be interdependent and allow others to support you if they can.

- **Interpersonal Skills:** These social skills help you build meaningful relationships with others. Examples include learning how to communicate effectively, joining different hobbies and doing volunteer projects, offering to help people in their daily challenges, loving others in their preferred love language, and having good boundaries.

- **Empathy:** This refers to your ability to step outside your perspective momentarily and put yourself in other people's shoes. It's hard to be in a relationship with someone who is always self-absorbed and unwilling or unable to show any consideration for your perspective. You can end up feeling alone and underappreciated. Children who face negligence often struggle to empathize since they don't see that behavior being modeled to them. If that's your case, please don't be hard on yourself. It just means that now you have to accept that you lack that skill and be open to learning how to develop it. Don't insist on being right when people tell you they don't feel loved or heard when they are with you. A great place to start is to watch fictional movies or real-life stories that have characters who are good at practicing empathy. Even reading or listening to podcasts can help you develop your critical thinking skills, which in turn opens your mind to understanding perspectives other than your own. Working closely with a therapist can also help you harness cognitive behavioral therapy (CBT) to break free from negative behavioral patterns and adopt new healthy relational habits.

- **Motivation:** What usually gets you pumped up to get things done and achieve better goals? Do you always have to wait for something outside yourself to inspire you to take action, or are you able to stir yourself into action? People with high EQ tend to be very good at motivating themselves. You, too, can develop that skill by believing more in yourself and harnessing the tools you have around you. For instance, listening to music, reading encouraging quotes, watching an inspirational movie, or exercising can get you motivated to take action on your goals and dream bigger. Lean in more into those activities and more instead of only waiting for someone else to make you feel good and get you ready to be productive. Childhood trauma can cause you to learn helplessness, whereby you believe that you can't do anything to change your life. You start to expect someone else to be your hero. What if that person never comes? Will you just keep waiting? Even if they do, expecting other people to be responsible for your success is unfair. Take ownership of your life and realize that you are born with greatness within you. It's just waiting for you to put in the work of unlocking it and letting it shine.

Practice Setting and Keeping Healthy Boundaries

Not sure if your boundaries are good or not? Asking these leading questions can help you understand your strengths and weaknesses when it comes to boundary setting.

Do you have a hard time standing up for yourself, especially when people catch you off-guard? Do social interactions overwhelm you, maybe due to feeling like people end up invading your personal space and privacy? Do you feel like people tend to try to control you or even tell you how you are supposed to feel? Does your family or loved ones have many unhealthy expectations for you and punish you in some way if you don't fulfill their needs? Are you often abandoning yourself just to please others and be liked? Do you speak up for yourself when people are making false or rude claims about you? Do you always feel the need to say yes because you think saying no might reinforce your fear of being seen as a bad person? Do you over function in your relationships and attract people who tend to be takers rather than mutually reciprocate love and respect? Are you always overworking to try to prove your worth? Do you suppress your true emotions just to "keep the peace and not upset others?" Does your life reflect your true potential, or do you just settle for less? Do people respect your time and presence?

As a child, your core wound might have been being told that there is something wrong with you. Believing this makes you feel defective and not worthy of love or respect. It creates a core belief in your psyche that you aren't worth much. This belief is what then makes you enable others to treat you badly. It makes you settle for less even though deep down in your soul, your inner child might remind you from time to time that you are believing lies.

You can even believe another malignant idea that no one will ever love you. This can make you settle for toxic or abusive relationships, because in your head, being with someone even though they mistreat you is better than not having anyone loving you at all. That's why it's important to uproot all negative limiting beliefs you might have, that cause you to have weak boundaries. Whatever we believe about ourselves is what people will sense and reflect on us. Just like how most dogs tend to be aggressive when they notice that you are afraid of them...

Believing the worst about yourself also makes people mistreat you. That's why the first step in building healthy bboundaries is letting go of toxic beliefs and adopting healthy core beliefs. Let's explore more on that.

Uproot Unhealthy Limiting Beliefs and Build Empowering and Positive Beliefs

Do you remember what you were told about how you were treated, which made you feel like you were less than good enough? Who said those mean words to you? Do you think that person loved? Chances are, they were only projecting their self-hate or bitterness on you. So, you took things personally and were conditioned to believe that what they said about you was true. You might have even convinced yourself that you deserved to be neglected, abused, or given breadcrumbs in your childhood.

Letting go of that negative conditioning can free you from other people's baggage you might have taken as your own. Write down what those negative beliefs were. Also, try to trace the root cause of your behavioral patterns. For instance, why do you avoid social interactions or fear intimacy? Asking these questions can help you find certain answers like perhaps you were made to believe that you aren't lovable, or you will just embarrass yourself. So, you end up settling for a life that feels like you're imprisoned and trapped in many limitations.

Replace every core belief you have with positive and empowering beliefs that can help you counter the counterproductive activities or habits you have. Use affirmations to plant those new beliefs in you. Also, practice being the person you wish to be; doing this consistently will eventually rewire your brain programming and make you an entirely different and healthier version of yourself.

Set New Values for Yourself

If you don't have standards for how you want to be treated by others, people will just do whatever they want with you. That's why it's important to have clear values and communicate them in advance to others. There should also be consequences for those who happen to violate those values and boundaries knowingly. If you don't exercise the consequences you announced, people won't take your boundaries seriously anymore. It trains them to keep repeating the very behaviors that hurt you. They do that because they know they can get away with it.

An example of value and boundary you can set is saying something like, "I don't respond to that volume and attitude," when someone is yelling at you. Further, communicate what the consequences of them yelling to you will be, such as "If you keep raising your voice at me and being rude, I will walk away. Only speak to me when you are ready to have a respectful conversation." The time will certainly come for you to be tested. People will watch to see if you will honor your words. The moment you stay there and allow people to yell at you without walking away as you promised, that's going to be your recurring reality for a long time unless you put your foot down. It takes practice to get comfortable with applying healthy boundaries. At first, your voice might be shaky as you assert yourself, but more practice makes things perfect. Your inner child will also be watching you stand up for yourself, and this will build self-trust and bring healing to your soul. Keep repeating your boundaries until it's clear to others what you stand for.

Don't Dim Your Light to Make Others Comfortable

Another way to set healthy boundaries is to respect your greatness and potential. When you play small, you are dimming your light just to try to get validation from others. Think about it: If someone truly cared about you, would they be happy with seeing you undermine your worth and potential? No. They will encourage you to do your best and shine your light. This means that you have to have healthy boundaries with yourself. Know your worth and accept it. Know what you are capable of and go for it! Don't put off what you can do today until tomorrow that will only delay your success. The more you own your greatness and let go of the need to impress people who might not even care about you, the more you will set yourself free from living in mediocrity. Better to be alone or have few friends than to be surrounded by people who put you down and feel comfortable when you downplay yourself.

This brings us to the conclusion of this chapter. Learning how to have a healthy relationship with yourself is an ongoing work with no end. Each day is a new opportunity to show up for your inner child like you have never done before. You can break free from self-hate or toxic relationships by learning to love, appreciate, and respect yourself. Let's now move forward to the next chapter, where we will explore how you can populate your new life with pleasant memories and worthwhile pursuits.

Chapter 5:
Building Healthy Relationships

Trauma makes us have tumultuous relationships. It's hard to have stable connections when you don't know how to be authentic with yourself and others. This brings tremendous anguish to our souls. Human beings have an inherent need for connection. When we are deprived of true connection, we become anxious and unfulfilled.

Sometimes, we may try to replace that pain with chasing after material needs, trying to be hyper-independent, or using career success as a cover for our pain. However, none of those things can fill the void in our hearts, which can only be filled with authentic and healthy bonds.

After having a childhood that made it hard for you to trust others and also doubt your worth, how do you heal and transition into building healthy relationships? The previous chapters helped us recognize how important it is to nurture your self-love. That becomes the foundation of building healthy relationships. It's utterly impossible to attract healthy interactions when we don't interact with ourselves in healthy ways. Implementing the knowledge in the previous chapters and starting to love yourself first will make it possible to change your frequency and vibration such that you will be able to enjoy secure and lasting relationships.

Think about how the television works. If you want to listen to the music channel you can't stay on the cartoon network. You have to change the channel for you to hear music. Waiting for hours and days watching cartoon networks won't allow you to get what you want just because you are waiting patiently for it. You have to take action and go to the channel that allows you to access music. Similarly, not loving ourselves and expecting healthy and authentic bonds is futile. No matter how hard you chase people, sacrifice yourself, and try to please others, you won't have true and healthy connections unless you bridge the gap of self-love deficiency.

This is in line with the universal laws of nature. For instance, if you jump up, you will certainly fall because of the law of gravity. It doesn't matter who you are or what you believe about that law. It will still apply to everyone because it's the law of nature. The same goes for the law of attraction. We can only attract what we are. Our lives and relationships become a reflection of how much we have worked on ourselves. It's also like the principle of sowing what we reap. You can't expect to reap cabbages where you planted kale seeds. These examples help us understand why having a healthy relationship is impossible when we haven't learned to have a healthy relationship with ourselves first.

Nurturing Self-Love

We now know that self-love is key to healthy relationships. But you might be asking yourself what self-love practically looks like. *How do I love myself?* That's the big question. For starters, you might want to know that the answer isn't very far from you. Learning and applying all the things we have discussed so far is part of nurturing your self-love! If you didn't love yourself, you would have just remained in your comfort zone and stopped fighting for freedom and the life you deserve. The fact that you are here doing inner child healing work proves that you do love yourself and care about your well-being.

Nevertheless, you can still do plenty of other things to develop a loving, fun, and healthy relationship with yourself. There is also no limit to the number of things you can do to invest in your life and build yourself up such that when you contemplate about your life, you will be proud of the reality you see.

So far, what do you see? Chances are that you mostly see the pain and all the damage that your childhood wounds caused you to have. You feel robbed of the life you could have had. However, self-love demands you to face your past with compassion and use it as a catalyst for achieving the life of your dreams. Instead of being bitter about what you went through, you can choose to look at things differently and use your experiences as a springboard for reaching greater heights. Think about it: There are so many people you can help and connect with because you probably went through what they did, too. It's hard to have a lot of influence on people when all we do is just live a soft life. People won't be able to relate to you. Thus, your hardships and adverse childhood can widen the circumference of people that you can connect with.

Your past only represents a fraction of your lifetime. That time is over. What remains is an infinite number of years ahead that await you. You can get to choose how you will harness the rest of your life. What you create today and, in your future, can become your new story. Let's now dive into exploring how you can create a great story by employing different habits and practices that help you nurture your self-love.

Refrain From Comparing Yourself to Others

Everyone is running their race. It's utterly unfair for anyone to compare themselves with any other person because we all come from different backgrounds. Start to love yourself by accepting that being different from others is okay. It's okay to not have the same growth pace as others.

The danger of comparing ourselves to others is that we hold ourselves to unrealistic standards of perfection. Especially with the prevalence of social media, people must just show the glamorous side of their lives. You don't get to see how much struggle and pain they are dealing with behind closed doors. You may think that only you have it hard, but life is challenging for everyone. Thus, accept your cross and carry it with grace. Not comparing yourself to others will also help you to accept others for who they are and have compassion for them.

Start to focus more on injecting your time and energy into running your race. As long as you stay in your lane and practice contentment, nothing will easily phase you.

Begin to Value Your Opinion of Yourself More

What caused us incalculable wounds are the unkind opinions from others which, we soak in. We may have believed our caregivers, friends, or family members when they belittled us or called us certain mean names. However, now it's time to declutter all that baggage. You get to chart your course and form your beliefs and values of what you stand for now. No longer allow anyone's opinion of you to define you.

Decide whatever you want to achieve and become in this life and go for it. Let the voices of other people in your head quiet down. Embody everything you envision yourself as and own that truth. Remember that no matter how much success you achieve in this life, people will always have something negative to say anyway. Taking people's opinions to heart will only hinder your growth.

Accept That You Can't Make Everyone Happy

Just as you had to learn to take responsibility for yourself, you also have to allow other people to be responsible for their happiness. Only children deserve our undivided care and protection since they are dependent on us. However, all adults have to take responsibility for themselves. Yes, it's okay to depend on each other in healthy ways. What's wrong is when people disable themselves and expect you to do what they are supposed to do for themselves. If you take it upon yourself to always be responsible for providing everything that people ask you for, it can take a toll on your health. It doesn't also create room for developing healthy relationships with reciprocal support.

Accept that you won't be able to make everyone happy, and that's okay. Do your part to convey your love to others, but know and respect your limits. Sometimes, when people notice that you are willing to abandon yourself to please them, they can take advantage of that and keep exploiting you. Be okay with saying no and show up for yourself more. The more you make sure that your cup is filled first before trying to pour it into others, the easier it will be for you to have a lot more to give without straining yourself.

Permit Yourself to Make Mistakes

Think about how often babies make mistakes while they are growing up and exploring the world. It's what makes them able to learn so much in a short time. However, you may have been reprimanded harshly when you were young for making any mistakes. Maybe it caused you to experience rejection or abuse. That may have made you develop a core belief that you have to be perfect for you to be lovable and accepted. That thought has to be uprooted for you to heal. Whether you make mistakes or not, you are lovable and loved! You are worthy of love and acceptance because you are you.

Start allowing yourself to make mistakes more often. This won't happen if you hold on to being a perfectionist. Most perfectionists hardly take any risks because of failure. Even if they do take risks, they have a hard time accepting their efforts and being proud of themselves. They still feel inadequate. Break free from that vicious cycle by learning to be content with just doing your best one day at a time. Whether things go well or not, that's not what should matter most to you. What ought to be your pride in knowing that you left your comfort zone and dared to try something new? That alone is worthy of praise and honor. Remember that for babies to walk, they had to be willing to fall many times and make mistakes until they figured out how to do it. Similarly, embrace that way of life and also see mistakes as part of your growth process.

Your Body Image Does Not Define Your Worth

Our bodies are just houses where our souls and spirits live. The real you is your spirit, and you have a soul. However, society can put lots of pressure on you to believe that your worth is all about how your body looks. Don't fall into that trap. Love your body, yes, but realize that you are more than what you too like. What makes you special is your spirit and what you bring to this world. Make that your focus and watch how your worth remains solid and unwavering.

Don't Accept Toxicity From People

Remember that people can only treat you the way you allow them to. If someone crosses the line with you, stand your ground and make it clear to them that you aren't a dumping ground for their unacceptable behavior.

People will test you. Make sure you don't fall for any animosity. If someone refuses to respect and honor your values, it's okay to let them go. If it's family members or co-workers, you can keep your distance and refuse to engage in unhealthy behaviors. Asserting your boundaries doesn't make you a bad person. Maybe as a child, you might have been told that you are being selfish by standing up for yourself. Don't fall for those lies anymore. You owe it to yourself to take care of your mental health and sanity.

Face Your Fears

A crucial part of loving yourself is to face your fears and not allow them to control you anymore. Common fears that arise from childhood trauma include fear of abandonment, rejection, failure, and so on. Ask yourself what's the worst thing that can happen if you try to face your fears. When it comes to abandonment issues, remember that as a child, it's valid to have such fears because your survival depends on your caregivers looking after you. However, as adults, it's not okay to continue thinking that you *need* someone to survive. That belief creates an unhealthy dependency on people. As a grown adult, you can look after yourself. Other people's presence in your something should be a pleasure to you. You *want* them, not need them for survival. Being able to accept the difference between needing and wanting someone can help you lessen the extent to which you fear losing them. If they choose to abandon you, reassure your inner child that you will always be there to protect and care for that child.

Any fears we don't face and overcome become the very obstacles that limit us from growing. Usually, fear is all in the thoughts you come up with in your mind about something. It's usually just an illusion. When you do face what you are afraid of, chances are that you will realize that it's not as bad as you imagined it to be.

Rebuild Your Self-Trust

Living a life of dismissing your needs and feelings causes your inner child to not trust you. To rebuild your self-trust, start being fully present with yourself. Practice emotional attunement and listen to how you feel. Think about an appropriate way to respond to your emotions. Whenever you respect yourself, your inner child learns to trust you more.

Self-trust is also built through keeping your promises to yourself. Start setting goals and going after what you truly want. The more you stay disciplined and keep your word, the more your brain learns to also trust you. You begin to also feel great about yourself. Your confidence to achieve higher goals also grows when you continue to show up for yourself.

Seize and Create Opportunities for Success

One mistake many people usually make is waiting for "the right time" to do something. This is a trap to make you waste valuable time. There are always growth opportunities that will arise in every domain of your life. Seize as many as you can. Even though you might have a plan for what you need to do each day, you should still maintain cognitive agility and be open to seizing any opportunities you might not have expected to see.

Having a fixed mindset and only sticking to how you planned everything to work out can make you miss out on important things that come when you don't expect them.

If you notice that opportunities you want aren't showing their face, harnessing your creativity and creating opportunities is okay. There isn't only one way to make it in life. Be open to exploring various ways to get where you want to be, like using a car, bus, bicycle, or motorbike to reach a specific destination. You can also get where you need to be using channels you don't think you would. It might take longer and sometimes faster, but what matters most is that you do make progress.

You Should Always Come First

It's not selfish to ensure that you are fine before you try to look after everyone else. Think about it: if a mother struggles with mental health issues and neglects herself because she is always busy looking after her child, what happens? Although the child will appreciate her help and devotion, the child will still suffer from the wounds the mother has. Hence, loving herself is also a way of loving and protecting her loved ones. You, too, need to be okay first. Whatever is going on inside you will come out one way or the other. If your heart and spirit are full of joy, you will have a lot of joy to give to others. However, if your spirit is broken and full of bitterness, you will also pour that hurt to others. That's why there is a common saying that "Hurt people are prone to hurt other people too."

Practice Bravery and Boldness

It's easy to practice bravery in secret. However, being bold in public can be challenging. Start to face that fear. For example, when someone is disrespectful to you in public, practice being assertive and standing up for yourself in public, too. This will also teach other people a lesson that you are someone who respects themselves and won't allow people to just get away with unkind behavior towards you.

Social bravery is also something worth practicing a lot. Instead of isolating yourself or only talking to people you are comfortable with, start conversing with new people. Expand your social circle and go out more. Even if you may feel excluded in some conversations, find a way to politely join in. Walk with confidence, and always remember that anyone who gets to know you is greatly lucky. Don't treat yourself like a fan. Instead, own your uniqueness and treat yourself like someone you admire and love.

Appreciate the Beauty Around You

Sometimes, we live years of our lives tied to the belief that if only we have a nice house, nice car, great romantic relationship, and money, then we will be happy. Attachment to such beliefs can make you fail to see the beauty that's already around you. It blinds you from seeing the beauty in simple things. For instance, being able to wake up healthy, having great weather conditions outside, having food in your pantry, and so on. Start to recognize and be grateful for what you already have. This makes you make the most of all that's already in your hands. Which in turn brings forth more abundance unto your life.

When we take what we have for granted, it doesn't grow, and we don't grow. We also risk losing what we have if we are careless and ungrateful. Thus, let go of your attachment to what life was meant to be like. Accept what you can't change and humbly work on what you can.

Make Kindness One of Your Core Values

Being subjected to abuse or any continual mistreatment makes us more tolerant of bad conduct. It makes us accept being treated unkindly. That pattern now has to stop. Loving yourself means you no longer have to condone any kind of mistreatment either from yourself or others. The world is already full of so much negativity that you don't have to add to it by being critical and harsh to yourself. Cut any negative self-talk and make use of positive affirmations to help you plant new core beliefs and thoughts that bring you peace and harmony.

Celebrate Yourself Often

Celebrating yourself shouldn't only be limited to your birthdays! Find something to celebrate about yourself each day. You can do this in creative ways like making a delicious meal, pampering yourself, watching your favorite shows, buying yourself cool clothes, upgrading your look, and so on. The more you treat yourself like royalty, the more you will also attract royal treatment from others. Remember, whatever we sow, we always end up reaping that too!

Creative Ideas for Building and Maintaining Great Relationships

All relationships require effort. Just like how you are supposed to plow the ground, weed it, and look after it for plants to grow well, relationships, too, require a consistent effort to grow. People you might have thought you could never be close to may surprise you when you start believing in them and putting in consistent effort to grow better relationships with them.

Is there anyone in your family or friendship circle you wish you had a better relationship with? It's not too late to make that dream come true. Below are some ideas to get you started.

Mutual Support

Healthy relationships require both parties to be there for each other. If only you are giving more while the other is just taking, it will be hard to be happy. To foster mutual support, be authentic, and don't pretend to be okay with everything. Express your needs and try to match each other's energies. Give more to people who invest more in you.

Mature Conflict Management

There are healthy and unhealthy ways to manage conflicts. Unhealthy ways to handle conflict involve things like yelling, gaslighting each other, stonewalling, gossiping, name-calling, threatening to end the relationship, being controlling, and so on. Doing these things doesn't make things better. Rather, focus on healthy conflict management habits such as creating a safe space for open and peaceful dispute settlement, listening to each other, making ground rules for the relationship, having regular emotional check-in sessions to talk about ways to repair things and grow more, being respectful, being assertive, and privately addressing your concerns instead of embarrassing each other in public.

Respect

Respect means learning what the people you are in relationships with value and don't accept. It's honoring their values and boundaries. It's also not trying to control or force them to do what they aren't comfortable with.

Respect also goes along with appreciating someone's contribution to your life. When you always take people for granted, they cease to feel loved and respected. Thus, ensure that you express your gratitude for what others do for you. Politely ask for what you need instead of demanding. Respect also means viewing others as your equal—not assuming that you are better than others. It also involves communicating with decorum and not being passive-aggressive or rude. Things like lying, not keeping your word, and one-sided effort are all signs of disrespect.

Respect should be both ways. You can't just be the only one respecting someone while they trample all over you. If you notice that someone isn't reciprocating your respect, be courageous enough to speak up about it.

Have Balance

Relationships are indeed important, but they can't be all you invest your time in. You have to manage your life in a way that allows you to have holistic success. Make time to nourish your relationships, but also have ample time to attend to your personal needs and other aspects of your life. You don't have to lose yourself in relationships. Maintain your individuality and also respect the other person's self and interests.

Make Honesty Your Policy

It's better to be disliked for who you are than to be loved for wearing a mask. Allow people to know the real you. This helps you get rid of patterns of isolation and disconnection in your life. Allow people to also show you their authentic selves. Expect to see flaws. There isn't anyone without flaws. Only expecting to be in relationships with perfect people will leave you waiting for a very long time. The key to successful relationships is both parties being willing to work on themselves and put effort into keeping the relationship strong. Be honest and take accountability for any poor decisions or choices you make.

Express Affection

Relationships deprived of affection feel dry and almost robotic. Be in touch with your emotions. When you love someone, show them. Don't just keep that love to yourself. Use varied ways to express your affection. You can either give a physical touch when it's appropriate, give words of affirmation, help them solve their problems, give gifts, or always carve out quality time to nurture the relationship. Something as simple as greeting your friend with a warm, big smile the moment you see them will make them feel loved and wanted.

Support Each Other's Vulnerabilities

When people are vulnerable with you, don't use what they told you against them once you argue. That can kill trust. Be emotionally available for people and even ask them how they would want to be supported by you. Sometimes, you won't have to ask. The more you spend time with someone, the better you know what they need. It's also more special when you surprise people with what they need when they least expect it.

Be Fun and Spontaneous

Relationships get boring when everything is all serious and gloomy. If you constantly have fights, it can strain the relationships and even breed resentment. Be open to exploring activities to do together. Routines are good, but balance them out with spontaneity, and go out to explore various adventures together. The more pleasant memories you have, the stronger your bond will be.

Accept Each Other's Differences

You won't always see eye to eye with people, and that's okay. Learn to see each other's differences as valuable assets to learn from. Don't use them as weapons against each other. Imagine how boring nature would be if there was only one type of plant or flower. It's the diversity that makes things even more breathtaking. Thus, see how you can use your friends and family members' differences to edify each other.

Another good example is how the body works. Many of your body parts are different, but they work and co-exist well. If everything had the same function, you couldn't do different things.

Work on Effective Communication

Without effective communication, it's impossible to hold up a healthy relationship. Both parties have to learn to communicate in a way that fosters understanding. Don't communicate to hurt the other person. Rather, take a break and get some space to cool down. It helps you avoid doing or saying things you might not be able to reverse. Great communication is all about being a good listener and also effectively making known anything you want to share. This means learning to choose the right time to address certain topics. Speaking in a respectful tone and voice projection. Your body language also has to convey respect.

Practice Self-Regulation

As shared earlier, it's unfair to expect people to always be responsible for how you feel. You, too, shouldn't take responsibility for someone's feelings. If you aren't feeling okay, practice self-regulation exercises to help you clear your mind and cool down. Examples include talking through your feelings with someone, having nature walks, sleeping, swimming, or journaling. Be careful of burdening others with your unprocessed hurt to the point where you end up making people suffer for your wounds. Take active responsibility for your growth and consider doing therapy or listening to self-help content regularly to help you grow and overcome your weaknesses.

Travel Together

Traveling to different cities, countries, or local places together helps you to build memories. Work on saving funds well in advance of your travel date and plan together activities you would like to do. Challenge yourself to include activities you are afraid of.

Give Each Other Constructive Feedback

Relationships give us a great chance to learn a lot about ourselves and grow. When you are isolated, you are unlikely to know in full what your triggers are. You may assume that you have healed from your past. But that only happens because you are secluded. Once you interact with people, that's when you are likely to be triggered sometimes. Don't see this as a bad thing. Your triggers help you to know that something still needs your attention. You can then take action and examine areas in your life where you still need healing. The more triggers that get revealed sooner, the better and faster you will grow!

Empathy

This is one of the most important skills to help you connect deeply with others. Empathy just means understanding where someone else is coming from and feeling what they feel. This makes it possible to be compassionate and more accepting of them. When we only see things from our perspective, we can be judgmental and lack compassion for others. Practicing being a deep listener is a great way to grow your empathy. Take time to understand people's side of the story with an open and curious mind. Ask questions and offer to give your practical support when you can.

Shared Goals

Relationships that last long are those where you have shared goals and learn to work together to accomplish them. The struggles of getting things done bond you even more. Knowing that you are building something with someone makes you find more value in those relationships. Give yourself a timeline for when you would like to have accomplished specific goals. This will also increase your level of interaction since you will have to collaborate to get things done. Continue to challenge yourselves with bigger goals every time you achieve smaller ones.

Small Thoughtful Gestures

Showing people that you are thinking of them and giving pleasant surprises adds sweetness and warmth to relationships. It doesn't have to cost a lot. Even doing something small like writing on the bathroom mirror that you love someone before they wake up to go brush their teeth can be heartwarming. Do more of these small gestures whenever you can. The kindness will always return to you when you also least expect it.

Grow Together

For relationships to last, both parties have to grow. If only a person grows, soon, they may start to feel like they have outgrown the relationship. This can make it hard for you to still get along well together. So, encourage and hold people's hands so they can also grow with you. If they, too, have their own growth goals, take an interest and learn from them. Growing together also keeps the novelty alive in relationships. You continue to be fascinated with each other. Lastly, growing together also means always encouraging each other to never lose sight of how important the next person is. Never allow appreciation and gratitude to be extinct in your relationships. That's the glue that will help you to stay close to each other in the long run.

This chapter has shown us the importance of cultivating self-love to have a strong foundation for healthy and lasting relationships. Whatever you wish to have, envision it, and go for it. As long as you put in effort, the relationship will come alive. Be intentional all the way. There is no limit to how much depth and success you have when you wholeheartedly devote yourself to showing up as the best and most authentic version of yourself. It's only a matter of time before the landscape of your life starts to sprout with beautiful flowers of healthy and fulfilling relationships.

Chapter 6:
Fostering Lasting Holistic Personal Growth

Change and growth take place when a person has risked himself and dares to become involved with experimenting with his own life. -Herbert Otto

Achieving holistic success is one of the greatest ways to overcome the pain of a broken past or past failures. Filling your life with much to be grateful for is a great way to live an enriched and fulfilled life. In this chapter, we will be unpacking different ways you can grow in the various aspects of your life.

There will be days when you might glance back at your past and feel sad. However, if you fill your present life with the fruit of your toil and disciplined living, your present joy will supersede any past failures or disadvantages you faced. Let's explore the different strategies you can use to create a robust and successful life across every domain of your life. This way, your past doesn't have to hold you back anymore or be blamed for any current lack of progress or productivity you might be facing.

Being committed to personal development should be a lifelong promise you make to yourself. This is because there is so much potential locked up within us. One of the best gifts we can ever offer ourselves is to harness that potential, even though we might not always be confident to do so.

Pursuing holistic growth will help you to feel like you have achieved true healing inside out. It's one thing to feel great about ourselves, but it's another thing to wake up each day to a life we love. Therefore, your biggest responsibility is to create that life for yourself now. Write down whichever areas of your life you feel unhappy about and set clear goals of what you would like to achieve. It's time to take charge and invite more abundance into every angle of your life you can think about. Let's get started!

Financial Growth Strategies

Financial education is not just reserved for students who take on board that subject at formal institutions. It's a subject everyone has to learn since we live in a world where we rely on finances to look after our livelihoods. Below are key strategies you can use to develop a successful financial habit.

Diversifying Income Streams

Relying on one source of income can put a massive strain on you. It also brings with it lots of anxiety because there is always a level of uncertainty about the longevity of that income source. Think about different ways to grow your income base. It helps with financial security. For instance, you can use your savings to start a new business project, invest in a company by buying shares, or start an online e-commerce business.

Open a Savings Account and Pay Yourself First

Avoid overspending on unnecessary things by deciding on a practical percentage of your income you will save every month. Wouldn't it be good to pay yourself a lot? See it that way. You can save perhaps 40% of your income and keep it safe in your savings account. Doing this every month will put you on the route to achieving financial freedom.

Budget and Stick To What You Planned

It can be tempting to always slide into your savings account just because you know that it's your money. That habit leads to financial strain. Practice leaving below your means. Don't just buy something simply because you can. Plan how much you will spend, save, invest, and give to other courses or emergency things each month. Respect your budget. You make a financial boundary to protect yourself from yourself and others draining up your finances unnecessarily.

Invest for Your Retirement Funds

Imagine being in your 60s or older and still having to wake up and work all day. How is that fair? Love yourself enough to give yourself a timeline for when you will put up with toiling. You can secure funds for your retirement funds starting as early as possible, even in your 20s. A hustle-free way to do so is to find a good investment plan and stick to it. If you invest your money, it allows you to gain profit over a long period. Imagine how much you would have raised by the time you are 60 years old if you started in your 20s. Even if you invested a small percentage of your income, it would still count over a long time, especially if you take an investment plan that involves compound interest.

Don't Take High-Interest Loans

A lot of loans are just a way to imprison yourself in financial debt. If you are unable to pay off things within five years, think twice before taking any big loan. If you need a loan, rather consider going for a lower-interest loan. Take your time to research; don't quickly accept any offer that first comes your way.

Pay Your Expenses on Time

When it comes to paying off things, avoid procrastinating. Paying bills on time helps you boost and keep your credit score good. When you have a higher credit score, you get more opportunities to get lower interest rates when you need to lend some money. You can use apps that will give you payment reminders to ensure that you will do everything on time.

Continue to Invest in Financial Education

There is so much you can learn about finances. Continue to read financial education newsletters and books about finances, and reach out to a financial advisor to learn new ways to make better financial decisions.

Look After Yourself

Yes, saving and spending less is important. However, it's also crucial to remember that you worked hard and deserve to treat yourself and celebrate your hard work. Each month, make it a ritual to do something special for yourself. Pamper yourself or get yourself something that you like. You might not feel like you need it, but it's still important to remind yourself that you are worthy of anything good in this life.

Achieving a Healthy Lifestyle

Living a healthy lifestyle will help you enjoy the quality of your life. Let's review some strategies to keep your body and mind in shape and also maintain a productive lifestyle.

Let Go of Ultra-Processed Meals and Sugar

Sadly, many highly palatable foods tend to be ultra-processed foods (UPFs). These are foods that have modified ingredients. Unfortunately, the things added are usually harmful to the body. Examples include frozen meals, processed cheese, and a lot of packaged cookies. Studies show that they often contain excess calories, which leads to obesity problems (Gunnars, 2023).

The same study also indicates how sugar-sweetened beverages can contribute to high blood pressure and type two diabetes. Examples include sodas, sweetened teas, and even fruit juices! You can opt for healthier options such as having spring water, unsweetened teas, and blending your juice from raw fruits.

Let go of eating too many refined carbs; rather find food with whole grains. Examples of refined carbs that can give you problems include things like added sugars, white flour, candy, pancakes, chocolates, and so on. Getting rid of refined carbs will also help you get rid of excess belly fat and reduce the production of stress cortisol.

Sleep Hygiene

Being awake between the hours of 11:00 p.m. and 4:00 a.m. can strain your brain and cause hormonal disruption. Have you ever felt sad for no reason when you stayed up late for hours? Chances are that it has a lot to do with your body being strained because it *needs* sleep to function well. You negatively affect your mental and physical performance when you deprive your body and mind of enough rest. Dim your lights or switch them off to help your body produce more melatonin (the sleep hormone) around the time you head to bed.

Take Care of Your Gut

Your body works hard day and night to keep you well cared for. Imagine how grateful it would be if you could only put more effort into supporting the hard work it already does. You can start by including in your diet-friendly bacteria that will promote optimal gut functions and prevent diseases. Examples include taking prebiotic supplements, eating yogurt, kimchi, feta cheese, and sauerkraut.

Majority of What Constitutes Your Meals Should Be Fruits and Vegetables. You probably heard it many times while growing up, but it's important to hear it again. Instead of making carbs a huge part of your meal, switch it up and make vegetables and fruits the main character. Your body needs more of those than carbs. They are packed with many minerals, antioxidants, vitamins, and more.

Avoid Substance Abuse

Drugs and alcohol only numb pain for a short while but keep you imprisoned for a painful life you won't like. Now that you have taken the path of holistic healing, it's time never to allow alcohol, cigarettes, or drugs to be a part of your life. If you don't have those addictions, think about any other unhealthy addictions you might be suffering from. For instance, binge eating, sex, gambling, and so on. Start practicing living a sober life you will be proud of. The more you face your wounds from the core, the easier it will be to live a free life because you won't have anything to hide or run away from anymore.

Become Friends With Spices and Herbs

Spices aren't just good for making your food taste great. They are also packed with lots of anti-inflammatory and multiple health benefits! Start applying as many species as possible because your meals will significantly boost your immunity.

Meditation and Journaling

Take time to look after your mental health by spending quality time with yourself. In the same way, it's important to do regular emotional check-in sessions with your loved one, the same way you should also do so with yourself. Journal how you feel. Think about different ways to problem-solve any concerns you may be having. Use your mirror to remind yourself how valuable and special you are. Look directly at yourself and repeat positive affirmations until you sense no resistance to what those statements are planting in your soul. Avoid overthinking. It's better to brainstorm solutions during your meditation sessions than allow anxious thoughts to distract your peace throughout the day.

Achieving Social Success

Social success involves how well all your relationships are doing. This includes your family life, work friends, and other acquaintances you might have. Let's review some ways you can boost the quality of all your relationships. Most of the things about relationships were already covered in the previous chapters. However, in this section, we will explore more tips to get your social life soaring.

Research Places to Visit

Not sure what to do with your friends or where to go? The phone in your hand can solve your problems. All you have to do is research to find out more about events or cool locations to visit in your area or wherever you can afford to go. Make sure to pitch in on time so that you can have the entire time to socialize and make new friends. Take the initiative and make the first move to get to know someone.

Treat Yourself Well

People tend to be more attracted to someone who treats themselves well. Don't wait for others to make you feel good. Just show up for yourself more and prove that you already have your back. Change your closet from time to time. Don't compromise when it comes to self-care.

Talk to People You Don't Know

It feels a lot safer to just stick to someone we know whenever we go out. But that doesn't allow us to grow that much. When you visit social gatherings, mix and mingle. Don't just stay glued to someone you know. Allow yourself to feel awkward and make mistakes while attempting to make new friends; that's how you grow.

Join a Social Club

Having a group of friends whom you can deem as your support network in some way can help boost your mental health. Think about something you enjoy doing. For example, reading or dancing. Join a book or dance club where you can meet regularly and create lasting relationships.

Meet Up With Online Friends

You might have hundreds of thousands of Facebook or Instagram friends by now. Regardless of the number, try to build real-life relationships with people you notice can be a great match for you. You can challenge yourself to meet at least one or two new friends in real life every month. Keep an open mind; even if things don't go well on certain meet-ups, don't give up! Things will gradually fall into place if you keep trying. You soon meet people you can create unforgettable relationships with.

Plan to Meet Up With Old Friends

Another great idea is to resurrect your old relationships. They might be feeling stale or dry by now, but don't give up on them. Plan to stick to a specific date when you can meet up and bring a new lease of life into your connections.

Work on Your Active Listening Skills

When you feel nervous, it's usually because you are too focused on your insecurities and worried about what to say. Start to do the opposite. Instead of bringing the attention to yourself, actively focus on what others are saying. This will give you a better chance to hear what's being said and respond appropriately.

Give Genuine Compliments

People can usually sense flattery or a sense of compliment. Connect to people in authentic ways. Focus on what people do well. Compliment their true strengths. This will make them gravitate more towards you. When you give fake compliments, it breaks rapport and makes someone not trust your words anymore.

Spread Kindness

Whatever you give out tends to come right back at you. Start to show people more kindness and compassion. You are likely to be treated with the same level of courtesy most times.

Be More Approachable

When you walk into a room, don't you sometimes scan people's faces and body language to see who you can go to talk to? Some people's body language can make us uncomfortable talking to them, while others are good at being approachable.

You, too, can choose to become an approachable person by working on open body language and charismatic skills. You can smile more and make good eye contact. Hug and wave at people more. Instead of talking a lot about yourself, make the other person feel like the main character and allow them to talk about you. Treat other people kindly. When others watch you do that, it assures them that you will also give them the same treatment if they engage with you. Try not to be argumentative during discussions. When conflicts arise, try to de-escalate them by making others feel heard and respected.

Overcome Your Insecurities

People can sense how you feel about yourself and others. When your friends or family members detect that you are jealous of them, it can make them feel unsafe around you. Avoid having an unhealthy competitive spirit that makes people feel like you are always trying to be better than them. The only person you should be racing against is yourself. Focus on winning your race instead of trying to raise by dimming other people's light.

Invest in Yourself

Manage your expectations of their people. We often get disappointed when others don't meet our expectations and get bitter about it. However, it's important not to place this burden on others. Don't expect people to give you what you haven't learned to give yourself first. If there is something you deeply crave to have from others, look within and see if you have been depriving yourself of that thing. Work on finding ways to invest in your needs and dreams. Take responsibility for your happiness, and don't leave others to be responsible for it. When you always wait for people to look after you, you set yourself up for disappointment because the reality is that everyone is worried about their own lives. Work on having interdependent relationships instead of expecting too much from others.

Get What's Important Done First

You will feel less guilt about investing in your social activities if you first learn to manage your time effectively. Work on getting the five most important things done before mid-day. This will free your space up and also make you feel less stressed throughout the day. When you are less stressed, you will have better energy to put out in your relationships.

Forgive

You will err, and so will others too. Make it a happen to accept other people's attempts to repair broken relationships. If someone is showing remorse and trying to make it up to you, don't punish them more and continue to be closed off. Practice telling people that you accepted their apology. Once you do share that you have forgiven someone, be careful of bringing up what they did when you have future conflicts. That will only prove that you didn't truly forgive them. It makes it hard for relationships to grow because you will always be judging people for the mistakes they made ages ago. Let go, and don't hoard people's errors anymore. It will also free your heart from carrying so much anger and resentment.

Support Your Friends and Family Members

Just handling your own life can be very busy and even overwhelming. However, that shouldn't be the reason why you fail to show up for others when they need you. Find ways to always serve your tribe. The more you sow in other people's lives, the more they, too, will be inspired to be concerned about your affairs. If there is any relationship you wish could grow, start to become the change you wish to see. Lead by example and be forthright about your intentions.

Find Ways to Make People Smile

You might be surprised to realize how very little encouragement people get even though it's something priceless we can always gift to others. Find ways to surprise people from time to time with unexpected gestures of love and goodwill. For instance, fix someone's makeup if you notice that they put it on the wrong way. Send a warm text to encourage your friends to study for exams or offer to help with cooking. Being more generous with your spirit will open people's hearts to loving you even more.

Challenge Yourself

You can do 30-day challenges to push yourself to become a greater version of who you can be. Each day can have at least one new thing you have to do to improve your social life. For example, have a difficult conversation with someone you don't get along with, or visit your grandmother's house and offer to give her a massage. Think about thoughtful ways to show your heart toward people. The only way people will see the goodness in your heart is if you dare to prove it through your actions. Mere words won't make a true difference. Always ask yourself how you can practically show up for others. Life has a beautiful way of mirroring back to us just how much effort we put in.

This chapter has shown us ways to boost the quality of your life and attract more success from every angle. Approach each day with a positive and grateful mind and see it as an opportunity for growth and enjoying the gift of life. Decide for yourself what each day is going to be like. Say out loud and declare exactly what you want to achieve before the end of each day. Setting specific, measurable, attainable, realistic, and time-bound goals will help you evaluate your success level. It will also help you stay motivated because nothing feels as good as seeing so much growth in your life.

Conclusion

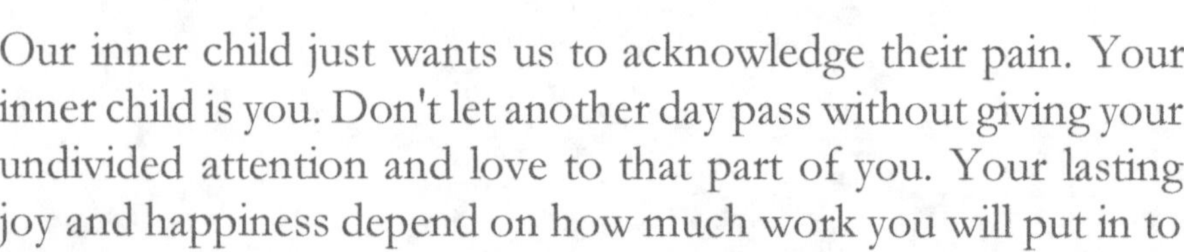

Our inner child just wants us to acknowledge their pain. Your inner child is you. Don't let another day pass without giving your undivided attention and love to that part of you. Your lasting joy and happiness depend on how much work you will put in to free that child and prove that you care about their pain and dreams.

As we are nearing the end of this journey, it's time for you to think about the dreams you forgot along the way as you were chasing after survival. What did you use to dream of becoming as you were young? How did you envision your future? What were some interesting things you enjoyed doing in your childhood that you might have forgotten about as time elapsed?

If you were to relive your childhood days? What would you do right? Now, you can sit down like an architect and plan exactly what you want the rest of your life to be like. You may not have had much of a say in the life you got to live before, but guess who's in charge now? You are.

Take some time to write your vision and create a clear blueprint of who you will now choose to show up as. We become who we are meant to be by showing up as that person. That means that if your dream was to be a medical doctor, there's no use for you to go study accounting. If you love nature, why live in a city full of pollution and buildings only?

It's now time for you to connect to your authentic self and live a life that's true to the core of who you truly are. The fear might still exist, but don't let it stop you from moving forward. All it takes is bravery and a made-up mind to get things done. You have already made it all the way and finished reading this book. For that, I sincerely commend you. The time has now come to use all the knowledge you are equipped with to create the life of your dreams. Your inner child deserves to be given that gift.

Thank you for reading this book. I trust that it has been a wholesome and therapeutic journey for you. I look forward to reading your reviews on Amazon. May your journey ahead be full of countless success stories. Keep tapping into your greatness!

References

Aletheia. (2019, April 6). *25 Signs you have a wounded inner child (and how to heal)*. LonerWolf. https://lonerwolf.com/feeling-safe-inner-child/

Cherry, K. (2022b, May 26). *The different types of attachment styles*. Verywell Mind. https://www.verywellmind.com/attachment-styles-2795344

Danielsson, M. (2022, September 23). *How to reach financial freedom: 12 habits to get you there*. Investopedia. https://www.investopedia.com/articles/personal-finance/112015/these-10-habits-will-help-you-reach-financial-freedom.asp

Grist, A. (2023, December 13). *Defining boundaries with inner child healing*. Amy Grist. https://amygrist.com/defining-boundaries-with-innerchild-healing/

Gunnars, K. (2019, June 7). *27 Health and nutrition tips that are actually evidence-based*. Healthline; Healthline Media. https://www.healthline.com/nutrition/27-health-and-nutrition-tips

Indeed Editorial team. (2022, November 30). *Career Development | Indeed.com Canada Self Development Quotes*. Indeed Career Guide. https://ca.indeed.com/career-advice/career-development/self-development%20quotes

Mandriota, M. (2021, October 14). *4 Types of attachment: What's your style?* Psych Central. https://psychcentral.com/health/4-attachment-styles-in-relationships

Merck, A. (2018, February 6). *4 Ways childhood trauma changes a child's brain and body*. Salud America. https://salud-america.org/4-ways-childhood-trauma-changes-childs-brain-body/

Miller, R. (2023, October 6). *Healing from childhood trauma: The process & effective therapy options*. Choosing Therapy. https://www.choosingtherapy.com/healing-from-childhood-trauma/

Moore, A. (2020, July 28). *Do you have an insecure attachment style? What it means + how to heal.* mbgmindfulness. https://www.mindbodygreen.com/articles/insecure-attachment-style

Ohanyan, V. (2021, April 22). *Build better boundaries with inner child work.* Womanly Inspiration. https://womanlyinspiration.com/articles/health/build-better-boundaries-with-inner-child

Perry, E. (2023, June 21). *Healthy relationships: 13 Valuable tips.* BetterUp. https://www.betterup.com/blog/healthy-relationships-in-life

Raypole, C. (2020, July 8). *8 Tips for healing your inner child.* Healthline. https://www.healthline.com/health/mental-health/inner-child-healing

Raypole, C. (2021, February 5). *Habit Loop: What it is and how to break it.* Healthline. https://www.healthline.com/health/mental-health/habit-loop#takeaway

Stewart, A. R. (2017, November 17). *13 Habits of self-love every woman should adopt.* Healthline. https://www.healthline.com/health/13-self-love-habits-every-woman-needs-to-have#13.-Be-kind-to-yourself

Verity, S. (2022, November 14). *8 Tips for social success.* WebMD. https://www.webmd.com/balance/social-life-success

The Shadow Work Workbook

Finding and Healing Your Unconscious Self | A Journey to Self-Discovery, Boosting Self-Esteem & Mastering Your Emotions

Sofia Visconti

TABLE OF CONTENTS

Introduction

Welcome to *The Shadow Work Workbook: Finding & Healing Your Unconscious Self—A Journey to Self-Discovery, Boosting Self-Esteem, & Mastering Your Emotions.* All of us at Relove Psychology are thrilled that you've chosen to embark on your journey into your shadow work. You have made a decision that will change your life forever. Your shadow uncovers secrets to the richness of life that, up until now, you may have not been able to reach. And I know your arrival to this point has not been easy. Just as Theodore Roosevelt once said,

> "Nothing in the world is worth having or worth doing unless it means effort, pain, difficulty..."

And he was right. The only things worth doing in this lifetime are the challenges where you struggle, resulting in a bitter-sweet victory because you've had to battle to reach your goal. And that's the road you will take with shadow work.

Is it worth doing? Yes.

Is it going to be hard? Yes.

Have you ever had a goal or dream, but no matter how hard you tried, you couldn't make it happen? Have you wanted something so bad, but for some reason, it never worked out?

This is the effect of the shadow self. An unintegrated piece of yourself that will remain a block to many of the things you want to do in life until it is successfully integrated into your mind, body, and soul.

You see, early trauma and conditioning can create a limited version of yourself. And past experiences and trauma can affect the way you perceive the world around you.

We all have personality traits we're proud of; and we all have traits we cover up, hide, and feel embarrassed about. Those can be impulsive, toxic, and shameful, exposing ourselves as out of control, triggered, and lacking self-awareness. These are not just traits we don't feel confident about; these are aspects of our personality that throw us under the bus. So, we go to endless lengths to avoid certain people and situations, trying to hide our behavior from public view. These parts make up your shadow self, and they long to be heard.

And when you finally listen, the whole world will open up for you.

How to Use This Workbook and Audiobook Version

Now that you are ready to begin, find a quiet space where you will be undisturbed. Light a candle and bless the space with peace and love to carry you on this journey.

Have a pen and notebook ready—a special notebook to journal and jot down things that stand out for you.

And don't forget: This workbook is designed to be used time and time again. However you traverse this journey, each time you do it, it will be very different.

If this is the first time you are using the book, certain things will be poignant depending on your current emotional state. If you decide to do the workbook again in a few months, your emotions will be different once more, and other particular features will resonate with you.

There is something to be gained every time you work through this interactive guide and undertake shadow work.

Before we begin each chapter, you are going to create a small ritual. This will help you complete the work inside this book and support you on this path.

Get ready to observe your journey and apply the following steps:

1. **Set your intention.** What do you want to achieve in each part of this workbook? What are you going to focus your efforts on? If it helps, journal on this so you can reflect on how far you've come.

2. **Take your time.** If you need to pause at any time during the workbook, please do so. Allow yourself time to think about what is coming up for you. But be mindful of

getting stuck in emotions. Shadow work is deep and introspective. If you need help moving past an emotion, journal what feelings are taking over and continue with the workbook. Remember, this is a complete process—once you begin, it is important to continue to the end.

3. **Self-reflect.** Throughout the workbook, there will be places for you to pause and journal, paying attention to self-reflection. Again, give yourself time, patience, and compassion. Your truth holds the key to advancing your self-awareness; if you need time to self-reflect, take it.

4. **Journal.** This is a very important part of the workbook. Make sure you write down every thought and feeling that comes up; this helps in the process of reflection, release, and integration. Everything you feel is part of you and should not be ignored, however distressing. This will ease your journey of integration as we move forward.

5. **Seek support.** At any time during this workbook, if you feel you need to gain clarity over an emotion or ask for a second opinion—ask a friend, mentor, coach, or therapist to hold space for you, so you can share these experiences and gain insights. This can be a huge step in helping you advance further in this self-care practice and ease your challenges at the same time.

6. **Integrate.** Your shadow needs to be integrated to allow you to regain yourself and move into full physical, emotional, and spiritual alignment. Acceptance is key to integrating anything you've feared, hidden, and avoided. By integrating lost pieces of yourself, your future self will be ever-evolving. Just watch your daily life improve!

7. **Celebrate.** At the end of each chapter of the workbook, I want you to celebrate yourself. Whether that's lighting

a candle on a cupcake to pat yourself on the back, buying a new outfit, or going out for dinner, mark your journey with celebratory milestones. This is a must as part of the shadow work practice you are navigating.

And don't forget, at all times, I'm with you.

Getting Started With Shadow Work

Are you ever triggered by something? Sometimes, it can be a behavior trait that you've seen in another person. For me, beginning my shadow work was tough. I was triggered by two things: a lack of respect and inauthentic people. This followed me around for years. I couldn't look at someone who had been rude or disrespectful to me and quietly think, "That's your problem." I would explode and shout or ghost them, punishing them with the silent treatment.

When I met a seemingly fake or inauthentic person, a similar thing would happen. I could feel my toes curl, and I'd be overcome with dislike, which almost felt like hatred. Physically, I needed to exit their company almost immediately, and I'd be angry with my friends if they continued with a friendship with them. What was happening to me?

I was looking in a mirror.

These aspects of people who, to be honest, I didn't know well or care too much for, were sending me spiraling. But all they were doing was showing me pieces of myself that I disliked. And using the word "dislike" is way too gentle. They were showing me pieces of myself I couldn't stand. I hated these parts of myself that I desperately tried to cover up.

As I took a more prominent role in my work, I had to come face-to-face with more people, and I started to feel exposed. What if others noticed these things about me? I was terrified, and so my journey into my shadow work began.

So, when you ask, "Where do I start with shadow work?" the fact that you're here means you've already begun. You've yearned for change, and deep down you know that you must walk this path if you ever want to truly have fulfillment and reach your goals.

The Importance of Self-Discovery

Self-discovery isn't just knowing who you are, it's knowing exactly what makes you tick. Emotional intelligence will get you a lot further in life than any set of qualifications will, and that's a fact. You can have all the money and the best job in the world, but if you can't regulate your emotions, or choose a partner who can regulate theirs, it's likely your life will be full of hurdles and chaos. You'll make poor choices and bad financial decisions and destroy things you've worked hard for. Sound familiar?

Why are some of the world's wealthiest people unhappy? Because they lack emotional intelligence.

So, to stop you from wondering what self-discovery is, let's look at what it encompasses so you can have a good idea of where you are on your own journey of self-discovery:

- Being in tune with your intuition, listening to your body, and feeling gut reactions
- Understanding your emotions when they come up and being able to identify why you are feeling them
- Expressing your opinions and defending yourself
- Stopping comparing yourself with others

- Setting boundaries with yourself and others
- Understanding what holds you back
- Acknowledging and understanding your fears
- Understanding when you are slipping into negative self-talk
- Developing compassion for yourself and combining it with self-love
- Identifying bad habits
- Starting to work on your bad habits because you know they don't serve you
- Setting heartfelt goals that are soul-desired and aligned
- Making a list of your strengths and weaknesses so you spend more time working with your strengths to avoid frustration
- Living intentionally in alignment with your values and belief system
- Fostering, developing, and cherishing relationships and exploring healthy new ones
- Learning from your past and forgiving yourself for the choices you made when you didn't know any better
- Looking objectively at your self-esteem, identifying where it could be improved, and accepting what you can't change
- Taking steps to work toward your ultimate dream or goal in life

How many of these can you say apply to you? Go back through the list now and check off the ones you can, making a note of the ones you want to work on, too.

The Importance of Self-Esteem

Self-esteem controls your decision-making; it is the power that fuels your choices and affects your motivation. When self-esteem is low, it can feel like you're batting the whole world.

Your standards are built on your level of self-esteem, and low self-esteem means low standards. Let's take the example of toxic relationships. When your self-esteem is at rock bottom, you will accept having a relationship with someone disrespectful, argumentative, aggressive, or who asserts coercive control.

However, when your self-esteem is high, you don't tolerate any of these bad behaviors because you know you're worth more than that. You are not attracted to people who don't have the same basic standards, so you don't welcome them into your life. You are not desperate to cling to bad relationships because you don't fear being alone. You walk tall in your skin and hold yourself accountable to a high standard.

So, you can see that when you have low self-esteem, it's easy to make poor choices. When your self-esteem is high, you make better, less emotionally charged decisions.

Make no mistake, self-esteem is your biggest driver in every aspect of your life.

The Importance of Emotional Mastery

Do you ever feel like you can't get control of your thoughts or emotions? Do you suddenly get angry or easily triggered by a negative behavior trait? Do you sometimes think so much that you become physically disabled by your thoughts and you can't continue a task, feeling overwhelmed?

These are all signs of not having emotional mastery. Emotional mastery is when you are in control of your feelings and you have achieved complete emotional control.

Is this a place that is easy to get to? No, not at all; but you can get there if you begin regular self-awareness practices that you continue to add to your life. Emotional mastery is a journey with no set destination, simply a path that evolves, shapes, and grows over time. Emotion mastery leads to emotional intelligence and is one of the most beneficial skills you can acquire in your lifetime.

Heartfelt Checkpoint 1

One of the features of this interactive workbook is to check in with yourself after each chapter. Before we begin your deep work, it's important to know where you are right now in your journey of self-awareness. Your self-awareness and emotional intelligence are the assets that will carry you through on this path when times get rough and you feel like giving up.

And feeling like giving up is normal on this path of improvement.

Remember, shadow work is the work we leave until last. It's the work we do usually because we have to; it is rare that we willingly walk into this arena. It's the work that if we don't do it, will trip us up and keep us from the work and mission we are meant for.

You are strong.

You are brave.

You can do this.

Self-Discovery Milestones

Answer the following statements honestly, using your heart as a guide to feel into your responses. Remember, there are no right or wrong answers:

I understand my emotions when they come up, and I'm able to identify why I am feeling them.
Always
Often
Sometimes
Not often
Never

I can express my opinion and defend myself.
Always
Often
Sometimes

Not often
Never

I do not compare myself with others.
Always
Often
Sometimes
Not often
Never

I know my own boundaries.
Always
Often
Sometimes
Not often
Never

I set boundaries with others.
Always
Often
Sometimes
Not often
Never

I know what's holding me back.
Always
Often
Sometimes
Not often
Never

I acknowledge and understand my fears.
Always
Often
Sometimes

Not often
Never

I know when I am slipping into negative self-talk.
Always
Often
Sometimes
Not often
Never

I have compassion for myself, and I feel self-love.
Always
Often
Sometimes
Not often
Never

I can identify my bad habits.
Always
Often
Sometimes
Not often
Never

I am working on my bad habits because I know they are not serving me.
Always
Often
Sometimes
Not often
Never

I set goals that are good for me and are aligned with my dreams.
Always

Often
Sometimes
Not often
Never

I know my strengths and weaknesses, and I steer my actions so I'm working on the things I am good at.
Always
Often
Sometimes
Not often
Never

I make intentional decisions that align with my beliefs and value system.
Always
Often
Sometimes
Not often
Never

I nurture my relationships, and I explore new ones.
Always
Often
Sometimes
Not often
Never

I can forgive myself easily for choices I made in the past when I did not know any better.
Always
Often
Sometimes
Not often
Never

I know myself and my worth, and I accept the things I cannot change.
Always
Often
Sometimes
Not often
Never

I take steps to work toward my ultimate dream and goals in life.
Always
Often
Sometimes
Not often
Never

Results

Always: If you scored mostly always, you are on the right track toward complete self-discovery. Well done, you! You've put in the hard work, and you're now reaping the benefits of understanding yourself better and working toward total alignment and fulfillment.

Often: If you score mostly often, you are on an enlightened path of self-discovery and you're understanding more about yourself daily.

Sometimes: If you scored sometimes, you've started your journey into self-awareness and now you need to practice consistency. Create a routine so you can further your exploration.

Not Often: If you scored not often, it's okay. What will help you get on the path to self-discovery is taking the time for self-reflection so you can understand yourself better.

Never: If you scored never, then this is the perfect time to start. Don't worry, we all started at the beginning, and this is the introduction to a beautiful, uplifting journey for yourself!

Now that you've firmly accepted where you are in your self-awareness journey, let's move on to deepen your connection to your shadow by understanding what it is and how it's affecting your life.

Celebration 1

Now that you've completed the very first section of your shadow work workbook, put on your favorite movie or show and relax, congratulating yourself for taking the first step!

Chapter 1:
Understanding the Shadow Self

Nobody wants to look at their dark side. We are willing and curious to unpick the dark elements of others' characters; but when it comes to our own, we often view ours with fear and shame.

So, what you're embarking on is brave—extraordinarily brave.

In this section of the workbook, we are going to take a deep look at what exactly is the shadow self. By truly understanding the key to unlocking your limitations, you will be able to take your life to the next level.

The next level of health, wealth, and happiness. Let's get started.

Defining the Shadow Self

The shadow self is also known as your dark side, the side of you that you are hiding from, have disowned, or repressed. The reason why we have unclaimed pieces of ourselves is that these are very often undesirable character traits. To explain what shadow aspects are, can you identify a time when you have acted out of character? Or is there a relationship where you feel embarrassed by your behavior? Check out the following list and ask yourself if you recognize any of these aspects in your character:

- greed

- jealously
- anger
- selfishness
- power hungry
- desire
- arrogance
- manipulation
- dishonesty
- cruelty
- stubbornness
- impulsivity
- impatience
- indecisiveness
- rudeness
- narcissism
- pessimism
- entitlement
- closemindedness
- egotism
- laziness
- intolerance

It is hard to face up to some of these characteristics, and not all of them are negative. However, the truth is that we all have many of these facets showing up in our personalities, and we don't want others to notice them. They creep in and seep out when we are not being our best selves. We need to mindfully communicate with others and work on increasing our emotional intelligence.

In a nutshell, we actively disown any characteristic that does not align with the way we want to be perceived. This forms your shadow self.

These disowned parts of you sit in your unconscious and usually show up when you're triggered or unable to master your emotions. If we own and acknowledge these pieces of ourselves, they don't interfere too much in our daily lives. However, when we fail to see them, that's when they creep up and cause chaos.

How the Shadow Self Is Formed

As a human, we come into this world with a whole range of emotions, both good and bad. If we are born with all these traits, you would think we should be able to use all of them, right? But from early childhood, we are punished for displaying negative emotions. For example, if you shouted or got angry with a sibling, were your toys taken away? Or, were you grounded for "talking back," to your mom or dad?

At this time, you were expressing an emotion you were feeling, but societal norms and socialization dictated that it was not good to express these emotions. It's likely you would be punished if you decide to display them. So, you hid them. Your primary caregivers, most likely your mom or dad, would have discouraged you from anger, shouting, crying, or even questioning. You were guided to hide or disown these emotions. And these created the shadow self.

So, for the first part of your life and education in this world, you believed you had a shadow, or a dark side, your bad side—the part of you that was not going to be liked by yourself or others. By hiding these aspects of you, you became unconscious of their presence and when they show up now, you deny them. You refute them. You blame others. You can't get rid of these features of your character, you simply bury and ignore them. This is your shadow self.

To accept this part of yourself—your shadow—you have to begin the process of unlearning everything you've learned so far about emotions.

The Impact of the Shadow in Your Life

"Unless we do conscious work on it, the shadow is almost always projected; that is it is neatly laid on someone or something else so we do not have to take responsibility for it." –Robert Johnson.

Your shadow will show up like a mirror. The things you dislike in another person are very often hiding in your shadow self. This is a gut-wrenchingly difficult statement to digest, as oftentimes, you will feel so strongly about these personality features that you become triggered and react badly to others who show you these traits.

Let me tell you a story about Melissa. Melissa always prided herself on being calm and patient, letting others speak first and remaining quiet and composed in the face of challenges, especially at work. Melissa had never undertaken any shadow work before.

One day, during a team meeting, one of her colleagues spoke up passionately and confidently about a project Melissa was also involved in. As a result of that, a lively debate took place between coworkers. Melissa instantly felt angry and upset with her colleague for not remaining calm and collected. There was no confrontational situation during the meeting, so Melissa couldn't understand why she had these emotions. She was confused and couldn't pinpoint where her feelings were coming from, especially since this was one of her favorite colleagues to work with.

This was Melissa's shadow self at work. Melissa had suppressed being outspoken and passionate as a child, as her parents favored calm, quiet, "speak when you're spoken to" behavior. Melissa had denied her voice. In this work situation, Melissa's shadow showed up very strongly, as Melissa had denied these aspects of her character. Her anger came from not being able to express herself in the way she needed to. Her anger was also fueled by knowing these are positive personality traits that someone can be rewarded for having, just like her colleague was during the team meeting. This sparked jealousy and resentment in Melissa. In truth, the emotions Melissa was feeling about her colleague were all about herself and her lack of being able to express herself in alignment with who she felt she really was.

In Melissa's case, we can see that the shadow created negative feelings about herself and her colleague. These feelings were hard to resolve and stayed with her in the days ahead. But it didn't end there. This reaction created more problems in feelings of guilt and shame for reacting this way about a friend and not having the courage to do the shadow work to retrieve these pieces of herself. From this one small incident, the shadow not only appeared but grew in size, too.

So, how does your shadow impact your life? Let's look at it in two ways.

The Negative Impact of Your Shadow Self

Your shadow self, if left hidden and ignored, will trip you up. Imagine it as a secret or a skeleton in your closet. At some point, it will expose you, and your reaction to it will be to run as fast as you can.

Your shadow, untamed, will cause chaos in your life. We gently touched on the negative impact of the shadow self that results in being unable to reach your goals fully or having a life of chaos. Your shadow will subconsciously attract the wrong people and, subsequently, your judgment won't be based on your whole, complete character. You'll make bad decisions and poor choices, and your alignment will be off. You'll struggle to feel fulfilled, perhaps always getting so far up the road and then having to give up. Not accepting your shadow is reflected in an incomplete life and life mission.

The emotional impact of this is usually reactive, impulsive behavior, feeling triggered, and shutting down further parts of yourself to cope with what's happening to you. In addition to that, you might be experiencing feelings of guilt or shame, knowing that you have character traits that you feel are ugly and should not be exposed to others.

If you have toxic behaviors, self-sabotage, or even more advanced mental health concerns—for example, hoarding—these can be part of the negative impact of the shadow self. Not dealing with them causes shame, anxiety, and further negative emotions to increase over time.

The Positive Impact of Your Shadow Self

"Authenticity" has become a bit of a buzzword recently and probably for the wrong reasons. However, it is the word used to describe how your character will become once you've accepted and understood your shadow self.

When you welcome in all the unwanted, undesirable pieces of yourself, your character becomes whole. Your interactions with others are genuine, and you are naturally calmer and mindful.

Your emotional intelligence increases, and you sit within your skin comfortably.

You rarely experience the impulse to overreact and create drama, accepting what is and living in the present moment. Owning your shadow is deeply empowering and boosts your confidence, too.

In the process of accepting your entire being, warts and all, your path to fulfillment starts to open up to you. You make better decisions, focus on what you truly want, and set life goals that are aligned with your dreams.

Life is calmer, more peaceful, and more mindful when you take time to enjoy breathing, a sunset or sunrise, and simple moments of pleasure found in the joy of being alive.

And the good news is you've already started walking this path, right here, right now.

Well, that was a lot to take in, and I want you to pause before we assess how your shadow self is showing up in your life right now.

Grab a coffee or your favorite herbal brew, snuggle under a blanket, and relax as we check into your heart space with Heartfelt Checkpoint 2.

Heartfelt Checkpoint 2

This is your next checkpoint. You must follow up on your shadow work learning with opportunities to explore what is happening for you. Remember that you are on this journey here and now, as this is part of your evolutionary path. Everything is right. Everything is as it should be. Nothing is given to you that you cannot deal with. You have everything inside of you that you need. Your time to explore, rest, and restore is now.

To go back in time to your childhood, I want you to find a quiet corner, where you can light a candle and lie down to gently journey back to your childhood years.

We will go on a pathway to meet your inner child and see what emotions they are feeling.

We will greet them in love and spend a little time with them.

When you're comfortable, your phone is on "Do Not Disturb," and you're ready, let's begin.

Guided Meditation: A Visit to Meet Your Inner Child

Find a comfortable space. Lie down or sit back in your chair if you can. Close your eyes and take a walk with me, back in time.

Breathe deep. Feel your body, each limb heavy and relaxed.

Relax your forehead and your mind, and release the tension in your face, especially around your jaw.

Connect your safety line to the present moment and gently close the door to now.

Let's begin our journey.

Close your eyes.

Take a deep breath in for 6. 1, 2, 3, 4, 5, 6.

And out for 6. 1, 2, 3, 4, 5, 6.

And again, in for 6. 1, 2, 3, 4, 5, 6.

And breathe out for 6. 1, 2, 3, 4, 5, 6.

One last time, breathe in for 6. 1, 2, 3, 4, 5, 6.

And slowly out for 6. 1, 2, 3, 4, 5, 6.

Today, we are on a journey into a timeless dimension to meet your inner child.

This space is free from fear and sadness. It is a space filled with love, compassion, and appreciation for your younger self.

You will meet your inner child today. They may be alone or with others; they may be able to speak; or they will talk to you through sounds and signs. They may not even notice you are there. All settings and scenes are okay. You are safe.

Breathe in again for 6. 1, 2, 3, 4, 5, 6.

And slowly out for 6. 1, 2, 3, 4, 5, 6.

This is a safe place. You and your inner child are protected and loved.

As you slowly take deep breaths in and out, fill your aura with love in a beautiful white light.

Watch as the light grows and grows and fills your aura, from the tip of your crown to the ends of your toes.

Let all that white light and love spill out of your aura and into the space around you.

Your inner child is here. Greet them with love.

Say hello to your inner child. Hold out your arms and let them come to you. Hold them close and fill them with love.

Apologize to your inner child. Tell them you're sorry for not visiting them sooner.

Say "I love you," to your inner child.

Now, what can you feel?

What emotion is your inner child experiencing right now?

Feel into that emotion. You may ask them questions if you want to.

Spend a few moments with your inner child to feel the emotions they are feeling.

What is coming up for them?

Let them talk to you if they can.

Take a few moments to feel deeply into this.

(Pause for two minutes or stop the audiobook and take your time.)

Say to your inner child, "It's okay to feel this emotion. It's okay to feel any emotion." Stay with your inner child while you feel the emotion together; watch it rise like a cloud in the sky, and let the gentle breeze blow it up and away until you can no longer see it.

Hold your inner child and say, "Well done for feeling and releasing that emotion. I'm proud of you. I'll come back soon to spend more time with you."

Tell your inner child you love them and what a good job they've done today.

Say goodbye to your inner child.

Close the door to the world of the past.

Take a moment to transport through time, back to the present.

Back to now. To this very moment.

You arrive at the door now. Open it, walk through it, and release your safety tether.

You are home.

Start to wiggle your fingers and toes.

Slowly open your eyes.

You are back in the present moment. Look around you and ground yourself in the now.

Repeat after me: "I am back in my body, in the present moment. I am complete."

Follow Up: Journaling Exercise

Once your meditation is complete, it's important to record the findings of your inner child meditation for reflection and progress checking. You can do this immediately after your transcendental journey or after a night's sleep. You may need time to process the journey you took with your inner child, and sleep helps us process many thoughts and emotional states.

If any distressing feelings come up during the meditation, remember to always ask for help. Talk to a friend, counselor, or therapist if you need to, especially if it has brought forward an emotion that you cannot release.

Your care and safety are the most important things right now; treat yourself with love and compassion.

If you are ready to continue with the journaling prompts, let's begin.

Take no more than 15 minutes to complete this task, so it remains something you can include in your daily actions and you can stay accountable to your self-awareness work.

Get a journal, specifically for recording your inner child work. Open it up and write down the following five questions about your inner child:

1. What emotion did your inner child feel today?
2. Why did your inner child feel that emotion?
3. How did that emotion make your inner child feel?
4. What do you wish others understood when you were feeling that emotion?
5. What words did others use to describe you when you were growing up?

Once you have answered all five questions, write down in a few sentences what you would tell your inner child now, so they could feel healed from that experience.

For example, you could write:

"It is okay to feel angry when your toy breaks. It's okay to feel frustration and sadness when something you love is broken. Let that emotion rise up and watch it float by. Do not hold on to that emotion. Feel it and let it pass on by. Everything will be okay."

Remember, if you are holding on to a negative emotion or sadness following your guided meditation, seek help so you can move past it. In the next chapter, we will begin a journey of self-discovery. We will begin your reflection journaling, and I would urge you to start that now, especially if you have some difficult emotions surfacing.

See you in the next section. Remember, I'm with you.

Celebration 2

But before you continue, it's time to celebrate again. Tonight should be filled with self-care. Run a warm bath, light a scented candle, and relax, comforting yourself for a job well done!

Chapter 2:
Your Journey to Self-Discovery

Have you ever been curious about your astrological sign to learn about the facets of your character? Or have you explored numerology to reveal your personality traits? Or maybe you've gone a step further and explored human design to work out how you operate when responding to others? These are all ways we try to discover ourselves and learn what makes us tick. Rather like layers of an onion, there are many ways to access ourselves; and the more we peel back, the more we discover who we truly are, beyond social conditioning and traumatic childhood experiences.

Assessing Your Current Self-Awareness

In the introduction to the workbook, you took part in a self-discovery assessment.

How did you do? What came up for you?

Today, we're going to take that a little bit further and look at ways you can regularly assess your current self-awareness. You may already be enjoying some of these techniques as part of your journey toward increased emotional intelligence.

Journaling

This technique has to be one of the simplest and most effective ways of assessing your self-awareness because it focuses on reflection. It also provides a diary of how much improvement you've made over time. This becomes an invaluable resource that you can use to measure how far you've come and empower yourself on your journey of self-discovery.

Journaling provides the space for you to be honest and open. It can also help in de-stressing and promoting feelings of improved well-being.

Very often, when you write down a feeling or situation you struggled to deal with, you gain a lot more clarity by expressing the feelings around it in a safe, personal space.

Mindfulness Practices

Mindfulness is simply the art of watching what you say and think, and there are many ways you can do that. Let's take a look at some of these tools, and while we're doing that, imagine the practice in your mind and feel into which ones you'd like to explore:

- **Breath Work:** Self-discovery practices with shadow work can unpick some delicate wounds. First and foremost, it's helpful to have a breathing practice you can fall back on, especially if your thoughts become too overpowering or you've suffered from racing thoughts and overwhelm before.

- **Body Scan:** This is an extremely effective way to see if you're physically holding on to stress related to your shadow. Very often, you can find online guide programs to walk you through body scans to see where you are holding stress. Work through this, adding it to a weekly practice of mindfulness on your self-discovery journey.

- **Shadow Walking:** Developing a process of shadow walking is similar to mindful walking. Set your intention before you begin your walk and decide on pieces of your shadow you want to work on. Think without judgment and pay attention to any thoughts or insights that come up for you.

- **Present Moment Sensory Awareness:** As you journey through pieces of your character, it can be a delicate time filled with thoughts of the past. Introducing present-moment sensory awareness can keep you from falling into old memories and a negative mindset. Focus on eating, bathing, looking around you, and saying what you see, smell, hear, and feel. This will help to keep you grounded, calm, free from distress, and in the present moment.

- **Walking in Nature:** Walking in nature with your shoes off is a very grounding experience, and it doesn't matter where you do it either—local park, forest, or even the beach. Flip off your shoes and ground yourself on the earth, there's nothing quite like it.

- **Mindful Movement Release:** Very often, it is only in the process of physical movement that we uncover parts of ourselves that have been buried deep, as far as our tissues and cells. Practicing movement—dance, sports, working out—can help in the process of bringing emotions to the surface and releasing them naturally into the ether. Set your intention before you begin and get ready to release what comes up.

Any one or all of these practices help you to assess your current self-awareness. If you can begin to create a schedule where you fit one or more of these routines into your daily life, your self-awareness will be constantly evolving.

Techniques for Uncovering Your Shadow: Journaling Exercises for Self-Discovery

Shadow journaling is one of the most important techniques you will use on this path of self-discovery. But to journal effectively, you need to get to the core of your shadow self. In this section, we will create the questions you need to ask yourself for effective answers that hold the key and get to the heart of your shadow. It's time to unpeel negative feelings you have connected and attached to your emotions.

Take a deep breath and remember that this introspective work will help you become aligned and complete with your true, authentic self. It will be tough, so thank yourself for taking the steps to create a better version of yourself and your life.

Remember that all emotions have positive and negative features, every emotion carries light and shade. There is no need to be fearful of anything that may arise.

If you need to take a pause and prepare your mind for the work that's ahead, then do so. Remember, these questions are wrapped in love and compassion, so you can create a whole, unfragmented version of yourself.

For the next 30 days, pick one of the reflective questions and journal the answers. It doesn't matter if you don't have clarity right now. What does matter is that you are walking the path to aligning yourself with your true character in acceptance and love. Some of these questions may touch a nerve; if so, make a note in your journal. What you are ready to face may hold a valuable key to aspects of your shadow. If not right now, you can come back to these prompts and deal with them when you feel ready.

Open your journal and write down the following questions, leaving yourself plenty of space to journal under them:

1. What personality, character traits, or strong emotions in other people trigger you? These can be either positive or negative.

2. Are there any recurring patterns and conflicts in any of the relationships you have with others?

3. Are there any aspects of your personality or character that you have from others, like your mom or dad?

4. Remember back to the role models you had as a child, what qualities you admire in them, and how they connect with your shadow.

5. Consider your feelings connected to authority figures, how do you feel around teachers, bosses, or people in positions of power? How do you connect with them, through respect or rebellion, or does any other emotion come up?

6. Consider your feelings connected to your parents. Are there any unresolved issues that could be connected to your shadow self?

7. Have you ever compromised one of your values because of another person? Why did you make this choice at that moment?

8. Do you find forgiving others hard to do or do you hold a grudge? Are these still affecting you and stopping you from healing?

9. Do you compare yourself to others? Does this cause envy, inadequacy, or competition that may hint these may also be hidden in your shadow self?

10. What emotions come up when someone criticizes or challenges you?

11. Do you ever wear a mask or take on a role to please or communicate with another person?

12. What emotions do you try and hold back or hide from other people?

13. Do you remember something that happened in your childhood that affected your self-worth (the feeling that you're a valuable and unique person, no matter what)?

14. Do you remember something that happened in your childhood that affected your self-esteem (the range of your happiness that can increase or decrease based on what you do and how you see yourself)?

15. What do you think the biggest problem is in your shadow self?

16. Do you suffer from recurring patterns of behavior or patterns in relationships, which may indicate your shadow holds these aspects of yourself?

17. Do you modify your behavior daily to fit in with people at work or in another setting?

18. Have you ever had an experience where you felt total resistance to something or someone?

19. Do you ever have a recurring dream or nightmare, and is there anything symbolic about these experiences that you could look into to discover what's hiding in your shadow?

20. Is there anything in your identity—religion, sexual orientation, ethnicity—that you choose to hide and not show others?

21. What self-limiting beliefs do you hold?

22. Have you ever felt like an outsider or that you didn't belong? How did that make you feel?

23. What does your negative self-talk sound like? Give as many examples as possible.

24. How do you cope with stress? What emotions come up and how does this change your behavior?

25. Is there a goal or dream you have not pursued because of feelings of self-doubt?

26. What is your behavior like during an argument, disagreement, or challenge with family or those close to you? How do you show up?

27. Do you have any fantasies about your life that you feel are completely unattainable?

28. What triggered moments of massive personal growth in your life? How can you build on those?

29. What is your version of success, how does it look, and do you expect to achieve it?

30. If you could remove the limitations of your shadow, what would your character be like? What strengths and unique qualities would you have?

Heartfelt Checkpoint 3

Already you have held yourself accountable by reaching Chapter 2, and you must be feeling a huge sense of relief and determination to continue uncovering your shadow.

Just by being here, you have achieved something remarkable, and I know how much effort and strength this journey takes.

You are determined to see this journey to the next level, and your heart must be bursting with pride right now.

To stay on this road takes great courage; courage I know you have. But life has a funny way of throwing us a curveball or two sometimes, and I want to ensure that you walk this journey to the next stop and feel an amazing sense of self and renewed pride.

So, let's begin our accountability schedule to cope with unreleased trauma, past emotions, fear, and negative thinking.

Take out your diary or calendar and mark down an ideal mindfulness schedule. We are consciously not going call it to shadow work because of the negative connotations; this can lead to avoiding doing the work. Most people throw themselves into personal growth without even undertaking shadow work, which leaves them incomplete. You're not going to be one of them.

Mindfulness Transformation Schedule

To make you more comfortable, we will use the umbrella of Mindfulness Transformation Planner.

Ideally, you should have check-in points every day:

- **Morning:** On waking, check in with your mindfulness for the day. You can choose from morning meditation, reflective journaling, priming yourself with breathing exercises and visualization, setting intentions, and positive affirmations. Make sure to acknowledge any feelings and emotions that come up overnight.
- **Midday:** Take a simple five-minute check to acknowledge any thoughts or feelings that have surfaced throughout the morning.
- **Afternoon:** Work on some of the journaling prompts. Don't go too deep, but continue with at least one question to move you forward on your shadow work journey.
- **Evening Reflection**: Use this opportunity to do reflective journaling about the day and to acknowledge and release any emotions before sleeping.

If you are not ready to embrace this journey fully, perhaps you have a very demanding job or family responsibilities, and that's okay. Do not be hard on yourself. However, the more points you have throughout the day, the faster your transformation will take place.

Make sure that you are accountable to at least one of the daily tasks, and if you can only manage one right now, ensure it is either the morning waking to check in or the evening reflection.

Let's look at how far you've come already. The next piece of the puzzle is self-esteem boosting, and we are going to find a way to immediately build strength and confidence—no matter what you have experienced in life this far. Join me in Chapter 3.

Celebration 3

Tonight, I want you to read a book for at least 15 minutes, snuggled up in bed or on a cozy chair, nurturing yourself with different thoughts and time out.

Chapter 3:
Self-Esteem Boosting Strategies

Do you wake in the early hours with racing thoughts, or do you sleep peacefully, like a baby, for a full 7-8 hours?

How do you sleep?

What's your bedtime routine?

And why am I asking? Because there are so many self-esteem-boosting strategies that make up your daily routine that you can fix right now without adding extra work into your day. So next, let's launch into strategies and exercises to increase your self-esteem naturally and simply. We can identify how you may have lowered it without realizing it, and then we can figure out what you can do it increase it effectively.

I want you to be mindful of the four main pillars that make up your life:

- sleeping
- eating
- spending time outside
- physical activity

Immediately, your brain is going to flag one of these four areas where you have a weakness. Perhaps your diet isn't good; maybe you don't get outdoors every day; maybe you can't sleep well or you've stopped working out.

And I'm sure you've heard it before, but these areas of your life are vital to master for the health of your mind, body, and soul.

Vital.

Each one of these categories shows the measure of self-love that you give to yourself:

- To eat nourishing foods is to treat your body, your temple, with love.
- To rest well is to gift your body and brain the correct amount of time to restore and heal daily.
- To work out is to cherish the body you have, push out all toxins, and build strength to keep your body's mechanisms working to support your life.
- To spend time outside is to gift yourself your home environment; you belong to the trees, the sea, and the wilderness. You will find restorative power here away from electric vibrations and the energies of the city or built-up areas.

Which of the above categories did you feel some resistance around when I mentioned them? Which areas do you feel proud of? Maybe here, it's time to take a moment to pause. If anything came up of you while you were in this section, add it to your journal. These fundamental pillars of life are the aspects that most people find hard to deal with, and we see this everywhere in obesity, health problems, depression and anxiety, and disconnection.

You are not alone.

So now, let's get back to your shadow and see how the shadow uniquely affects self-esteem.

Recognizing How the Shadow Effects Self-Esteem

Your shadow directly affects your confidence. Let me explain how.

When you hide parts of yourself and deny aspects of your character so you "fit in" or "get on" with people to make you "one of the crowd," your confidence bombs. You can't be yourself fully when you have to watch what you say and do. You show up as an incomplete version of yourself; and while you may be able to do this for a time, you certainly won't be able to sustain it. And eventually, others will also start to notice it.

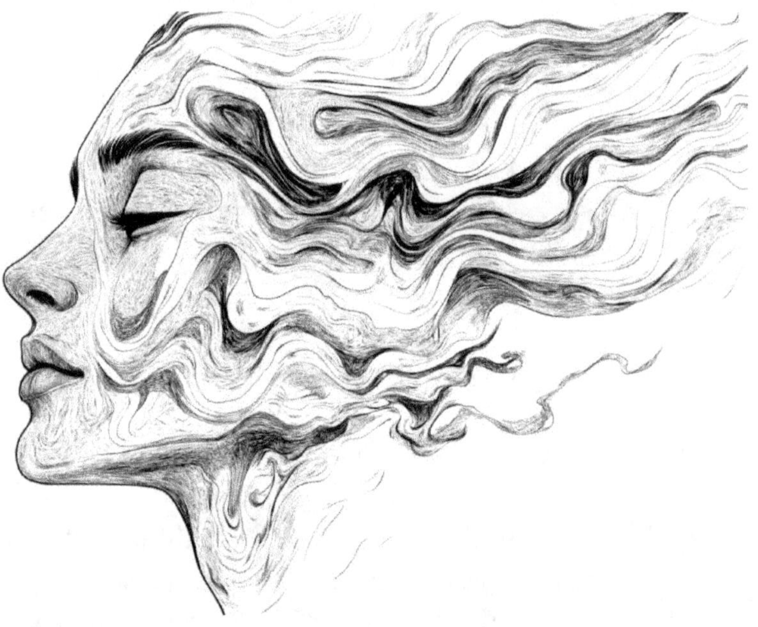

But when you can show your true face and voice to the world, you show up whole. You are fully integrated and who you are supposed to be. You are who you were born to be, and this version of yourself not only commands confidence but also attaches all that is good and plentiful to your being. This, in turn, creates your path of alignment; your path to fulfillment, and that, in turn, compounds you with more confidence.

Your shadow is vital to your self-esteem. Let's look at how it works.

When you accept parts of yourself you're not happy with, you dislike, or you feel shame about, it becomes easier to bring them into the light. By bringing them into the light, you can manage these aspects of your character better when they surface.

When you haven't accepted your shadow, do you notice any of these behaviors in yourself, where your confidence is directly reduced by your hidden shadow?

- You are happy to say hello and introduce yourself at gatherings but nervous to initiate conversation.
- You think people are judging the way you look or the clothes you are wearing.
- You think others are better than you or you think they think they are better than you.
- You have mild paranoia and think others are looking at or talking about you.
- You are reluctant to take food from a buffet or self-service area and wait for others to go first.
- You feel awkward for all, or a large part, of the time.
- You regularly second-guess yourself, and you think about your past actions, or what somebody said to you, over and over again.

Conversely, when your shadow is integrated and you are doing shadow work, you may behave differently:

- You are excited to go to social gatherings, even when you don't know anyone there.

- You are comfortable to eat alone in restaurants.
- You can go to the cinema alone.
- You can talk to others and initiate conversations without thinking about it.
- You don't dwell on what you could have said or done differently or over what someone said to you.

Where did you recognize yourself and your actions here? Remember, whatever comes up for you is valuable—add it to your journal, as this is another piece of your journey.

And don't forget to thank yourself for being honest and open about this. Compassion for yourself is the key to helping you continue this work. You've worked on some dark corners of yourself here; make sure you move on immediately to Building Self-Love and Self-Worth.

Building Self-Love and Self-Worth

What's the difference between self-love and self-worth? The best way to describe self-love is to think about how you treat your friends. Consider the way you want to make them laugh, have fun with them, treat them to gifts or days out, listen to them, spend time with them, and help them; that's exactly how you want to treat yourself. Behaving this way with yourself is self-love.

Now, this self-love builds self-worth. Self-worth is knowing that no matter what, you are amazing and you are valuable. Self-love is the road to self-worth.

Self-Love

Let's begin with self-love.

Pause here and take a moment to think about your typical day. What do you do each day to instill self-love?

Take a moment to think about the following questions:

- Do you write down gratitude statements?
- Do you say private affirmations out loud?
- Do you practice mindfulness to guard your brain against negative thinking?
- Do you pause, rest, and take breaks during your work schedule?
- Do you allow time to eat, away from all distractions?
- Do you do something you like each day, like reading, dancing, drawing, or listening to music? Something that connects you to yourself and lights you up?
- Do you limit time on social media and other screen-time entertainment?
- Do you celebrate your wins, even things as small as checking off your to-do list?
- Do you make time for yourself, instead of thinking "I don't have time"?

If you're not doing any of these, where can you make a start today? What small practice can you add immediately to your schedule? If you're finding yourself thinking, "I don't have time to do this," this resistance could be coming from your shadow self. Remember to jot this down in your journal, so you can explore what not making time for yourself means. For example, if you're so busy, does this stop you from thinking about other things in your life? Is being so busy and having no time simply a distraction from something you're avoiding?

Take another pause to clear your head. Notice what thoughts are coming up for you now, both the positive and the negative. It's in these moments that you will gain complete clarity, these moments when you are alone and can be completely honest with yourself. These moments are your lightbulb moments. These moments will move you forward.

So, think about your day and implement at least one practice to move the needle. Make sure you do it in bite-sized chunks, otherwise, you won't implement it and stick to it. Small, incremental practices are much easier to turn into habits.

Self-Worth

Now it's time to move on to self-worth. Increased self-esteem has a very different feeling from increased self-love. Self-worth is tied to your confidence and self-belief. You can have a strong sense of self-worth even if your self-love feels lower. For example, you can have undeniable self-beliefs even if you don't like yourself too much. But what increased self-love does is create an even stronger sense of self-worth.

Building self-worth works a slightly different way. Self-worth can emphasize personal attributes. Let's go through each one to fully understand how they connect to self-worth:

1. **Achievements:** This refers to your success and achievement. Things that you've done, and that could be anything where you have felt personal accomplishments, breakthroughs, triumphs, gains, or milestones.

2. **Recognition:** This centers on others' awareness of your abilities, being acknowledged for your skills, or being awarded for your efforts and contribution.

3. **Self-Respect:** The boundaries you set play a huge role in establishing and maintaining self-respect, and this also includes how you treat yourself generally.

4. **Inner Strength:** This touches on your mental strength, the way you deal with upset, and challenges when you're faced with adverse conditions.

5. **Faith:** Your faith is the belief in something you cannot see; this could be your higher self, religion, or spirituality and is usually at the core of your driving force.

Take a moment to pause here and think about your achievements, recognition, self-respect, inner strength, and faith. Do you feel that any one of these areas is lacking? Do you feel any resistance to these personal attributes? Remember to journal any feelings that are surfacing and pay attention to where you feel them in your body. This will also provide you with key insights into how your shadow is playing a part in your self-worth.

You've taken a lot in on self-esteem and self-worth, so before we leave this chapter, let's create affirmations that you can use immediately to reinforce positive language and emotions about yourself.

Affirmations and Self-Esteem Exercises

The next stop on your journey is to make authentic affirmations. Affirmations, when used with other self-esteem exercises, can significantly boost your self-worth.

Choose five of the following self-love affirmations, then choose five of the self-worth affirmations to make your own authentic list of confidence boosters. Remember, these strategies work better when they mean something to you, so if you can create more personal ones, they will have greater significance and work much faster:

Self-Love Affirmations

1. I love and accept myself fully.
2. I love myself just as I am today.
3. I love every part of my life, and I am grateful for each moment.
4. I am my own best friend, and it is natural to love myself.
5. I deserve a life filled with love and happiness.
6. I love being with myself, and I am kind to myself.
7. I choose to feel joy above any other emotion.
8. Great things happen to me.
9. I am in control and stand in my power.
10. I am beautiful inside and out.

Self-Worth Affirmations

1. I show up for myself every day in the best way possible.
2. I am confident and love myself and my body.
3. I am capable of achieving all my goals and dreams.
4. I forgive myself for making decisions when I did not know any better, and I trust all the decisions I make.
5. I am capable of achieving anything I want to.
6. I deserve love and respect from others.
7. I am enough, and I have always been.

8. I feel calm and peaceful and can handle any challenge that comes my way.

9. I praise myself and others all the time.

10. I redirect negative experiences into powerful opportunities for growth.

Now that you've created your own list of affirmations, let's put that into action with your next Heartfelt Checkpoint. Affirmations work well when combined with other practices, so let's jump into journaling prompts to help you firmly instill these self-empowering beliefs.

Heartfelt Checkpoint 2

In your next checkpoint, I want you to think back to Chapter 2 where we discussed checking in with yourself during different parts of the day. Now that you know how much your daily routine can affect your mindfulness, here are a variety of journaling prompts you can use to keep you on track, boosting self-esteem while working through your shadow work.

Pause before you begin this work and take time to set your intention, which will enable you to answer more honestly and in alignment with your goals.

Daily Routine Journaling Prompts

- What small change can I make to each of my meals to make them healthier?
- What can I eat less of?
- What can I eat more of?
- How can I get outdoors each day for at least 20 minutes?
- Where can I feel nature's strength, peace, and calm to help me feel good?
- Where can I include this in my day that doesn't cause me to feel stress?
- How can I include exercise in my day?
- How do I love to move my body?
- Where can I incorporate this in my day so I don't feel stressed and look forward to doing it?
- What bedtime routine can I create so I am fully rested and restored?
- How can I create a routine where I fall asleep naturally when the sun goes down and then wake naturally when the sun rises?

Pause again before moving on. Sometimes, when we go deep into our unconscious or belief system, we don't treat ourselves with enough compassion. Rest a little, unwind, take a bath or warm shower, light a candle, and take some deep breaths. Take out your journal, begin on your self-love journaling prompts, and finish with self-love affirmations up next.

Self-Love Journaling Prompts

1. Identify an underlying belief about yourself. Where does this come from? When was the first time you noticed this belief? Do you think it is stopping your healing process?

2. List the things you still have not forgiven yourself for. Why have you not forgiven yourself yet?

3. List the qualities the best version of yourself would hold.

4. Why do you think you struggle to love yourself? What is holding you back?

5. What is your biggest insecurity? How can you learn to love that?

Before moving on to self-worth journaling prompts, take a moment to pause again, make sure you won't be distracted, and have the time to answer openly and thoughtfully. Note that each time you do this exercise different things may come up, and that's okay.

Always close any hard work practice with self-worth affirmations so you can feel strong and empowered.

Self-Worth Journaling Prompts

1. What have I achieved that makes me feel proud of myself?

2. What comes up when I compare myself to others? How can improve this quality so I feel better about myself?

3. Did you feel unloved as a child? What can you do now to repair those feelings?

4. What is a consistent negative thing I tell myself? How can I change the wording to make this an empowering statement instead?

5. What is the one thing I love and appreciate in myself that does not come from any external source or validation?

Use these journaling prompts at your check-in points as part of your daily shadow work practice or create your own if you can develop more meaningful ones. Once you've finished your journaling prompts, remember to always close them with self-esteem-boosting affirmations. This way, while you've dived deep into personal areas of sensitivity, you close your mind with empowering, uplifting phrases of love and compassion for yourself.

Celebration 4

Today's celebration is to take all that love you've boosted in yourself and share it with a friend. Go for an empathy walk and talk and listen to a friend for at least 30 minutes. Let them share their issues with you, without you talking about yourself at all. Practice active listening; this is a beautiful gift to share now that you are creating an increased sense of emotional intelligence.

Chapter 4:
Emotional Mastery

Emotional mastery is not something you have; it's something you do. Nor is it a destination; it's a practice. Being able to manage your emotions, regulate them, appreciate that they are subjective, and understand everybody's interpretation of emotions can be different. It's the process of communicating effectively using the right emotion, and it's a practice that we all need to consistently work on.

Exploring Emotional Intelligence

Emotional intelligence is understanding your emotions and using them appropriately, and in the process, helping others do the same. It is an ongoing commitment you undertake to repeatedly produce a better version of yourself. Emotional intelligence will get you further than any level of qualification you hold, simply because you will have less destructive behavior in your life.

Emotional intelligence guides us to make better decisions and choices for ourselves. If we can look at situations with a calm, peaceful perspective, we are often better equipped to fine-tune our selection process and avoid chaos, drama, and self-sabotage. Emotionally charged or reactive choices often include all three of those.

Think back to a time when you made an emotionally fueled decision. What happened?

Let's take the example of Jess. After a heated discussion with her boss, Jess quit her job in a rage. She was solely responsible for the finances in her home, and as a consequence of her actions, her family sank into debt, and all family communication became strained. Her husband felt particularly pressured, and their relationship suffered.

Now, if Jess had been emotionally intelligent, what do you think she would have done?

Perhaps take a step back to gather her thoughts? Maybe she could have explained to her boss that the disagreement left her feeling unsure and she'd like time to respond. Both these actions are perfectly reasonable; and Jess, once she had calmed down, would have had the ability to talk things through with her superior in a much calmer way.

Now, in your journal, think of the last time you made an emotionally loaded decision and write it down. What emotions did you feel when this situation happened? Were these emotions directly related to the problem or were they connected to something else? What would you have done differently if you had not felt these emotions?

Pop the kettle on, and don't judge yourself, simply answer the questions without shame, guilt, embarrassment, or regret. Know that this is the first step to improving future choices for yourself and forgive yourself for not being the best version of yourself at that time.

Understanding and Processing Repressed Emotions

Understanding what a repressed emotion is can sometimes feel baffling. Especially since people who repress emotions tend to be forgetful. This type of emotion is one that's been pushed to one side. It's not been allowed to come out into the open and be felt. And that's okay for some of the time, especially if you are in a situation where your emotions can cause problems for you, such as in the workplace. However, in the long run, if the emotion stays shut down and cut off, it's going to come back to haunt you. Oftentimes, when you least expect it and at the drop of a hat!

This is why we sometimes see people explode.

A lot of repressed emotions have their roots deeply anchored in a childhood experience of trauma. That can mean that that emotion has been pushed down for a long, long time.

Have you ever watched a movie with an emotional scene that made you ball your eyes out immediately? It's like you are connected with the emotions in that part of the movie; the connection hits you deeply, and the movie acts as a floodgate, opening up your emotions with a very intense reaction.

But really the question is, how do I know if I have repressed emotions? Well, there are a few questions you can ask:

- Do I frequently feel numbness or emptiness?
- Do I often and without reason feel anxiety, sadness, or stress?
- Do I feel uneasy or uncomfortable when others start talking about their emotions?
- Do I maintain a cheerful and calm presence to avoid feeling anything else?
- Do I get annoyed when someone asks me how I'm feeling or enquires about my emotions?

The repression of your emotions probably happened most when you were a child, and you would have acted swiftly, as you may have been punished by your parents for expressing certain emotions. You may have been told to "buck up" when feeling disappointed or been scolded for being angry when you were filled with rage. Rather than your primary caregiver explaining what was happening and why you were feeling that emotion, you were instructed to cut it off. You may have even told yourself to shut down and deal with your feelings at a later point. Compartmentalization can happen as a consequence of this and, of course, this also makes up part of your shadow.

The question now is, how do you go about accessing those parts of you that are closed off or buried so deep, that you don't even know what's in there?

Techniques for Managing and Mastering Your Emotions

First of all, it's important to understand that managing and mastering your emotions is an endless exploration of the self.

Some techniques will work well for you, others may not, and that will also change over time.

It's also a good idea to try different techniques. You may not vibe with some of them now, but as this journey takes you into different emotional states, your needs will also change and your practices will develop, too.

Let's look at the different techniques and ways to manage and master your emotions:

Naming Your Emotions

This is the process of saying out loud "I am feeling sad," or "I am feeling angry" when this feeling rises within you. This is the first step in becoming emotionally aware, and it's something that many people avoid. There is calm and clarity in being able to say how you're feeling and ask yourself, *Is this emotion relevant right now or is it connected to something deeper?* Either way, you'll get an answer that enables you to move past the feeling and get clarity on your thoughts.

Emotion Observation

This technique focuses on watching your emotions rise and float away like clouds once you've acknowledged the feeling. It's a mindfulness practice that's helpful to do in a quiet space, similar to meditation, or you can do it with a guided meditation. Allow yourself to feel into the emotion, visualize it rising into the sky, then floating away in the breeze. This a very helpful technique that pushes you toward increasing your emotional intelligence.

Deep Breathing

Deep breathing calms the nerves and your body and helps to regulate your nervous system. When you experience an emotion, slowly breathe into it and try not to let it overcome you. Do this as many times as you need to be able to think clearly.

Body Scans

Body scans are perfect for identifying where you may be holding stress in your body. You can use a guided meditation—there are many free ones found easily online—or try the one below that we will use in our interactive Heartfelt Checkpoint 5. The benefit of a regular body scan is bringing awareness to how your emotions affect your physical body, bringing back your mind swiftly to the present.

Journaling

As we've touched on before, journaling is possibly the most beneficial of all the shadow work practices. There is something that connects your soul to your mind when you put pen to paper. There are other methods too; speaking out loud and voice memoing your journal can be full of release. You also have the option of online apps and programs to journal in. Journaling is so powerful because it holds a record of reflection, a history of how far you've come, and that's hard to record anywhere else.

Empathy Walks and Talks

Have you ever taken an empathy walk with another person and just listened to what they say? Have you been able to put yourself aside for 30 minutes or an hour and pay attention to someone else's thoughts or problems? In this space, you can offer your thoughts and perspectives on an issue and help someone else see things from a different point of view. This is an extremely cathartic experience and allows you the peace of mind to put yourself aside for a while.

Conflict Resolution

Asking for help when you need to resolve difficulties is a constructive way to move forward if you have conflicts in relationships, especially personal ones. You can learn effective communication practices, problem-solving methods, negotiating, mediation, how to avoid conflict, and how to draw up a resolution agreement. The scope of conflict resolution goes far and wide, and they are all helpful ways to master your emotions and push you toward greater emotional intelligence.

Emotion Regulation Techniques

Think of emotion regulation techniques as you would for a small child. What comforted you then and what comforts you now? I know for me, a hot bath, essential oils, and a lit candle are all soothers and stabilizers of my emotions. What is personal and works for you? How can you distract or soothe yourself in or after a challenging situation?

Positive Coping Strategies

What makes you laugh? What makes you smile? What makes you light up inside? Think of activities, such as listening to music, dancing, or going to the gym, that you can add to your schedule to avoid negative coping habits, such as drinking alcohol, substance abuse, or overeating.

Therapy, Counselling, or Seeking Help

Last but not least, don't forget how important it is to seek help if you need it. Continued support can be very effective if you are struggling to move past emotions.

Heartfelt Checkpoint 5

It's your fifth point to check in with yourself, and this time we're going to take the focus away from your mind.

Shadow Body Scan

Put on some restful music that makes you feel calm and at peace and listen to the following body scan guided meditation to watch and observe feelings in your physical being.

In this body scan, we are going to fill your heart with an intention and move that around the body. Light a candle, lean back, or lie down so your body is supported, allowing you to feel every corner of your physical being.

Let's begin.

Take a few deep breaths in and slowly let the air flow out of you.

Breathe deep into your stomach again, allowing the air to blow up your stomach like a balloon, and breathe out.

While you're breathing slowly in and out, think about your intention.

Let's set an intention for today. It can be anything you want, but let's set one before we start.

Notice how your body is feeling right now. Acknowledge it and accept it. Whatever feeling it is, it is perfect for now.

Everything is right and as it should be.

Notice as I'm saying these words if your body is distracted at all or moving you away from your thoughts. Don't judge it, simply notice and acknowledge it.

If you could choose any feeling today, what would it be?

Take a few minutes to decide.

Own that feeling, claim it, and decide to feel that feeling today.

Notice again if any part of your body is distracted, pulling away, or feeling resistance.

Everything is right and as it should be.

Take a few deep breaths in and out.

Welcome all the feelings in your body—peace, resistance—all feelings are welcome. Notice where you feel these feelings in your physical body.

Welcome everything in, even if it is numbness or nothing.

Now, focus your attention on your forehead and feel your intention spreading across or shooting out of your forehead.

Feel as that intention drifts from your forehead down your face into your jaw area and throat.

Is your body resisting or relaxing now?

Is the feeling spreading or can you only manage to spread it in drops?

What feelings are coming up for you?

Let's try again and move that intention from your forehead, jaw, and throat down toward your heart. Can you feel it fill your heart space?

Ask and invite your body to feel your intention; don't force it.

Feel your intention in your heart, filling it with love and beautiful white light flowing from your forehead to your throat and down to your heart.

Now, take a few deep breaths.

We're going to move that glorious white light into your stomach, your emotional center, the place where you store all pain and worry.

Your power is created here. Fill it with beautiful yellow light to empower your gut instincts, your decision-making center. Fill it with sunshine light that radiates directly from your stomach.

Observe any feelings you have in your body. Don't judge. Welcome them all; watch and observe.

Take a few deep breaths and repeat.

Fill your stomach with beautiful yellow light to empower your gut instincts, your decision-making center, and fill it with sunshine light that radiates directly from your stomach.

Breathe deeply into the light.

Now move that beautiful yellow light down your body to a warm orange light, and move it into your sacral area, lower abdomen, and intimate anatomy.

This is your area of creativity, passion, and play. Fill it with warm orange light, letting that intention spill into this area and flow gently further down your body.

Welcome all feelings without judgment; simply watch and observe.

Take a few deep breaths.

Repeat again.

Move that beautiful yellow light down your body to a warm orange light, and move it into your sacral area, lower abdomen, and intimate anatomy. Your place of passion, creativity, and play.

Your passion for life!

Now, we are going to change the warm orange light to a deep red light and connect it to our base, your root, and feel it in the base of your spine and the backs of your legs.

Feel it in your connection with the ground, anchoring you; feel the earth under your feet, supporting you.

Watch and observe how our body feels when we move this invention to your roots, with no judgment, just peace.

Take a few deep breaths.

Repeat again.

Feel the warm, deep red light and connect it to our base, your root, and feel it in the base of your spine and the backs of your legs.

Feel your deep connection with the earth, your spirit lifted with your feet anchored safely in the ground.

Feel the energy of the earth fill your body with support and love and ground your energy into the earth, anchoring this feeling you chose today.

Remember feelings are a choice; you get to choose every single day.

Take a few deep breaths in and out.

And in love and light, connect yourself with the space you are in. Listen to the sounds of the room and the smells; wiggle your fingers and toes and slowly open your eyes.

You are one with your intention. You are complete.

You will feel a deep sense of relaxation in your body following the body scan. Thank your body for letting you into the untold stories and emotions it holds and allow grace to flow in for a body that supports and nourishes you on this journey.

Celebration 5

Today, a slice of your favorite cake or specialty coffee is on the list of rewards. Your body has done well, and you deserve a little treat for all that hard work!

Chapter 5:
The Shadow Work Process

Working in the unconscious can be a scary concept, and that's where you're going when you work on your shadow. Many practices of psychology, therapy, and even spirituality promote the benefits of shadow work. However, few welcome it in because it is not perceived as the uplifting side of personal growth and healing. Even fewer stick to it. But without practicing shadow work, you will rarely reach the complete version of yourself, as this work is fundamental to finding wholeness within yourself.

Is there a process? Yes, but that process can be different for everyone. In the section of the workbook, we will go through a step-by-step guide to shadow work to get you underway. Let's begin our walk into the shadows.

Step-By-Step Guide to Shadow Work

The process of uncovering parts of yourself that you have hidden through shame or trauma is never going to be an easy one. However, at this stage, you have learned many self-care tips and practices that will lift you on this journey; and I recommend practicing those even if this journey is lighter than expected. This will lead to greater self-discovery and ultimately increased emotional intelligence, no matter how your passage unfolds.

Any one of the following practices can be used in any order. I will provide you with a step-by-step guide that you can follow;

however, during this process, if you change direction and feel that some of the practices mentioned further down the list would help you sooner, feel free to deviate and explore what works for you.

The final process of integration is very important to move past old triggers and hidden behaviors. Integration of the denied pieces of yourself reduces your shadow. Your shadow becomes filled with light and dissipates, and this is your end goal.

Step 1: Set Your Intention

Before undertaking any self-care practice, it helps to set your intention. An example of this might be, "I no longer want to feel anger when someone is rude to me" or "I want to heal my relationship with my mother." This will help you to stay on track and keep you guided when delving into different emotions that have brought about negative feelings and experiences.

Step 2: Feel Into the Feeling

Try to feel the emotion or the feeling the emotion generated if you can. If it's hard to get there, go back to a place in your mind where you first felt that feeling. If that's impossible, go to the next step of identifying triggers.

Step 3: Identify Triggers

This is a slightly different way to tackle shadow work and get to buried emotions, especially if they came about due to trauma. Try reverse engineering to get to the core of the repressed emotion. Think about your triggers, dealing with just one at a time. Tap into the last time you were triggered. What feeling arose? Was it relevant in that moment or tied to an experience? If it was an experience, what words pop into your mind? For example, Jane was abandoned by her mother at an early age, creating feelings of being not important. Jane is triggered when someone is very rude to her, and she reacts badly and often aggressively. This is not because of the rudeness of the other person, who she cares little about. It is because the rudeness makes her feel unimportant, and this feeling connects back to her childhood.

Step 4: Mediate to Find When You First Felt the Emotion

Now that you've found the origin of the feeling, either from memory or trigger work, try to go back and recall when you first felt that emotion. You want to get a clear picture in your mind of its origin. This will help you accept this feeling and forgive yourself for not managing it better sooner. Thank you past self for sharing it now and helping you to resolve it.

Step 5: Name the Feeling

Give this feeling a name. This is the fastest way to make this emotion disappear. And you know what? By doing this, you take all the power away from that emotion. Once you recognize it when it surfaces, it's so much easier to handle, and you'll watch yourself become less reactive.

Step 6: Emotions Leave Feelings in the Body

One of the reasons why you have to do shadow work is because emotions and experiences don't leave thoughts in the body. They leave feelings, codes, signs, and symbols. For example, ill health, shyness or awkwardness, lack of confidence, depression, anxiety, and many, many more. None of these are thoughts; they are symptoms of this experience. This is especially important to recognize and practice regular body scans to fight this issue head-on.

Step 7: Inner Child Meeting

This can be very difficult for some, and don't expect to meet your inner child straight away. Don't put pressure on yourself to have a conversation with your inner child either. Sometimes, we expect way too much of ourselves, especially if our childhood has been filled with trauma after trauma. You are not alone. Inner child work can take a lot of time. Initially, your inner child may still not want to be found or communicated with; whatever happens, be patient and fill this space with as much love and forgiveness toward yourself as possible. When you get to meet your inner child, ask them questions. For example, what emotion are you feeling today? Or mention an experience to your inner child and ask them to describe how they felt at that time. Remember, patience is key; this part of shadow work is hugely impactful and life-changing.

Step 8: Journaling

Have you ever looked at an old photo of yourself and noticed how much you've changed? The impact of it is quite incredible; sometimes, those old photos take your breath away! And it's the same with journaling. Flipping back through an old journal, even two or three months previously, it's amazing to see how much your thinking and thought patterns change. For this reason, it's important to document your work. There is also something deeply satisfying in writing your feelings down; by making them real, giving them life, and allowing them to breathe, you can identify their strengths. Where negative feelings are concerned, as soon as they are written down, they lose their power and dissipate fairly quickly.

Step 9: Recurring Patterns

Another deeply effective way of getting your shadow work underway is looking at recurring patterns in your life. For example, do you always choose the same type of partner—maybe you get stuck in recurring abusive relationships. Or perhaps you always end up chasing a love interest and they repeatedly ghost you. Maybe when things are going well in your life, you blow them up and destroy everything before you reach your goal. These are all signs of recurring patterns of behavior and signs that shadow work needs to be done! Journal on the patterns you see in both your life and behavior and observe how you change these over time.

Step 10: Reframe Inner Dialogue

Once you've started this journey, you can now begin to understand the triggers better and how you'd like to reframe them. Think of changing every "can't" into "can"—reframing is the same kind of process. For example, when you think, *I'm overweight and ugly*, flip the thought to *I love myself just the way I am and feel good about working on the areas of myself I want to improve*. Make the reframing of the thought realistic and you'll believe and be guided by these re-routing statements.

Step 11: Affirmations and Acceptance

At this next stage, you've undertaken a lot of heavy emotional work, and that takes its toll on you. That's why affirmations serve you well; they bring you into the present moment, connecting and grounding you, and reinforce believable, compassionate, and empowering statements of improved self-worth. These should be repeated throughout the day, so pin them somewhere you can see them regularly and read or say them out loud as many times a day as possible. These move your thinking into a different version of yourself and are extremely effective. Affirmations bring you toward greater self-acceptance and a more positive self-image.

Step 12: Integration

This is the final step in the shadow work practice. Integration is fundamental to breaking the chains of unwanted behavior and moving you into alignment with who you are supposed to be and your purpose in this life. You take back the missing pieces of yourself, becoming whole and complete. This stops the shadow emitting frequency that attracts more negative things; better things start happening in your life.

Are you still stuck wondering why some people get everything they want and attain abundance? They integrated their shadow work!

Practical Exercises for Confronting Your Shadow

The first question is, should I confront my shadow or embrace it?

Embracing your shadow is exactly how you approach your shadow work, and I'll show you tips on how to embrace it to bring it out into the open.

Remember, confronting your shadow will make it bigger. You want to bring light to your shadow so you can reduce it and ultimately integrate those lost or discarded pieces of yourself.

The best way to access your shadow is to journal on the following three questions (*What is Shadow Work?* 2020). These questions will tap into your shadow immediately and bring force to the system. However, when answering these questions, you must do so without judgment, as criticizing them—criticizing yourself—will increase the size of your shadow. Be mindful of this!

Write down the questions and answers to the following questions in your shadow work journal:

1. What parts of myself do I dislike?

2. What parts of myself do I judge?

3. What parts of myself do I fear?

If you want to go a little deeper and include your inner child work—where most of your shadow will have been created—respond to the next set of questions:

1. Was I completely accepted as a child?

2. What was expected of me as a child?

3. What behaviors and emotions were judged by my parents when I was a child?

Lastly, an interesting question that arises from the spiritual side of shadow work may help you to shift some beliefs. I want to include it, as it has an important impact on where you are headed in your life.

- If I wasn't afraid, what would I do with my life?

This last question can be tricky and leave you feeling a little lost, as it's such a big life question. The best way to tackle it is to try some guided visualization exercises to help you see the things you are good at and what you bring to the world.

Tips for Staying Committed to the Process

Having the staying power to continue ongoing shadow work is a skill in itself. Don't forget, you are extremely brave and one of the few who remain committed to this work! The key to staying on track is to remember why you began shadow work in the first place, and that could have been for many reasons, such as:

- repeated abusive, toxic relationships
- self-destruction and self-sabotage
- failure in manifesting abundance or simply not being able to reach your goals
- healing from unresolved trauma
- self-discovery to increase emotional intelligence

Take out your journal and write down your "why." What brought you to shadow work? What triggers kept coming up that drew you to shadow work in the first place?

Once you fully understand this, it will be much easier to stay committed to the process.

Another way to keep skin in the game is to create your shadow work journals from day one, so you can keep a record of how far you've come and celebrate all your wins. This is a journey you have to actively fill with love and compassion, so go out for dinner, buy that outfit, take a friend for coffee, or treat yourself. Whatever it is, celebrate it! These will become milestones in your journey, and celebration is a pure act of love.

Always stay focused on your transition when doing shadow work. Keep your eye on the end goal. Imagine the new improved version of yourself and visualize it in your mind every chance you get. During visualization, imagine yourself achieving success and feel this and the emotions you'd experience when celebrating. Imagine the celebration of achieving your goal, having the relationship of your dreams, working in your dream job, and living life on your terms. Attach the emotion to your visualization and feel it. Your mind will want to replicate that feeling as fast as possible and will help you get there without you even realizing it.

Heartfelt Checkpoint 6

It's important to balance shadow work with goals and dreams. And this is the best way to stay committed to the process of shadow work. You have to be working toward something more than just a better version of yourself. You need to see a goal or a vision of how your life might look in three years.

So, in this heartfelt checkpoint, we're going to do a visualization that tells us exactly where you want to be in three years. What's changed since you started doing your shadow work? What dream or goal do you have for yourself? In this visualization, we'll find out, so I want you to light a candle. Sit back in your chair where your body can get nice and heavy or lie down. Make sure the door is closed so you won't be disturbed. And let's begin.

Three Years Future Visualization

Close your eyes and take a few deep breaths in and out, nice and slow.

Let all your limbs relax.

Feel your legs and feet getting heavy.

Feel them firmly on the floor. Feel your buttocks in your chair.

Your back pressed against the back of the chair or on your bed, your arms, and shoulders heavy; your fingers just weightless.

Take a few deep breaths in and out again.

Make sure your eyes are closed and you're in a place of stillness a place of safety.

It's three years in the future.

Imagine you're just waking up; you haven't opened your eyes yet.

You're just lying there, warm and safe.

What can you smell in the room around you?

What can you sense?

What can you hear?

Can you hear cars on a road nearby? Or maybe you can hear birds tweeting outside?

Can you hear water from the ocean or a river?

Or is it complete silence and you're in the mountains?

Feel your arms and your legs; your body feels heavy.

And I want you to slowly open your eyes. What colors can you see?

What can you smell?

What can you hear now?

Pause for a moment.

Think about the sounds and sensations. Now, I want you to sit up slowly.

Put your feet on the floor and slowly look around you.

What can you see? Is there a bed? Maybe a wardrobe, a chest of drawers, and a mirror?

Maybe there's nothing, and your room is empty. What can you see around you?

What colors are the walls? Is there a window? Maybe a balcony? Are you upstairs? Are you downstairs? Where are you?

Take a few deep breaths in and out and completely relax.

Now you're going to walk to the bathroom.

Clean your teeth, wash your face, and feel fresh.

You're slowly going to make your way to the kitchen.

How do you get there? Is it a long hallway? Is it next door? Is it upstairs? Do you walk downstairs? How do you get to your kitchen?

Before you open the door of the kitchen, what can you smell? What can you hear? Is silence in your home or is it laughter?

Do you hear other people? Maybe an animal, a dog barking, a cat meowing?

What do you hear as you open the door? What can you see inside your kitchen?

What colors are here? Who is here? What can you smell?

Is someone making you breakfast? Is bacon sizzling, bread baking, or coffee brewing?

Take a few moments to pause and understand who is here. Or are you alone?

Take a mental note of the colors; take note of anything significant that stands out for you.

As you make your favorite drink, make your way back to your bedroom.

Think about putting on your clothes for the day.

What clothes are you putting on? Maybe an outfit for the gym or to work out. Maybe a dance class.

Maybe your business suit. Maybe you're going to speak on a stage.

Are you putting on comfortable clothes and going to your living room to relax and wake up and read a book?

What clothes are you putting on?

What kind of day are you having?

What kind of day is ahead of you?

How do you start your day?

Take a few moments to think about it.

Now, we are slowly going to come back to the present moment. Start to wiggle your fingers and toes; feel your limbs and slowly open your eyes.

You are back in the now.

How do you feel?

And this is where visualization ends.

This visualization should give you enough clarity on what kind of day you desire. Make notes of all the things that you noticed in the visualization and see if they are connected to a current dream or goal you have in mind. Journal about everything that stood out to you in your visualization: colors, people, sounds, where your home is located, its surroundings, what clothes you wore, and where you were heading that day. This gives you significant insight into where you want to be in three years.

A very good way to see a glimpse into the future you desire!

Celebration 6

Congratulations! You stepped into the future version of yourself. Today, to mark this significant goal, buy something that reminds you of this future self. Did you see a cup in the kitchen, can you go and buy that cup or one similar to create the connection between you and your future self? Were you wearing a particular item of clothing? Can you buy an item similar to that, again, to remind you of the future and hold that vision alive?

Chapter 6: Healing and Integration

We've touched on the best orthodox ways to heal your shadow throughout this book. All of these practices take time and are the most effective if they are practiced regularly. However, both healing and integration have some unorthodox practices you may have already heard about and find helpful to explore.

Alternative Methods for Healing and Transforming Your Shadow

During the process of healing, your shadow will begin to transform; it will reduce in size and power. Different people find different ways of successfully reducing their shadow from many practices, including alternative ones. Some of those could be useful to you, too. Let's check them out.

Past-Life Regression

There are two perspectives on shadow work. The first, held by psychologists, is that your shadow is created in your childhood. The second perspective, held by the spiritual community, is that your shadow is created in all of your lifetimes, in any dimension. What this could mean is if you are aware of a piece of your shadow that you find impossible to connect to any experience, perhaps it was created previously in a past life. Past life regression may hold the key to helping you explore that.

The process of past life regression is very simple. It involves using meditation or hypnotherapy as a tool to go back through time to find untapped memories and experiences. In that space, there may be a piece of your shadow, created from an experience that your conscious self cannot access.

The practice itself can be done through guided meditation or with a practitioner; if you choose to work with someone personally, make sure you get a good recommendation beforehand.

Akashic Records and Shamanic Journeying

Another way to connect with your shadow is by using Akashic records. These records refer to a place thought of as the library of thoughts from the past, present, and future, which can be accessed by anyone, or any other life form, in this dimension or the multi-dimension. Using a meditation process, it's very easy to get there, and your experience in the Akashic records can be facilitated by a guide.

Again, you can do this practice alone or with a practitioner. This is often helpful, as they will guide you through your visualization and help you ask the right questions while inside the records to retrieve aspects of your character you may have lost or denied. They are also useful in helping you feel complete, which means that you've integrated this discarded piece of yourself successfully before you leave the meditation space.

Shamanic journeying can also take you into your Akashic records with the shaman as your guide, usually using distinctive drumbeats or specific musical sounds.

Artistic Expression

A beautiful way of accessing your shadow and expressing it positively is through artistic expression. That can be dance, art, music, writing, or anything that has artistic release. In this way, you'll find a way to let go that lights you up inside and helps you to become a next-level version of yourself. The more you shine brighter by doing the things you love, the smaller and smaller your shadow will become, and this process will help you love yourself and all that's inside your shadow.

Holotropic Breathwork

This practice can help you access parts of your unconscious by using different breathing patterns. While it's recommended by many, it is beneficial and safer to work with a practitioner who can guide you as you try to tap into higher states of consciousness. The effects of breathwork are said to be deeply healing, but be mindful of any breathwork practice, as you can feel side effects, including nausea and dizziness.

Sound Healing

Many forms of sound therapy help with shadow work, such as sound baths, singing bowls, shamanic beats, and more. What these sound experiences do, similar to listening to any song you love, is allow you to release emotion. Sound has an energetic level that can help you heal and restore energy in the body, while at the same time releasing tension.

Family Constellations

This kind of therapy looks at the family dynamic, the family you have now, and the family from past generations. It seeks to identify where aspects of your shadow have been created, and some find it a beneficial way to work through shadow work. Choose a practitioner who has experience in this field.

Mandalas and Symbols

Mandalas and symbols can be found in all cultures, religions, and timelines across the world and have significance in healing and ritual practices. The practice of working with a mandala or drawing a geometric symbol helps to harmonize all aspects of the psyche—and that includes your shadow.

Integrating the Shadow Into Your Conscious Self

All of the shadow work practices we've explored inside this book will begin the journey to integrating your shadow self. Many of these practices will help you integrate your shadow fully, especially if you keep up a continued practice of reflective journaling and mindfulness. Working through thoughts and feelings will keep you in the present moment and increase your self-awareness, preventing the shadow from growing or responding.

However, an interesting shadow technique from philosopher Ken Wilber is the 3-2-1 method (Hussain, 2020). It focuses on looking at yourself in three ways and how you fit into the world.

- In the third person, *we:* What do you make of the world? What's happening out there, with your friends, your wider community, and the world as a whole? What's your perception of life in general?
- In the second person, *you:* Consider how you interact with other people. How do friends and family see you? What would they say about you?
- In the first person, *I:* How do you see yourself? What do you notice about yourself? Jot down all the things about yourself that are significant.

The simplest way to imagine this process is to think of it as a puzzle, with you playing the roles of I, me, and we, just like you do in real life.

Alternatively, the Bhavana Learning Group has a very interesting way of interpreting this directly for shadow integration. Let's take a look at confronting your shadow:

1. Face them. Imagine a situation when someone was emotionally charged—this can be a positive or negative emotion.

2. Talk to them. Face this person and fix them in your mind; speak to them and connect with them and ask them how they're feeling during this emotional charge.

3. Be them. Be this person and talk about what you're going through using "I."

This can be a fun and empathetic way to reduce your shadow, and this process will help you stay calm and objective when you face challenges.

Personal Story of Transformation

This is the story of Sadie. Sadie was abandoned by her mother at the age of five. Sadie learned quickly that she wasn't allowed to cry, as this upset her father even more. He was already devasted, and Sadie did not want to make it worse. She closed down her sadness, which also shut down part of her voice.

As a child, she became afraid to speak up. She dreaded being asked a question in school or having to talk in front of other people. She would even skip school to avoid this.

And she continued to skip many things right into adulthood.

This impacted Sadie in several different ways. She began substance abuse at the age of 14; she became an addict for 11 years. Twice during this period, she tried to take her own life, and eventually, she asked her doctor for help, and he suggested psychiatry for her.

Sadie took the clinical help and got better. But she was still afraid to be sad in front of her dad, and this created a false relationship between them. Sadie also found it difficult to speak up, even to the extent of not being able to ask for help in a local store when shopping.

Forty-three years after her mom left, Sadie finally started to do shadow work. She experienced extreme anger and rage throughout her life; in her younger years, she would get into physical altercations and argue with everyone.

She also found it difficult to sustain friendships; she felt she always said the wrong thing and had no confidence in her voice.

Sadie tried many different types of shadow work. Journaling was particularly helpful, especially when she reflected on how far she'd come.

Body scans were also her favorite for opening her heart and creating more light and power in herself, and they also made her feel relaxed after doing the deep work.

But there were aspects of herself that Saide couldn't access. After 12 months of shadow work and not being able to access her inner child, Sadie sought the help of a shadow work coach and tried several different practices to integrate her shadow. It was only after telling the story of her upbringing to her mentor that Sadie made some realizations. It was the first time that she had ever named the feeling she was experiencing and she named it "not important." As soon as she did that, they went on a guided meditation to meet her inner child, and she appeared for the first time.

Sadie was able to commute with her younger self and tell her that she was important. For weeks after this experience, Sadie saw her inner child in a few visions and dreams, and finally, her connection to this abandoned aspect of herself was being integrated. She slowly lost her sadness and rage and forgave her mom.

Out of all the practices that Sadie tried, naming her emotions was a turning point for her.

Heartfelt Checkpoint 7

In this checkpoint, you will see another step toward emotional mastery and self-discovery. Very often when people ask you

"What do you like to do for fun?" you have no idea and have to think hard about it. The next two exercises are going to work on your shadow and at the same time, identify how you can increase joy, fun, and good energy in your daily life.

Claim Your Emotions

Emotional processing is something that we perhaps think about but never physically do. And naming your emotions is like calling them out. This incredible power of knowing how you feel and being able to describe it removes the personal connection to the emotion and allows you to see it as something exterior; not just a feeling you're experiencing and internalizing.

In this next interactive task, we're going to work through a range of emotions. I want you to journal which of these emotions you are feeling frequently that show up in patterns of behavior.

I want you to also journal which emotions you are fearful of feeling. We can learn so much about how we operate on a day-to-day basis when we can name the emotions that we are avoiding.

Eventually, you'll get to a point where you feel the emotion and name it, and recognizing it reduces in size and impact. This level of emotional processing expedites your journey to healing and emotional intelligence. It's something very simple but very, very effective. So, let's get started.

When looking at the emotions, see if there's one that isn't on the list and add it to your journal. Let's begin by identifying categories of emotions.

Sad

- guilty
- ashamed
- depressed
- lonely
- bored
- tired
- remorseful
- stupid
- Inferior
- isolated
- apathetic
- sleepy

Mad

- hurt
- hostile
- angry

- selfish
- hateful
- critical
- distant
- sarcastic
- frustrated
- jealous
- irritated
- skeptical

Scared

- confused
- rejected
- helpless
- submissive
- insecure
- anxious
- bewildered
- discouraged
- insignificant
- inadequate
- embarrassed
- overwhelmed

Peaceful

- content
- thoughtful
- intimate
- loving

- trusting
- nurturing
- relaxed
- pensive
- responsive
- serene
- secure
- thankful

Powerful

- aware
- proud
- respected
- appreciated
- important
- faithful
- surprised
- successful
- worthwhile
- valuable
- discerning
- confident

Joyful

- excited
- senseless
- energetic
- cheerful
- creative

- hopeful
- daring
- fascinating
- stimulating
- amused
- playful
- optimistic

Step 1

First, I want you to begin with the negative emotions. List all that have been coming up for you. Some will resonate with you immediately, and you'll find yourself thinking, *I feel that one; I feel that regularly*! Some may be more challenging and harder to accept, and that's okay. Treat yourself with compassion as you work through this process.

Step 2

Then, I want you to work through all the positive emotions. This is going to be a very positive process that will make you feel amazing and empowered. It will also help you identify which emotions you enjoy!

Step 3

The next part of the task is to work through naming your emotions again, working on the negative ones first. Think back to a time or a situation where this emotion came about. Why did it arise? What triggered that feeling? Be specific.

When you finish that task, I want you to do the same with positive emotions. Look at each emotion independently and relate it to a person, task, or situation where you felt the sensation of this emotion.

The purpose of this task is important. When you can identify where you feel good emotions, you can practice more of that in your daily routine, even when you're working on your shadow. In this way, you'll be bringing light into the shadow. So, while we're accepting negative emotions, we're owning them; and by working on the positive emotions and doing more of the things you love, you're bringing so much more light into the shadow, decreasing its size and helping it dissipate.

When you can work inadvertently on your shadow by simply operating from the heart space in the things you love to do, there is no hardship, dreading, or tough days. This is another of your ultimate goals.

I'm so proud of you for undertaking this task. It's never easy looking at yourself. It's one of the hardest things that you'll ever do. But the work that you're continuing to undertake is commendable. And the things that you'll be able to achieve right now may seem unbelievable. But just watch as with each step of this workbook, you transform yourself a little bit more each time

Claim Your Emotions Journaling

As part of your ongoing self-discovery in shadow work, I want you to journal on your emotions for the next seven days.

Before going to bed each day, write down what emotions you experienced. Ask yourself how they made you feel and identify what brought about the emotion.

This is also an excellent place to note if you are not feeling any emotion. Ask yourself why you feel the absence of emotion and record your daily activities to see if there's something that you can change or do to either increase or decrease a certain emotion.

This is a seven-day task. On the seventh day, use this day for reflection and answer the following questions:

1. What patterns of emotions can I see regularly occurring within me?

2. What can I do more to increase positive feelings within myself?

3. What can I do less to decrease negative feelings in myself?

4. What is one activity that I can add to my weekly schedule that improves my joy?

Celebration 7

Today, I want you to try something you've been longing to do but have been putting off. If it requires planning, you must agree to do it within the next seven days. Enjoy!

Chapter 7:
Maintaining Your Shadow Work Practice

When we think about positive thinking and mindfulness, we often reject the thought of diving into the dark stuff that drove us toward the need for change.

We dip in; we dip out.

And we still find that we're not quite where we want to be. We join programs, take coaching, and find healers and healing therapies.

But we regress.

We see glimpses of our shadow creeping in: An overheated argument or a jealous moment with a partner. We ghost someone on social media or run a few fake posts about ourselves. We start a new coaching program and never finish it. The list goes on. Maintenance and discipline is the key to success, and that includes shadow work.

Creating a Long-Term Shadow Work Routine

Shadow work isn't something you can pick up and put down. It's a lifelong journey of repairing and moving forward. People, relationships, and circumstances will bring challenges to your life—that is the very essence of life. At this moment, there will be opportunities for your shadow to surface, and keeping your shadow in check will be your priority. If you don't, you will inadvertently grow your shadow—making it bigger—and all the hard work you've done will need to be unpicked again.

The tough truth is that your shadow has probably been with you for a long time. And like most people, you've also put off working on it for a long time. Or you may have started and just given up. Without the right support, shadow work can feel impossible, especially if negative thoughts and feelings surface and you start dreaming about them or feeling low. There has to be a way to pull you out of getting stuck or a pick-me-up when you begin to feel like you're falling.

Recognizing Ongoing Shadow Issues

There are several ways to recognize if you still have your shadow showing up and preventing you from becoming the best version of yourself and succeeding in your goals.

Here are some things to look out for:

- You exhibit reactive behavior, such as jealousy or anger.
- You have impulsive behavior, such as blowing all your money and making hasty decisions without giving yourself time to think about them.
- Indecision. You're unable to make any decisions and play the waiting game.
- You have emotional outbursts or cry at the drop of a hat.
- Relationship difficulties. You choose the same partner over and over again or fall into recurring patterns of behavior in you or your love match.
- You play the victim. Are you now showing up as the victim in situations and feeling hard done by?
- Insecurities. What are you still insecure about?
- You dwell on the past. Are you spending hours lost in past experiences and thinking, *What if?*
- Are any big emotions surfacing regularly? What are they and how do they play a part in daily life?
- You're blocking your shadow and convincing yourself you don't have one. Everyone has one; what matters is the size of it.
- You have recurring or disturbing dreams. What's happening in your dreams?
- Your inner dialogue is negative. Are you continuing to talk yourself down and run a negative script in your head?
- Self-sabotage. Do you find yourself going so far with a person or project and then destroying your progress?
- You're labeling yourself and using labels to create your identity to avoid owning parts of yourself that need work. For example, saying you have adult ADHD or bipolar disorder when you haven't been diagnosed.

- Projecting. Are you projecting your issues by pointing out someone else's?
- Do you find yourself being defensive about your actions? Or denying that you have certain destructive behaviors?
- Are you a fake person? Are you showing up as inauthentic on social media and posting fake aspects of your life? An example of this in your character would be continuing to make the wrong connections with the wrong people.
- Are you still a perfectionist? Maybe you never finish projects or tasks because you have to get them better and better and they never see completion.
- What about addiction? Overeating, alcohol, or substance abuse. Porn addiction or gambling? Obsessively working out or going to the gym? What addiction can you pinpoint in your life?
- Time deficient. Are you telling yourself you are too busy and have no time; unable to make time for short spurts of regular self-care work?

If any one of the points struck a chord with you or you could immediately say, "Yes! I still do that," then it's likely that shadow work needs to be regularly continued.

And don't worry, you are not the only one.

Spend a few moments now thinking of the close people in your life. What can you identify about their personalities that show you they have shadow work to do, too? This will help you feel less isolated and alone. After all, everyone has a shadow, but only some take the responsibility and courage to change it.

Balancing Shadow Work With Self-Care

If you think about bad things all the time, you're going to feel bad.

And that goes for shadow work too. You can't think about the things you want to change about yourself without bolstering yourself with powerful, empowering work, too.

If you don't, you'll stop doing the work and just feel bad.

Period.

So, instead of teaching a balanced shadow work self-care approach, let's build one together.

Start here by choosing one of the shadow work practices and then coupling it with a self-care practice:

1. Journal about five negative beliefs, then write five positive affirmations about yourself.

2. Explore past trauma, then create five gratitude statements.

3. Call out your triggers, then sink into a mindfulness guided meditation.

4. Find repressed emotions and journal on them, then choose one form of creative expression and go do it.

5. Identify recurring patterns in relationships, then call a friend and go for an empathy walk.

6. Observe negative inner dialogue, write it down, and then reframe each negative sentence positively.

7. Work with your inner child. Write a letter to them to tell them what you love and have learned about yourself.

8. Work through limiting beliefs, then set three goals to achieve within three months.

9. Identify unconscious bias by learning something new about another culture or volunteering.

10. Face your fears through self-reflection journaling to celebrate your bravery and acknowledge your accomplishments.

Balance is the key to success in anything in life, and you'll see that the more you nurture yourself with an exercise that promotes self-love and increased self-awareness, the easier it will be to stay on track with your shadow work.

Heartfelt Checkpoint 8

Self-Date

The second part of our heartfelt checkpoint is to take yourself on a self-date.

This entails taking a shower, putting on your nicest outfit, and taking yourself, alone, for a coffee or a slice of cake or somewhere where you can spend some time to appreciate and celebrate yourself.

It doesn't matter where you go, but you should take the time to get yourself ready. Pamper yourself and then go and celebrate yourself.

This exercise is a deeply empowering exercise that also increases confidence.

Remember to journal about how you felt before your date and how you felt after it, too.

Not only will you have a great time, but you will increase your self-worth and emotional intelligence.

Celebration 8

Today, you have already celebrated yourself, so now I want you to plan a big celebration for the completion of this workbook. Go big! Invite friends and family and share your experience.

Chapter 8:
Relationships and Shadow Work

Relationships and shadow work are boldly intertwined.

They are often the very thing that brings the shadow out into the open; and anything that brings forth the shadow can end up in overreaction, impulsivity, emotional outbursts, and projecting when faced with a challenging person or situation.

The biggest relationship that the shadow will overtake is the one you have with yourself. And like Dr. Jekyll and Mr. Hyde, the shadow can overtake you if you're not careful. The shadow is easy to identify in relationships because it usually brings up negative or toxic behaviors. These can be such things as jealousy, rage, love-bombing, indecision, and many more character facets that can be noticeably regarded as out-of-control or intense emotions. They can be classed as out of the ordinary, over the top, obsessive, impulsive, or reactive.

The shadow can also bring about the victim. You may hear victim phrases like "Why are you always doing this to me?" "Why don't they love me?" "Why do bad things always happen to me?" and many more. The shadow isn't just the pieces of negative emotions— negative emotions also have positive aspects. The shadow is pieces of you that can arise in every situation and every relationship. Be it love, work, children, family, your relationship with food, alcohol, TV, and social media. Your shadow shows up in every single part of your life. There is no place for you to hide.

There is only one solution, and that is to work on reducing your shadow. So, let's dive deep into shadow work and relationships to see if we can navigate a way to allow the best version of yourself to come forward at all times. If we accept the shadow is always there, it prevents us from being naive and blocking more behaviors. You are going to love and embrace your shadow, that's the simplest way to reduce it. And when it does show up, you're going to deal with it calmly and mindfully because you know what the shadow is going to do next. Nobody knows your shadow better than you, and that's your weapon in taming it!

How the Shadow Effects Relationships

So, before we look at how the shadow affects relationships, let's first look at how the shadow shows up in relationships. See if you can identify one or a few of these ways of the shadow. Has your shadow popped up and attracted a certain type of partner? Think back to previous partners you've had. What exactly have you been attracted to?

- Have you been attracted to their childhood trauma? Was it similar to yours?
- Have you been attracted to a piece of their personality that you don't have like, for example, assertiveness? Maybe you want to see this in yourself and don't, but this quality mostly ends up becoming a trigger.
- Have you been attracted to anger and aggression? Because you want to release that anger and aggression to deal with the terrible trauma you've been through and you don't know how to deal with it.

These are all aspects of your shadow attracting their shadow. This is dangerously deceptive because when your shadow is attracted to another, it's wrapped up in a lot of negativity, conflict, and pain. Very often, those are the only things you're going to feel in that relationship, which leads straight to disaster.

Projection

Your shadow can also affect relationships through projection. When we have feelings of repressed anger deep down inside of us, we make the smallest disagreements everybody else's fault. And usually, that hits the closest person to us. We can destroy relationships through constant arguing, bickering, and conflict. And that's the shadow inside of us doing it. It's not us. It's the things from the past that you're still bringing forward into the present. This past experience means nothing in your present life, but every time we are triggered by it, we bring that shadow forward and increase its size.

Childhood Style

A popular belief held by some is that love relationships will always seek to mirror your childhood. For example, if you're always searching for the childhood you didn't have, you'll be unconsciously looking for it in your relationships. If you had areas of conflict growing up, then it's likely that you will bring those forward into your current relationships, even friendships, work relationships, and most definitely love relationships.

Self-Sabotage

Another way that the shadow shows up in relationships is self-sabotage. You may have been chasing the partner of your dreams. You may have won over that partner, and you may be in a loving relationship. But deep down, if you don't feel that you deserve the relationship and the love that goes with it, your shadow will seek to destroy it at every opportunity. This is typical of the shadow when there are feelings of low self-esteem and low self-worth. Your shadow will act out ways to destroy your relationship, create conflict, and bring you back to your most comfortable emotional state of low self-esteem and rejection.

Inauthentic Relationships

Fake relationships are a big thing. When the shadow is showing up in your daily life, you may think you're presenting the authentic version of yourself. But when the shadow is in control, you are presenting somebody who's inauthentic. Fake relationships can happen in love, work, and friendships. And what happens to relationships based on inauthenticity is that they fall apart quickly. The cracks begin to show, and when you spend more time with others, they start to realize that you are not who you appear to be.

These can be attributed to the shadow, and because you never seem to be able to maintain friendships, you can slip into the belief you can't make friends. This isn't true. But the missing pieces of your character need to be integrated for you to have genuine, authentic relationships with genuine, whole people.

Communication Difficulty

The shadow also shows up if you have difficulty communicating when you can't express yourself to your partner, your children, or your loved ones. Doubt becomes an area of strain within a relationship when things go unsaid. It can create resentment, disappointment, and a lack of connection, and all of those things lead to the breakdown of the relationship. This is primarily caused by the shadow, and the longer the problem exists, the greater the shadow grows.

Navigating Conflicts and Improving Communication

Undertaking shadow work can give you huge benefits in managing disagreements and enhancing dialogue. Work through the ways below; and in your journal, write down which ones you would find the easiest to work with to make a conscious decision in approaching conflict differently next time:

Switch "You" to "I"

When the shadow has been at work, causing mischief, conflict, and creating distance between two people, it's sometimes hard to find a resolution with words. However, one of the key ways to talk to somebody after you've argued is to change the way you frame your sentences. For example, instead of saying "you," change that to "I." In this way, you put yourself at the center of the conversation, instead of making the other person feel like the target and as though they are being attacked. This also helps you to avoid projection, too.

Journaling

Another important way to get to the bottom of why you have conflict in a relationship is to start journaling on the problems that keep surfacing. Very often, we think that when there is a problem between two people, it's the other person's fault. Journaling is the best way to look at yourself deeply; it's a private space for you to reflect and grow. You can ask yourself any questions and be honest about how you feel inside. It remains an underrated practice with huge benefits.

Mirrored Traits

When the shadow is at work, we are very often mirroring a character trait that shows up in somebody else. And that's exacerbated by the denial of that character trait within ourselves. So, we get angrier and angrier when we see this personality flaw represented in another human being because we dislike it so much in ourselves. This is evident in relationships with children. When we have a child who exposes key personality characteristics we hold and we've tried to either eradicate or disown them, this can send us into a mind-blowing rage within ourselves. We love our children so much that we don't want to see this negative part of their personality in them, especially because we passed it down, and now we feel responsible for it!

So, this is where a lot of conflict can arise in families. A really good way to combat this is through talking and verbalization. Talking through problems, sharing, and trying to find a resolution is the number one way to deal with any problem, trauma, or issue that causes distress.

Conflict Resolution

However, I appreciate that that's hard to do sometimes and even harder with the closest people to you. Especially when you see each other day in and day out. If it's impossible to find a resolution and get to that sweet spot that makes your family and loved ones tick, then try conflict resolution with a therapist or a mediator. What this does is help you create the space to listen to one another without making yourself the center of the issue.

For example, if you can listen to a problem from someone else's perspective, this induces empathy. Understanding how they feel and how the situation affects them increases your self-awareness and helps you to understand a wider view of the problem. If you can acknowledge somebody else's criticism without reacting or slipping into impulsive, explosive behavior, this helps you get to the bottom of the issue faster. It also helps you to deal with problems similar to this in the future. There are problems in every family structure, relationship, and situation, but it's how you deal with them that matters. Calmly talking things through without apportioning blame is the best way to try and find a resolution without increasing your shadow.

Increase Your Vulnerability

One of the hardest things to do in times of conflict is to be vulnerable in front of someone else. However, opening your heart in front of a loved one is something you should practice. Vulnerability helps to foster a connection between two people and breaks down barriers when anger, resentment, or fear stand in the way of good communication. Being vulnerable takes time, and the best way to increase this quality within yourself is to practice in small baby steps. In this way, you get to open your heart more, bit by bit, and let people into your heart space. You will find that in return, people will be vulnerable with you. Conflict and disagreements will be much easier to resolve. They won't get to the stage where emotional blowouts happen.

Setting Boundaries

Setting boundaries is also another important way to resolve conflicts and improve communication. Make sure that you have your standards in check. Having standards about the way you want to be treated reflects your self-worth and increases your self-esteem. Be mindful not to make boundaries that are so firm that you cut people off. This also increases the shadow because it's blocking and not dealing with the problem. Another way to look at it is that everybody deserves a chance and everybody makes mistakes. We are all human. But it's good to understand when you've reached your limit with another person and when it's time to say no and move on.

Practice Forgiveness

Practicing forgiveness is perhaps the number one way to improve communication. When the shadow has been at work, forgiveness seeks to release you from the burden of the problem. Never think that because you forgive another, the other person gets let off the hook or doesn't face consequences. Forgiveness is a gift you give yourself. Otherwise, you hold the anger, disappointment, jealousy, or resentment inside of you. This makes the shadow bigger and bigger and increases the space between you and improved emotional intelligence.

Forgiving yourself is always the first place to start when you practice forgiveness. Then, you can move on to forgiving others within your life. Remember that people make mistakes when they don't know any better at the time. You will have done this too; we all do. Accepting this stops you from holding the weight of others' actions, and acceptance permits you to release yourself from any bad feelings.

Practicing Patience

Have you ever wondered how some people are patient while others aren't? Patience is a skill that needs to be practiced. You will often see that mothers have an abundance of patience because they have practiced it over and over again with small children. When we have behaved badly, we long for patience and acceptance from another person, so why are we so bad at giving it ourselves? Being patient is not something that will happen overnight; but if you commit to the practice, you will be proud of yourself, and you'll find that others admire this quality in you, too.

Practicing patience is the gift you give yourself that increases your emotional intelligence. Your shadow self will always want you to react, explode, and be impulsive and not think about the consequences. And there will be an internal struggle when you begin to practice it.

Practicing patience takes time. But when you start being patient with others, you'll find you have that returned to you, as the energy you emit will attract the same energy back. It's a great weapon to have in your arsenal against your shadow, as the work you do on yourself will be the greatest key to unlocking and improving communication methods.

If you continue to practice self-awareness by journaling and mindfulness activities, you will see that you will naturally become a better communicator. You will be calmer, and you will think instead of emotionally reacting when you want to discuss a problem. Self-awareness is your greatest asset. It's also one of the shadow's biggest fears, so the more you improve this quality within yourself, the greater your ability to fight anything in life and gain more confidence in the process.

Healing Relationships Through Shadow Work

The amazing thing about shadow work is that it increases compassion. Your expansion in compassion will, in turn, help you to see things from your partner's point of view. This is important in healing relationships. Oftentimes, you'll find that when conflict is in a relationship, distance increases between two people. And working through your shadow work will help you to decrease that distance. It will bring you closer together. As a by-product of all the work you do in your shadow, your personal growth will expand and bring a positive impact to all relationships. If you remember, relationships are based on everything in life: work, money, food, health, community, and personal life. Your energy is your greatest asset, but it can be your worst enemy. Remember to nurture it.

It's also worth noting that while nobody wants to be called out and have their shadow work identified, it does give you the compassion to see when others haven't worked on theirs. This also gives you the ability to help them when they're going through a dark time and perhaps redirect them to something that will help them manage their emotions better.

But perhaps the most important thing to note is healing the relationship within yourself. You'll find that once you're on the right track with your shadow work, everything in your life will become a lot easier. There will be more ease in your work, home life, and your family and the day-to-day will become a lot more enjoyable.

Heartfelt Checkpoint 9

In this heartfelt checkpoint, I want you to write a letter of forgiveness to yourself.

First, we will go through some examples of things you could forgive yourself for.

Then, we will create seven statements of forgiveness as examples. After that, I want you to go on to create your own statements that are personal to you.

Remember that these will change over time. Maybe once a month, you can look at refreshing the seven areas you want to forgive yourself for. This will keep you constantly evolving and decreasing your shadow. Let's begin.

1. **Forgive yourself for poor decisions.** Think back to when you made a bad decision. What was happening in

your life at the time? Were you trying to please somebody else? Were you trying to keep the peace or was it just a simple error of judgement? Everybody makes mistakes. Looking at those mistakes, owning them, and seeing how you could have made a better judgment will help you move forward. It also really pushes your personal growth in the right direction.

2. **Forgive yourself for being your own worst critic.** No one will give you a hard time like you will. Forgiveness work provides major transformation and a turning point in your shadow work journey. By forgiving yourself, you will reframe statements or the negative dialogue that comes up when you start giving yourself a hard time.

3. **Forgive yourself for feeling regret.** Regret is a feeling that does not serve us in any way, and missed opportunities are just part of life. Fear often plays a part in us not seizing the day, and maybe this opportunity wasn't right for you at the time. Opportunity is always evolving throughout your life. Just because you missed one opportunity doesn't mean that you'll miss another. Forgive yourself for feeling regret and stay in the present moment.

4. **Forgive yourself for the time when you didn't know better.** This usually comes up in abusive and toxic relationships. Show forgiveness for not having stronger self-worth, knowing that you are worth more than being treated like a doormat or a punching bag. Forgive yourself for not feeling important and showing yourself the love that you deserve. Acknowledge that you did your best at that time.

5. **Use forgiveness to be compassionate about unrealistic expectations you've set for yourself.** We all expected to be further on than we are now. Forgive yourself for feeling that way. And know that just by doing these exercises, you are moving in the right direction now.

6. **Forgive yourself for negative inner dialogue and negative beliefs.** Forgive yourself for not attracting positive beliefs and positive things in your life. Forgive yourself for hindering your progress. Know that you won't do that again.

7. **Forgive yourself for not loving yourself enough and neglecting yourself.** You are the most important person to you, and no one loves you more than you will love yourself. Forgive yourself for not putting the correct food in your body, for not working your muscles correctly, for not connecting with nature. Forgive yourself and make sure that you are mindful of all those things in the present moment.

Next, look at the seven statement examples created below and say these before your affirmations each day.

My Forgiveness Letter—Example

1. I forgive myself for my bad decisions when I did not know any better.

2. I forgive myself for verbally beating myself up.

3. I forgive myself for feeling the regret of missed opportunities.

4. I forgive myself for lowering my standards in toxic relationships.

5. I forgive myself for putting expectations on myself.

6. I forgive myself for my negative thoughts and beliefs.

7. I forgive myself for neglecting myself.

Now, it's your time to create your own and say these before your affirmations each day.

Celebration 9

Forgiveness work is tough. Today, I want self-care to be optimized. Run a big bubble bath and soak, listening to your favorite soothing music.

Chapter 9:
Advanced Shadow Work Techniques

There is no one way to use shadow work to help you retrieve those lost pieces of yourself. We all veer toward different practices and rituals. The most important thing for you is to find one that you enjoy—that way you'll feel positive and excited about doing the work, which will keep you consistent and accountable. If you find a practice that you really don't enjoy, move on and explore another. And if you want to go even deeper, keep on listening.

Exploring Deeper Layers of the Shadow

During our time working through this workbook, we haven't considered how our shadow affects society at large. We've looked deeply at the layer of the shadow that affects us the most. We've looked at where it comes in to disturb our relationships with every part of our life, including health, wealth, and love. What we haven't explored yet is the deeper layer of the shadow that forms part of the collective shadow.

We enter this world with unconscious bias, which begins forming in our childhood with the effects coming from the society we live in. This means that we may not be consciously aware of our bias toward certain things. The culture we've grown up in gets instilled inside of us from an early age. For example, we may believe that people from developed countries are somewhat more civilized than those from developing countries. This happens in areas of race, religion, and many other areas of life. This isn't something that you can control. But being aware of it can help you reduce your reaction toward other races, cultures, religions, and other people in society at large.

When you feel an aversion to something, this is your shadow at work. And in this age of information, we are often given a lot of incorrect facts and media-biased opinions. It's important to be mindful of what we allow into our intellect, as biased opinion is set to unbalance us.

But there are always great ways to tackle this and educate yourself. You can travel to places you usually wouldn't or immerse yourself in volunteering or in simply learning about other countries, cultures, religions, and traditions. So, when you experience anything different from what you know and are comfortable with, you react in a very balanced manner with a much broader view of the world. This helps to reduce the collective shadow. While the collective shadow may seem enormous, if everybody can do their piece of work to reduce it, then we will all have a better world to live in.

Addressing unconscious bias will help you unlock stereotypes, diversity, inclusion, and equality; don't undervalue its effects on yourself or your community.

Working With Dreams and Symbols

Working with dreams and symbols to work through your shadow requires a very open mind.

Sometimes, it takes you to a different level within yourself. It can connect with your spiritual core and help to express pieces of your higher self and different levels of creativity. It can also be confusing and disturbing if not done in the right way. So, it's important to counterbalance working with dreams and symbols together with self-care practices.

You could begin by starting a dream journal, paying attention only to the emotions in your dreams. Write your dreams down regularly and see if you can find a pattern or reoccurring emotions that come up for you. Interpretation of these emotions is going to be subjective, and I recommend that you have a very balanced approach to interpreting what they may mean and get the help of a specialist if you need it—especially if you encounter areas that are worrying or make you feel uncomfortable.

Inside your dreams, you're often going to come across different animals, places, and people. And these can be viewed as symbolic depending on the culture and tradition you value. Symbols mean different things in different cultures and traditions, and perhaps here it's important to take a holistic view of what these symbols mean to you.

Never become obsessed or dwell on the negative aspects of these symbols; symbolism will give you both positive and negative viewpoints. If you inadvertently dwell on negative parts of symbolism, this is going to increase your shadow, and it's not going to help you. However, if you always look at symbols as something like a guideline or an indication of something positive, then that's a very healthy approach.

Remember, you will always find what you're looking for. If you're looking for deeper significance in something, you will always find it. We are attracted to what we think about, and this works in both positive and negative ways.

If you enjoy exploring your dreams, then it's quite easy to do. Sink into a meditative state by closing your eyes and going on an active journey back inside your dream to see what you can find, what resonates with you, and what helps you reach the resolution you are looking for.

I would stress that it is important to stay on top of positive significance and symbolism. If your shadow shows up in your dream as an aggressive person, a bad situation, or trauma, take a deep breath and try to engage with this person or this situation and ask it questions. Ask what it is trying to tell you to see if you can unpick the process in your mind. Your mind is taking you on this journey for a reason. What is it trying to say?

During your dream visitation, if you find aspects of yourself that you believe need to be integrated, go ahead and do so. Embrace these pieces of yourself with compassion and love. See if this is another doorway to working through your shadow work in a very positive manner.

Many therapists and alternative practitioners work with dream therapies. If you need help in this area or you want to go deeper, it's a great idea to get professional help and never be afraid to ask.

Shamanic and Therapeutic Approaches

Shamanic approaches steer you more toward the spiritualist side of shadow work. It's up to you to decide if this is something you want to explore and find a connection with. Let's go a little deeper:

Shamanic Approaches

Shamanic approaches to shadow work provide a different level of exploring your shadow. Many of these practices involve meditation. If you take shamanic journeying, for example, this is where you use music, or repeated rhythms like the beat of a drum, to go back on a journey to find aspects of your shadow. This takes you deep into your unconscious and helps you retrieve pieces of yourself that you have once denied or been ashamed of. Some call it soul retrieval.

This can be a deeply healing way to retrieve parts of your psyche, and it requires quite a lot of energy to partake in these rituals. Before you go headfirst into shamanic journeying, make sure that you are feeling well and that your energy level is high. You may feel a little depleted after doing this work. It's also worth bearing in mind that when you do any deep energy work, it can take a day or even a week to recover.

As part of shamanic approaches, you can also delve into the practice of animal work. This work is usually called animal guides. Animals represent a deep connection to the natural world, the original world where you began. Animals here are used in many different ways as symbols or as presentation of certain personality traits. Other animals are viewed as protectors or totems. You may even find yourself with an animal guide who will steer you and your shadow into the light.

Again, most of these practices will be through guided meditation or ritual, and you must balance this kind of work with lots of self-care. While exploration can provide deep insights into your psyche, and your shadow, it can also be uncomfortable and unsettling at times. You may feel slightly imbalanced when you finish doing this work. If you explore this journey, you must do it with a lot of time and compassion for recovery. Not everyone reacts in the same way to shamanic work and a deeply meditative state, so you must make sure you can feel and see a physical tether to the present world in the present moment. If you don't come out of deep mind exploration experiences properly, you can feel disconnected and foggy.

Therapeutic Approaches

Alternative therapies can be very simple approaches to healing the shadow. Let's explore some of those here, and while you thinking about them, see how they feel in your body as we go through each one:

Psychotherapy

Several therapeutic approaches are very interesting. One of them is psychotherapy. In this practice, you can go back in time and act out certain parts of your childhood to see what comes up and what emotions you felt as a child. Your relationship with time was very different from the relationship you have with time now. For example, one week may have felt like 12 months as a child, so unwrapping and unpicking things that happened in your childhood in a safe space can help you get a lot of clarity and shift some limiting beliefs that have helped to create your shadow.

Talking Therapy

Simple talking therapy is another way for you to express withheld or repressed emotions. By spending time with another person talking over your fears, emotional outbursts, and feelings, you can get to the heart of many problems and trace their roots, making them easier to dissipate. In the society that we live in now, we do very little "real talk" about the things that cause us a problem and affect the way that we live. With the constantly increasing use of social media, we have turned into a very inauthentic society that, on a collective level, has increased the collective shadow. That rebounds on us and increases our shadow. So, while talking therapy may seem like a very simple option, it's very, very therapeutic.

Art Therapy

Art therapy is a very popular way of expressing yourself in a nonverbal sense. Over the years, this therapy has become very popular because it provides release in artistic expression. This means that you can paint or draw anything you want to, as it's an expression of art, and free yourself of the dark side of your shadow in a beautiful context. This is often met with less judgment than if you were talking about the same emotional experience. Immersing yourself in therapy also gives you the time to disconnect from your thoughts. And if it's something you love, it's a beautiful act of self-care at the same time.

Gestalt Therapy

Gestalt therapy is also a therapeutic approach where you avoid going into past experiences and stay in the present. You may be worried or nervous about an upcoming task or event, and this may bring some feelings to you that you need to explore. A trained therapist will help you do that by staying in the present moment and talking about your feelings surrounding your worry. Bringing these out into the open helps you get more clarity on what's happening to you and why it's happening, and it helps you to neutralize and manage your feelings in a better way.

Heartfelt Checkpoint 10

In the last section of this book, we've been looking at alternative ways of exploring shadow work. One of these ways can be with artistic expression. In this final checkpoint, we're going to make the aspects of your shadow into characters.

Creative Shadow Characters

One of the most fun ways of doing shadow work is by making your shadow aspects into real characters. And you are going to give all the characters in your shadow a voice!

You will create characters for each one of your shadow elements and turn them into real people. This is a fun way to visualize the aspects of your shadow. You can even give them names and call them out when you feel that they're starting to rise within you.

Adding humor to painful aspects of life is a great way of dealing with challenging aspects of yourself. When you're lighthearted about facets of your character, you're eager to change, and it makes the process a lot sweeter. Step by step, we're going to dive into character exploration, and this helps you to externalize your shadow rather than internalize its negativity.

Step 1

Identify the pieces of your shadow. These can be anything from repressed emotions, fears, desires, inabilities, silence, or any aspects of your shadow that have been showing up for you. Write them down now.

Step 2

It's time to give your shadow aspects a name. Think about how they look. What physical features do they have? What other personality traits? Once you've identified these create a background story for each one. If you need to meditate on this that can be a fun way to do it. What's the backstory of this character? Who are they? What kind of life do they live? What kind of hopes and dreams does this character have?

Step 3

Create a short story. Once you have identified your characters and named them and you can see a picture of them in your head, it's time to create either a monologue or a short story about them. A monologue, for example, would be something typical that your shadow aspect would say. What kinds of words and phrases do they use? How do they express themselves? What are they thinking about? What do they fear? What do they desire? What are their dreams and goals?

You can also write a short story about them. What happened to this character? Where have they been? What have they suffered? What have they done to other people? Go through all their experiences, and keep it as amusing as possible.

Step 4

If you are creative, then paint a picture of your character. Draw them, paint them, or make a clay model of them. By doing this, it's again externalizing your shadow aspects and bringing beauty and light into them.

Step 5

What does your character want to achieve? What are they trying to express? How are they trapped inside? What's keeping them there? What's stopping them from moving forward and into the light?

Step 6

It's time for reflection. Now, how do these characters relate to you? Can you see a tie or a tether between you? What's your connection? How is this character playing out in your life? What would you like to see happen to this character? Usually by thinking about your character as someone else, it's easier to see a clearer vision of how their life should be lived beautifully.

Step 7

Now, you need to integrate this character. You know everything about them, what they do, why they react, what they want from life, and how are they going to get there. It's time to integrate them into yourself. You can do this through simple visualization or meditation. Spend time with them in your head. Make them feel loved because, after all, you're just loving pieces of yourself.

Step 8

Share your character. Find a community or share with friends and family how you explored your shadow work using this creative process. It will be really fun and interesting to hear if your family, friends, or community members use this form of artistic expression. This can provide a refreshing sense of release in an area of personal growth that is undoubtedly the hardest. We know that when we bring humor and light to the darkest of times, they're much easier to deal with, and this is a perfect way to explore an alternative practice of shadow work.

Take the 30-Day Shadow Challenge

Engaging in the 30-day shadow work challenge is going to make you feel motivated and inspired in an alternative way to address your biggest challenges!

Week 1—Self-Discovery

Day 1: Journal on your current state of emotions and where you are in your shadow work progress.

Day 2: Engage in a meditation of your choice for at least 15 minutes to establish your level of self-awareness.

Day 3: Set an intention. Choose one shadow aspect you would like to work on over the next 30 days.

Day 4: Stay grounded. Take part in breathwork, yoga, or any exercise or physical activity of your choice that makes you feel good.

Day 5: Tell a friend about your 30-day challenge and see if you can get them to join you.

Day 6: Make one affirmation specifically on self-acceptance. Pin it on a wall or somewhere you can repeat it at least three times a day.

Day 7: Spend some time outdoors reflecting on the week and your progress so far. Try and connect with nature.

Week 2—Connecting With Your Shadow

Day 8: Write a letter to yourself acknowledging the different parts of your shadow that you are currently aware of.

Day 9: Take a journey to meet your inner child. See how they're feeling and try and find out if they are directly connected to aspects of your shadow.

Day 10: Take part in the artistic expression of your shadow through writing, dancing, or music.

Day 11: Write a letter to someone you need to forgive. You don't need to send it, but write the letter for yourself.

Day 12: Learn something new about shadow work. Use the free resources on the internet or take part in a workshop where you can be active and present.

Day 13: Practice gratitude. Shadow work can make you feel low at times; balance that out with at least seven statements of gratitude.

Day 14: Look closely at your shadow aspects and see if you can identify any positives in the negative traits of your shadow.

Week 3—Integration

Day 15: Try a meditation on integrating parts of your shadow. Visualize yourself welcoming in aspects of your shadow.

Day 16: Try to explore or at least research something new that aligns with the potential your shadow aspect could have.

Day 17: List all the people who trigger your shadow and start to create boundaries for them.

Day 18: Look into getting more support from a mentor or a guide. If you need a free resource, go to YouTube and find a personal growth specialist, shadow work healer, or psychologist with whom you vibe.

Day 19: Write a letter to your future self. Tell them about the person you want to be.

Day 20: Work out, exercise, or do something that makes your heart rate increase and disconnects your mind from your body. This will help you release any emotions you are struggling with.

Day 21: Practice affirmations of acceptance. Create five affirmations about accepting where you are now and loving yourself as you are today.

Week 4—Growth

Day 22: Create a new vision board representing the desires of the person you want to be when your shadow work is complete and your shadow is as small as possible.

Day 23: Explore personal growth to greater depths. Which mentor do you resonate with? Start one of their programs and work through their books and videos.

Day 24: Practice random acts of kindness. Do something for someone else today. Even if you can only manage to smile or say hello to someone, engage in something for no personal gratification at all.

Day 25: Journal how you've come on this road and what parts of your shadow have now transformed.

Day 26: Share your experience online in a community or with your family or friends.

Day 27: What action can you take today to integrate the piece of your shadow that you are working on? Name that action.

Day 28: Reflect on all of your journal entries from the beginning of this challenge and celebrate yourself. Go for a coffee, go to a restaurant, go to the cinema, or book a holiday—whatever it is, celebrate yourself today!

Day 29: What self-care does your new version of yourself need? Make a list and practice one thing on that list.

Day 30: Write a letter to the person you were on day one. Thank them for taking part in this challenge. Thank them for growing and not being fearful and acknowledge their strength along this journey.

Celebration 10

Wow! Look how far you've come! Treat yourself to a spa day in total relaxation and reward for a job well done.

Conclusion

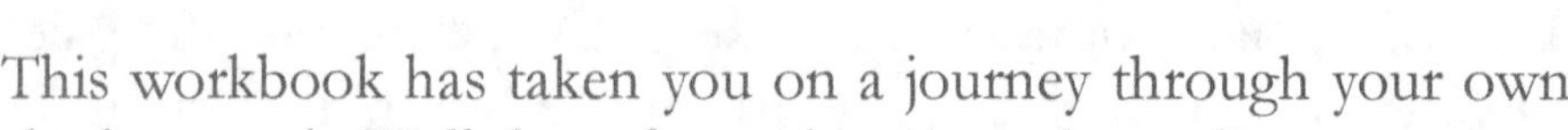

This workbook has taken you on a journey through your own shadow work. Well done for making it to the end!

I hope that during your shadow work practice, you have undertaken equal amounts of self-care to counterbalance bringing out and dissipating the dark side of yourself.

Remember that shadow work is an ongoing journey. This work is never complete. It would be wonderful to feel that there would never be another challenge or problematic person you would face for the rest of your life, but that's a dream. It is your job now to make sure that your shadow decreases and doesn't grow.

You can hide from your shadow. You can pretend it's not there. But remember those things grow your shadow. The best way forward now is to be completely responsible for keeping it as small as possible and bring in as much light into yourself to keep your shadow at bay.

From the very first chapter of this workbook, you started a process of transformation. What levels of transformation can you now see in yourself? Are you pausing to think before you speak? Are you taking a deep breath when an emotion arises? Are you an observer, watching an emotion rise, observing it, and then letting it float on by?

If so, this is a huge transformation and milestone, and I congratulate you on the personal growth that you now have achieved. This is the evolution of you; the evolution of your spirit and your soul. And as long as you keep practicing those rituals, you will keep on evolving and creating increased emotional intelligence.

When we have talked about integration, what have you managed to integrate? Have you integrated pieces of your inner child? Maybe you've managed to integrate your inner child completely. Have you integrated anger and jealousy and know that the next time that they both show up, you're not going to let them run the show? Integration is the absolute goal of shadow work. And now it's time to see what goals and dreams you can achieve in this new, whole version of yourself.

Shadow work is a lifelong exploration of the challenges of your dark side. Remember, there is nothing wrong with having a dark side. We have to have dark to have light; we have to have night to have day. But what we don't want is your shadow to ever take over the best version of yourself. We want to keep on receiving abundance. Keep on achieving goals. Keep on living life on your terms, the way we imagine it should be.

If you've reached the end and feel anything less than amazing, I would encourage you to spend more time in practices of self-love, self-esteem, self-worth, and self-care. This will increase your self-awareness, and you will create more compassion for yourself; the byproduct of this is your happiness.

Don't feel that you are alone on this journey. Everyone who undertakes shadow work does so knowing that this is the beginning of a road that never ends. You are brave, you are strong, and you can do this. Even if you have only taken one step in this direction, you have taken one more step that millions of other people haven't.

Maybe you're feeling now it's time to share your experiences or you need further support. Find a community that can hold space for you. If that's not enough, don't forget you can always seek out professional help. Combining professional help with therapies and practices we've already discussed is a great idea to move forward. Don't ever think of working on yourself as something negative. Those of us who want to move past our struggles and move forward in life with increased emotional intelligence are the ones who will succeed in health, wealth, and relationships.

So, now I'm curious to know what new goals you have. What can you achieve now that you couldn't when you started this workbook? Remember the big question: If there was no fear, what would you do with your life? How would you answer that differently now? Does that question feel exciting rather than scary? I'm excited about your future, and I hope it's one that you're excited about, too.

Before we close this chapter of your shadow work, remember to use this book whenever you want. Make it a point to journal about it in three months, six months, or even once a year to keep you on track. And don't forget to share it with your friends if you see them struggling with a shadow aspect they cannot shift.

Before we go, we're going to explore a questionnaire similar to the one that we did when you started the book. This is a perfect time for you to reflect on just how far you've come from day one. I bet it's miles further than you ever imagined!

Self-Discovery Transformation

Take the self-discovery questionnaire to document your transformation and take you to the next level of completeness!

1. What is your perception of yourself now?

2. What have you learned about yourself on this shadow work journey?

3. How is your self-awareness now different?

4. Has your shadow been triggered since the beginning of this book?

5. Did you find any recurring patterns of behavior in your shadow work? Are they still present in your life now?

6. Which parts of your shadow work have been the hardest?

7. What did you not enjoy delving into and how did you work through these?

8. Name three breakthroughs you had during the book. How have they impacted your life?

9. Can you identify any major changes in current relationships after working through this book? How does that make you feel?

10. What is the one technique you learned from this workbook that you are going to continue to practice?

11. What is the one technique that you did not enjoy from this workbook? And what does that tell you about yourself? Is that something that you can identify in your shadow?

12. How difficult was it to forgive yourself during the book? Does thinking about forgiving yourself still make you feel emotional?

13. What is now your favorite self-awareness practice?

14. What is now your favorite self-love practice?

15. Are your goals and dreams now clearer or different from when you began?

16. Do you have something that you want to aim for that was different from when you started the book?

17. Have you created a schedule where you have equal shadow work and self-care practices scheduled regularly?

18. Are there any new techniques you want to try but you are unsure of trying?

19. What advice would you give to someone starting their shadow work? Could you help them in any way?

20. What has been your biggest integration and is there anything left you feel you need to integrate?

Seven-Day Self-Care Checklist for Your Onward Journey

You didn't think I'd leave you here without helping you maintain all the good work, did you?

Let's create your checklist to keep you going strong in the days ahead!

Day 1: Spend time reflecting on how far you've come in your shadow work journey. Write a letter to yourself today that celebrates your courage and determination for your personal growth. Write down another aspect of your shadow that you want to explore in the future.

Day 2: Make a gratitude list today, especially taking into account the positive changes that have come from your recent shadow work. Write a self-appreciation list, identifying at least seven qualities or strengths that you've discovered as a result of this shadow work.

Day 3: Be mindful. Engage in any mindfulness activity that makes you feel good. It can be mindful breathing, mindfulness meditation, an empathy walk, or talking with a friend. Simply mindfully explore your thoughts and feelings by observation of your inner self today. You should pamper yourself with self-love and a comforting activity that makes you feel good and gives you space to think about something else.

Day 4: Get involved in a community project or work that encompasses shadow work. Talk to a friend about their journey. Talk to your family and see if they need help with that.

Day 5: Create a ritual for yourself. releasing parts of the shadow or letting go of people in your life who trigger the shadow. Say goodbye to things from your past. Find a way of letting go. That could be exercise, writing, and burning a letter. Throwing stones in the river, anything you choose shows you that you have released and let go.

Day 6: This is your celebration day. Treat yourself to a meal, take yourself out for a coffee, go for a walk, or get out in nature. Think about how positive your life could be if you continue on this path of growth.

Day 7: Set some goals and intentions for the future that align with your future self. Spend some time in nature and reconnect with the earth. Ground yourself; anchor yourself to all that is and all that you want to be.

I leave you in love and light and peace for the future. Good luck with your onward journey to being the best version of yourself.

References

Aletheia. (2020, April 25). *Breathwork: 11 magical techniques for spiritual healing.* LonerWolf. https://lonerwolf.com/breathwork/#h-5-intensely-transformative-types-of-breathwork

Cherry, K. (2021, April 24). *Why self-esteem is important for success.* Very Well Mind. https://www.verywellmind.com/what-is-self-esteem-2795868#:~:text=Why%20Self%2DEsteem%20Is%20Important

Clarke, J. (2021). *What is Gestalt Therapy?* Very Well Mind. https://www.verywellmind.com/what-is-gestalt-therapy-4584583

Editorial Team, B. (2023, September 27). *What is shadow psychology?* Better Help. https://www.betterhelp.com/advice/psychologists/what-is-shadow-psychology

Emotional intelligence. (2019). Psychology Today. https://www.psychologytoday.com/intl/basics/emotional-intelligence

Heyn, S. (2020, September 3). *Exactly how to do shadow work (an easy 6-step process).* Soul Scroll Journals. https://soulscrolljournals.com/blogs/news/exactly-how-to-do-shadow-work-an-easy-6-step-process

Hussain, S. (2020, June 21). *Ken Wilber's 3-2-1 process: A method for retracting shadow projections.* Ox-Head Psychology. https://oxheadpsychology.com.au/ken-wilbers-3-2-1-process-a-method-for-retracting-shadow-projections

Jeffrey, S. (2019, April 15). *Shadow work: A complete guide to getting to know your darker half.* Scott Jeffrey. https://scottjeffrey.com/shadow-work

Lamkin, W. A. (2020, August 24). *The mandala: An archetype of the self.* Medium. https://medium.com/@WilliamLamkin/the-mandala-an-archetype-of-the-self-72c30146d39d

LaVine, R. (2023, March 28). *100+ deep shadow work prompts to accept yourself and move forward*. Science of People. https://www.scienceofpeople.com/shadow-work-prompts/#:~:text=Shadow%20work%20prompts%20for%20inner%2Dchild%20healing

Lewis, J. (2023, July 29). *Shadow self: What is it and how can it help you?* Zella Life. https://www.zellalife.com/blog/shadow-self-what-is-it-and-how-can-it-help-you/

Lopes, C. (2020, June 9). *What is shadow work?* YouTube. https://www.youtube.com/watch?v=5kDN7g9kBAs&t=8s

Maria. (2021, January 4). *19 top reasons why self-discovery is important*. Aim Lief. https://aimlief.com/why-is-self-discovery-so-important/

McKenna, K. (2023, June 11). *Why naming your feelings matters*. Sit With Kelly. https://www.sitwithkelly.com/blog/feelings

Mind. (2019). *Tips to improve your self-esteem*. Mind. https://www.mind.org.uk/information-support/types-of-mental-health-problems/self-esteem/tips-to-improve-your-self-esteem

100 self-love affirmations for higher self-esteem. (2021, April 20). Gratitude Blog. https://blog.gratefulness.me/20-affirmations-to-say-to-yourself-when-you-need-support

Pahwa, V. (2023, January 1). *50 nothing comes easy quotes to deeply love hard work*. Uprise High. https://uprisehigh.com/build-yourself/nothing-comes-easy-quotes

Raypole, C. (2020, March 31). *Repressed emotions: finding and releasing them*. Healthline. https://www.healthline.com/health/repressed-emotions

Riopel, L. (2019, September 14). *17 self-awareness activities and exercises*. Positive Psychology. https://positivepsychology.com/self-awareness-exercises-activities-test

6 steps toward emotional mastery. (n.d.). Skills You Need. https://www.skillsyouneed.com/rhubarb/emotional-mastery.html#:~:text=Emotional%20mastery%20is%20the%20gradual

Solis-Moreira, J. (2022, August 12). *6 ways to practice self-love*. Forbes Health. https://www.forbes.com/health/mind/how-to-practice-self-love/

3-2-1 process for the shadow (n.d.). Bhavana Learning Group. https://bhavanalearninggroup.com/wp-content/uploads/321-Process-for-the-Shadow.pdf

Williams, K. (2022, May 16). *35 shadow work prompts for self-love*. KB in Bloom. https://kbinbloom.com/shadow-work-prompts-for-self-love/#:~:text=Deeper%20Self%2DLove%20Shadow%20Work%20Prompts%3A&text=Write%20down%20how%20you%20believe

Wooll, M. (2022, June 13). *8 benefits of shadow work and how to start practicing It*. BetterUp. https://www.betterup.com/blog/shadow-work

Work, I. S. (2021, October 13). *30 shadow work prompts for self-worth*. Inner Shadow Work. https://innershadowwork.com/shadow-work-prompts-for-self-worth/References